REMAKING CONGRESS
Change and Stability in the 1990s

REMAKING CONGRESS
Change and Stability in the 1990s

EDITED BY

JAMES A. THURBER
American University

ROGER H. DAVIDSON
University of Maryland

With a Foreword by Rep. David Dreier

Congressional Quarterly Inc.
Washington, D.C.

Book and cover design: Paula Anderson
Cover illustration: Marilyn Gates-Davis

Library of Congress Cataloging-in-Publication Data

Remaking Congress: change and stability in the 1990s / edited by James A. Thurber,
    Roger H. Davidson ; with a foreword by David Dreier.
        p.   cm.
    Includes bibliographic references and index.
    ISBN 1-56802-160-7 (hard) — ISBN 1-56802-161-5 (paper)
    1. United States. Congress—Reform. 2. United States—Politics and government—1993-
    I. Thurber, James A. II. Davidson, Roger H.
    JK1061.R46 1995
    328.73'07042—dc20

95-3110
CIP

For Claudia and Nancy

CONTENTS

CONTENTS

FOREWORD

On the morning of November 9, 1994, after a couple of hours of sleep, I contemplated the historic changes that were about to take place in our nation's capital. I was particularly excited by the prospect of making significant reforms to the organization and operations of the House of Representatives.

I had spent the greater part of August and September working with my colleagues in the House Gerald Solomon, R-N.Y., and Jennifer Dunn, R-Wash., to put together a comprehensive package of institutional reforms as part of the "Contract with America." That morning I received a telephone call from soon-to-be Speaker of the House Newt Gingrich, R-Ga., asking me to craft several specific proposals to reduce the number of House committees and realign their jurisdictions. Fortunately, like the authors of major reform legislation 50 years earlier, I was able to draw on the experience and objectivity of the academic world.

When the Legislative Reorganization Act of 1946 was passed, substantial credit went to congressional scholars at the American Political Science Association. They played an instrumental role in designing and marketing the reforms that would establish the framework for the modern Congress.

Today a new generation of activist scholars, such as Walter Oleszek, C. Lawrence Evans, Norman Ornstein, Thomas Mann, James Thurber, Roger Davidson, Barbara Sinclair, and Steven Smith, has performed an equally important role in shaping the House reforms that were adopted on the opening day of the 104th Congress.

Their initial platform was the Joint Committee on the Organization of Congress. It was created in 1992 in the wake of the House bank, restaurant, and post office scandals, and other perceived ethical improprieties by members of Congress. The real impetus for the Joint Committee, however, came from a desire among rank-and-file members to do something about a deeper, less visible institutional crisis.

Symptoms of this institutional crisis included restrictive floor procedures in the House that prevented Democrats and Republicans alike from offering germane amendments and debating alternative policy solutions; a lack of long-term planning by House and Senate leaders; erratic legislative schedules that placed terrible pressures on family life and district work schedules; a complicated and indiscernible federal budget process; an archaic committee system characterized by abuses of power, fractured attention, interest group dominance, and jurisdictional gridlock; and a large, unaccountable staff bureaucracy.

The solution to this crisis, many believed, could be found in a resolution sponsored by my former colleague, Bill Gradison, to create the Joint Committee on the Organization of Congress. That resolution, H. Con. Res. 192, was adopted near the end of the 102nd Congress by a unanimous vote in the Senate and a near unanimous vote in the House.

The Joint Committee consisted of 28 members, 14 from each chamber, equally divided between Republicans and Democrats. Rep. Lee Hamilton, D-Ind., and David Boren, then a Democratic senator from Oklahoma, served as co-chairmen. Both of them were extraordinarily committed to the reform process. Pete Domenici, a Senate leader with tremendous institutional knowledge, and I served as the co-vice-chairmen. The committee's mandate was to study the operations of Congress and to provide recommendations for reform no later than December 31, 1993.

It had been 47 years since Congress undertook its first comprehensive and bipartisan examination of the institution that led to significant reforms. As a result of the steady leadership of Kim Wincup and the intellectual strength of Walter Oleszek, C. Lawrence Evans, and Phil Grone, the Joint Committee did its task extremely well. Over the first six months of 1993, the committee held 36 hearings and took testimony from 243 witnesses—including 133 House members, 37 senators, 14 former members, 15 current and former staff members, and 44 outside witnesses, among them Ross Perot and former vice president Walter Mondale. The committee organized symposia, conducted surveys, contracted outside studies, and consulted with anybody who had anything to say about how to reform Congress.

In the end the Joint Committee compiled the largest information database ever assembled on the problems with the institution and options for reforming it. Many of the proposals discussed in the Joint Committee became the basis for the sweeping reforms enacted by the House on January 4, 1995. Those reforms sent a clear message to the American people that Congress was serious about changing the way Washington does business. They were intended to make the House more accountable, professionalize the administrative management, and rebuild public confidence in representative government.

Invaluable support was provided to the Joint Committee by Norman Ornstein and Thomas Mann, who together produced three reports as part of the Renewing Congress Project of the American Enterprise Institute and the Brookings Institution. These reports provided an independent assessment of Congress and offered recommendations for improving the effectiveness of the institution.

For example, Mann and Ornstein took the early lead in calling on Congress to comply with civil rights, employment, and workplace safety laws. These statutory requirements were signed into law by President Bill Clinton on January 23, 1995.

They called for the establishment of Oxford-style debates, and the House undertook three such debates in 1994. They also called for a reduction in committee sizes and assignments, a consolidation of jurisdictions, and the elimination of proxy voting, all of which were included in the opening day rules package.

The Joint Committee also drew on the extensive historical research of Roger Davidson, James Thurber, Barbara Sinclair, and Steven Smith to help steer the panel away from many of the political pitfalls that doomed previous reform efforts. Of course, their perspectives did not include the one sure-fire method of avoiding those political pitfalls: ending 40 straight years of Democratic control of the House of Representatives.

By no means did adoption of the opening day reforms in the House of Representatives complete the reform agenda. The House and Senate, for example, must jointly tackle substantive reforms to the federal budget process. The Joint Committee on the Organization of Congress and the Bipartisan Commission on Entitlement and Tax Reform have identified the major problems with the current budget process and outlined proposals for change. Must reading on the subject is James Thurber's chapter "If the Game Is Too Hard, Change the Rules: Congressional Budget Reform in the 1990s," which conveys an honest insight into how a future budget reform process may play out.

Major jurisdiction reform of committees is another area that continues to need serious attention. The early Congress routinely altered the committee system, generally after every census. They were not wed to a static view of the world. Unfortunately, the jurisdiction and structure of committees today have not changed in any meaningful way in nearly 50 years. As Roger Davidson states in his chapter "Congressional Committees in the New Reform Era: From Combat to the Contract," committee organizational problems, if unattended, will continue to plague Congress, and will be heard from again.

Many of the formal recommendations of the Joint Committee with respect to Ethics Committee reforms and Joint House and Senate operations could not be included in the opening day reforms and must be considered on a separate track. The new majority is committed to a long-term agenda to change the culture and customs of Congress. As that agenda accelerates, the research and analysis contained in this book will be a continual source of inspiration for activist reformers both in Congress and in the academic world.

Rep. David Dreier
Member of Congress

PREFACE

Changes are sweeping inexorably throughout the U.S. government. No event more unmistakably signaled these changes than the 1994 midterm elections, which reinstalled Republican majorities of both chambers of Congress for the first time in 40 years. Yet the period of instability and upheaval had begun long before voters cast their ballots that year, and it promises to stretch into the foreseeable future. Our political and governmental institutions are resilient as well as responsive to the forces driving change; continuity as well as innovation characterizes our institutions.

Believing that there was need for an assessment of the effect of these singular forces on various aspects of congressional operations, we planned and cochaired the Conference on Congressional Change, held by the Center for Congressional and Presidential Studies on October 8, 1994, at American University in Washington, D.C. The conflict-torn 103rd Congress was just adjourning, having adopted a number of innovations that left members and observers frustrated that an even longer list of agenda items was left unresolved. A month later, the congressional elections dramatically changed the market for innovation on Capitol Hill. As changes that promised to affect nearly every aspect of Congress were being discussed and implemented, we asked our authors to take a fresh look at their subjects. The result, we believe, is a revealing before-and-after examination of congressional reform as a work in progress, illuminating not only the specific innovations but also the contexts within which they developed.

Plan of the Book

This book is organized around the topic of congressional change in the 1990s. In describing and evaluating recent reforms, the authors also focus on the major sources of stability. To understand what has happened on Capitol Hill both before and after the 1994 elections, one must think about Congress as a complex organization responding to its environment. Most change is part of an ongoing struggle over coming to terms with external demands and internal stresses (Davidson 1992, 5-10). The institution adapts to outside environmental forces and public expectations, and to internal workload tasks and organizational arrangements. Actually, we should speak of two institutions, for the House and Senate respond differently to these contending forces. We attempt to set forth in Chapter 1 the framework for analysis.

The historical context for the remaking of Congress and the 1994 election is described by Leroy N. Rieselbach in Chapter 2. He analyzes causes and characteristics of congressional change in the twentieth century. Some reforms have been largely invisible, noticed only by the closest observers of Congress; others, like most of those in the 104th Congress, are highly publicized.

Congressional committees gather information, evaluate alternative policies, draft and refine legislation, oversee executive branch agencies, and educate members. As the nerve ends of Congress, committees respond to a wide range of influences from the public, interest groups, the executive branch, and members of the two chambers. In the story of congressional change during the 1990s, committees play a leading role. In Chapter 3 Roger H. Davidson examines reasons for and features of recent committee system reforms.

In Chapter 4 Sarah A. Binder and Steven S. Smith explore House-Senate relations and patterns of stability and change in rules and procedures. Walter J. Oleszek and C. Lawrence Evans, staff members of the Joint Committee on the Organization of Congress during the 103rd Congress, relate in Chapter 5 the inside politics of the Joint Committee—only the third such panel in history. The authors evaluate the successes and failures of the Joint Committee and assess its influence upon the major innovations adopted by the 104th Congress. In Chapter 6 Barbara Sinclair assesses the momentous shifts in congressional party leadership. She delineates criteria for judging Congress, using that framework to analyze and evaluate leadership reforms that have been adopted or proposed.

Political demands for congressional change have been building over the past decade. Public support for Congress dropped to historic lows in the 1990s, and Congress bashing became an irresistible sport of the media as well as members of Congress. Norman J. Ornstein and Amy L. Schenkenberg describe these external demands for institutional reform in Chapter 7.

Congress considered a wide range of reforms in the 1990s that would fundamentally change the way the institution makes decisions about taxing, borrowing, and spending. The political and historical contexts for the line-item veto, the Balanced Budget Amendment, unfunded mandates reform, and other proposals are discussed by James A. Thurber in Chapter 8.

Campaign finance reform and lobby reform—the "forgotten reforms" of the 1990s (always on the agenda but never passed)—are examined, respectively, by Candice J. Nelson in Chapter 9 and Ronald G. Shaiko in Chapter 10. Legislators' and scholars' attempts to monitor and assist in the process of change are portrayed by Thomas E. Mann in Chapter 11, "Renewing Congress: A Report from the Front Lines."

Just as the present era of upheaval did not begin when voters cast their ballots in November 1994, so it did not end when the ballots were counted and the victors proclaimed. Our analysis ends with our own reflections about what happened and why.

Acknowledgments

As coeditors of this volume, we have accumulated numerous debts that we wish to acknowledge. The Conference on Congressional Change that we cochaired in October 1994 could not have succeeded without the support and encouragement of Dean Neil Kerwin of the School of Public Affairs at American University. We also thank Sharon Drumm, David Farmer, and Mimosa Jones of the Center for Congressional and Presidential Studies for their excellent support with the conference and in the preparation of the manuscript.

At Congressional Quarterly Books, we have once again been privileged to work with an outstanding group of professionals—many of them old friends, some of them new. Acquisitions Editor Shana Wagger expressed confidence in the project from the beginning and supervised the work throughout. There is no better copyeditor than Barbara de Boinville, and we were gratified she was willing once again to wrestle with our prose. Book Editorial, Design, and Production Director Nancy Lammers and Production Editor Talia Greenberg kept the production process running smoothly and on schedule.

Finally, we want to thank our authors, who, having prepared papers for our October 1994 conference, responded swiftly to our post-election appeal to update their analyses, and in some cases to rewrite their stories' endings. Personal friends as well as valued colleagues, these individuals are exemplary members of that highly visible community of congressional scholars who analyze the institution dispassionately but who care passionately about its effectiveness.

Among the senators and representatives who serve at any given moment, relatively few of them take pains to learn systematically about Congress and to work to adapt its structures, procedures, and norms to meet altered circumstances. Most politicians, and indeed most citizens, care mainly about policies and programs and devote little thought to the processes through which those results are achieved. Fortunately, a few members choose to make the institution itself one of their specialties—to become, one might say, institutional entrepreneurs. Congressional scholars naturally feel a special bond to those far-sighted public servants, and so we hope this book will acknowledge and illuminate their efforts.

James A. Thurber
Roger H. Davidson

CONTRIBUTORS

SARAH A. BINDER is research associate in governmental studies at the Brookings Institution. Her work on procedural politics in Congress appears in the *Brookings Review,* the *Encyclopedia of the U.S. Congress* (1995), the *American Political Science Review* (forthcoming), and the *Journal of Politics* (forthcoming). She is currently coauthoring a book with Steven S. Smith on the politics of the Senate filibuster.

ROGER H. DAVIDSON is professor of government and politics at the University of Maryland, College Park. He has served as senior specialist in American national government and public administration with the Congressional Research Service, U.S. Library of Congress. His books with Walter J. Oleszek include *Congress and Its Members,* 4th ed. (CQ Press, 1994), and *Governing: Readings and Cases in American Politics,* 2nd ed. (CQ Press, 1991); other books include *A More Perfect Union,* 4th ed. (1989), and *On Capitol Hill,* 2nd ed. (1972). He is coeditor of the *Encyclopedia of the U.S. Congress* (1995) and a fellow of the National Academy of Public Administration.

C. LAWRENCE EVANS is associate professor of government at the College of William and Mary. He has written a book, *Leadership in Committee* (1991), and a number of articles about the Senate committee system. A former Brookings Institution fellow and APSA congressional fellow, he served on the Joint Committee on the Organization of Congress from 1992 to 1994 as the staff representative of Rep. Lee H. Hamilton.

THOMAS E. MANN is director of governmental studies and W. Averell Harriman senior fellow in American governance at the Brookings Institution. With Norman J. Ornstein he codirected the AEI-Brookings Renewing Congress Project, which produced three reports and two edited volumes: *Congress, the Press, and the Public* (1994) and *Intensive Care: How Congress Shapes Health Policy* (1995). He and Ornstein are now working on "Back to the Future of Congress," a popular treatment of the arguments developed in the Renewing Congress Project.

CANDICE J. NELSON is assistant professor of government at American University and academic director of the university's Campaign Management Institute. Prior to coming to American University she was a visiting fellow at the Brookings Institution. She is coeditor, with James A. Thurber, of *Campaigns and Elections: American Style* (1995); coauthor of *The Myth of the Independent Voter* (1992); and coauthor of *The Money Chase* (1990). She has been an APSA congressional fellow and a special assistant to Sen. Alan Cranston.

WALTER J. OLESZEK is senior specialist in American national government at the Congressional Research Service. In 1993 he served as policy director of the Joint Committee on the Organization of Congress. His latest book is *Congressional Procedures and the Policy Process,* 4th ed. (CQ Press, forthcoming). With Roger H. Davidson, he wrote or edited *Congress and Its Members,* 4th ed. (CQ Press, 1994); *Governing: Readings and Cases in American Politics,* 2nd ed. (CQ Press, 1991); and *Congress against Itself* (1977), as well as numerous other books and articles.

NORMAN J. ORNSTEIN is resident scholar at the American Enterprise Institute. He is codirecting, with Thomas E. Mann of the Brookings Institution, the Renewing Congress Project, a major, comprehensive examination of Congress. His books include *Vital Statistics on Congress, 1995-96,* 8th ed. (CQ Inc., forthcoming); *Renewing Congress,* with Thomas E. Mann (1993); and *Congress in Change* (1975).

LEROY N. RIESELBACH is professor of political science at Indiana University. He has written numerous articles and books on American national politics and political behavior, including *Congressional Reform* (CQ Press, 1994) and *Congressional Politics* (1973).

AMY L. SCHENKENBERG is research assistant at the American Enterprise Institute. She is working on the Renewing Congress Project.

RONALD G. SHAIKO is associate professor of government and academic director of the Lobbying Institute at American University. He received the 1993-1994 William A. Steiger congressional fellowship, awarded by the American Political Science Association. He is currently working on a book entitled *The Art and Craft of Lobbying.*

BARBARA SINCLAIR is professor of political science at the University of California, Riverside. Her publications on the U.S. Congress include *Legislators, Leaders and Lawmaking: The U.S. House of Representatives in the Postreform Era* (1995) and *The Transformation of the U.S. Senate* (1989). She served as an APSA congressional fellow in the office of the House majority leader from 1978 to 1979 and was a participant-observer in the office of the Speaker from 1987 to 1988.

STEVEN S. SMITH is professor of political science at the University of Minnesota and an associate staff member at the Brookings Institution. He served as an APSA congressional fellow from 1980 to 1981. His publications include *The American*

Congress (1994); *Committees in Congress,* 2nd ed. (CQ Press, 1990); *Call to Order* (1989); and *Managing Uncertainty in the House of Representatives* (1988).

JAMES A. THURBER is professor of government and director of the Center for Congressional and Presidential Studies and the Campaign Management and Lobbying Institutes at American University. He has participated in congressional reorganization efforts headed by Rep. David Obey and Sen. Adlai Stevenson, Jr. His books include *Rivals for Power* (CQ Press, forthcoming); *Campaigns and Elections: American Style,* with Candice J. Nelson (1995); *Setting Course: A Congressional Management Guide,* coauthored (1994); and *Divided Democracy: Cooperation and Conflict Between the President and Congress* (CQ Press, 1991).

1

REMAKING CONGRESS AFTER THE ELECTORAL EARTHQUAKE OF 1994

James A. Thurber

The 1994 midterm elections brought an overwhelming victory for the Republican Party and profound changes in the policy agenda and the structure of Congress. Divided party government returned to Washington. The 1994 election was the biggest midterm loss for an incumbent president since 1946 when President Harry S. Truman lost 55 Democratic seats. Democrats had controlled the House of Representatives since 1952, enjoying by far the longest period of single-party control in U.S. history. However one interprets the 1994 elections, they significantly altered how Congress operated, what policy issues were pushed to the top of its agenda, and how such policies were likely to be processed. The elections helped to set the foundation for remaking Congress, the topic of our book.

Eighty-six freshmen entered the House and 11 new members came to the Senate as a result of the 1994 election. The 104th Congress opened with 230 Republicans, 204 Democrats, and one Independent. The last time a Congress had such a split was in 1955 when the Democrats had 232 members and the Republicans 203. In the 104th Congress one-fourth of the Senate had less than three years of congressional experience. In the House almost half the membership had served less than three years. Well over half of the House of Representatives are new members since 1990.[1] The addition of a large group of freshmen in 1992 and 1994 shifted the chamber's center of gravity toward reform, reflecting what they thought the voters wanted.

The 1994 midterm election devastated the Democratic Party, which lost 52 House and 8 Senate seats. After the election it lost several more seats when Sen. Richard C. Shelby of Alabama, Sen. Ben Nighthorse Campbell of Colorado, and two southern representatives switched to the Republican Party. For the first time in 40 years, the Republican Party controlled both the House and Senate. For the first time in 60 years, the Republicans had parity with the Democrats at the national, state, and local levels of government with the loss of ten governorships, six state senates, and nine state houses. Every Republican incumbent who sought reelection to the House, Senate, or governorship won in 1994. Thirty-five Republican challengers beat House Democratic incumbents, and five Republican gubernatorial challengers defeated Democratic incumbent governors. Republicans also won a disproportionate share of open governorships and House and Senate seats. Republicans earned a net gain of 17 in the 52 open-seat House contests and lost only 4 Republican-controlled House open seats to the Democrats. A number of influential Democratic incumbents lost—including Thomas S. Foley, the first Speaker defeated for reelection since 1860; Jack Brooks, the chairman of the Judiciary Committee; Dan Rostenkowski, the indicted former chairman of the House Ways and Means Committee; Dan Glickman, Intelligence Committee Chairman; and Neal Smith, an Appropriations subcommittee chairman. The 1994 election was one of the most negative, most expensive, most anti-Democratic incumbent, anti-Washington, anti-incumbent president campaigns in modern times.

The 1994 vote revealed a continuation of southern incremental (or secular) realignment. For the first time in history a majority of the South's senators and representatives were Republicans. The election reinforced the hypothesis that a permanent shift or realignment of southern white males from the Democratic Party to the Republican Party is occurring. The 1992 supporters of independent H. Ross Perot voted more Republican than Democratic (68 percent in 1994). Independents also voted more Republican (57 percent in 1994 compared with 46 percent in 1992). Men voted more Republican (57 percent in 1994, up from 48 percent in 1992). Whites voted more Republican (58 percent in 1994, up from 50 percent in 1992). Ninety percent of those who said they identified with conservative religious groups voted Republican (Voter News Service exit polls quoted in Curran 1994C, 10).

The 1992 presidential election had called into question claims of Republican realignment or of a durable change in the distribution of party support by voters. But the 1994 midterm election confirmed the incremental realignment, especially of conservative southern Democratic white males moving permanently to the Republican Party. The secular realignment was a major reason Senator Shelby and Representatives Deal and Laughlin felt it safe to switch to the Republican Party following the move in 1983 of Senator Phil Gramm of Texas from Republican to Democrat.

President Clinton's narrow 1992 popular vote plurality of 43 percent raised questions about Democratic dominance; the 1994 Republican sweep in the House, Senate, gubernatorial races, and state legislative assemblies left little doubt that the Reagan Democrats had left home permanently. The three-way race in the 1992 presidential election was a dealigning election: old voting patterns broke down without being replaced by new ones. Nearly 20 million voters (almost 20 percent) rejected both major parties and supported Perot. This weakening party loyalty led to the overwhelming Republican victory in 1994 as significant numbers of independents and Perot voters elected Republican candidates at the national, state, and local levels. The 1994 midterm elections revealed a continuing change in the regional base of Republican Party support in the South. The harsh reality for the Democratic Party was that the 104th Congress had a majority of Republican senators and representatives from the South. The realignment is long term unless the Democratic Party can move to the middle ideologically to recapture the white southern male voters.

What was different about the 1994 election campaigns? Although simplistic and emotional appeals to the voters persisted, issues were extensively discussed through the debates and campaign themes and strategies. The news media covered the issues more thoroughly than they did in recent elections and the campaign turned more on issues and less on personalities.

The campaign was "nationalized" with a clear theme and message in House Republican candidates' "Contract with America," masterminded by Rep. Newt Gingrich of Georgia, who became Speaker in 1995. The electorate was angry at Congress and Washington; they voted for change, and they got it with immediate and long-term change for Congress. The 1994 election campaign continued the use of blatantly negative attack advertisements. Voter distrust of government and politicians continued in the 1994 elections with the growth of the term limits movement and high levels of cynicism expressed at the polls (see Chapter 7 by Norman J. Ornstein and Amy L. Schenkenberg).

The 1994 congressional elections also brought changes in the campaign landscape. Paid media saw the introduction of a technique called "morphing," in which one candidate's face was electronically transformed into another's face. This was most successfully done by Republican candidates attacking their Democratic opponents; the faces of Democratic congressional candidates all over the country were "morphed" into the face of Bill Clinton, the supposedly unpopular president.

The 1994 election also saw record spending in the congressional elections. Preliminary reports from the Federal Election Commission indicated spending increased 18 percent over 1992 (see Chapter 9 by Candice J. Nelson). Moreover, Republican challengers and open-seat candidates apparently had unusual financial success. In the past Republican challengers to Democratic incumbents were typically the most meagerly funded candidates, outspent at least four to one. In 1994 a particularly strong group of Republican challengers and open seat candidates were generously funded. Preliminary figures indicate that median spending by Republican challengers almost doubled from 1992, and median spending by Republican open-seat candidates increased 60 percent.

Nationalizing Congressional Elections

The late Thomas P. (Tip) O'Neill, Jr., former Speaker of the House, once said that "all politics is local." On September 27, 1994, the House Republican Party defied that statement. That day more than 300 Republican congressional candidates met on the steps of the U.S. Capitol's West Front to sign the "Contract with America." These Republicans together pledged that if elected they would support changes in congressional procedures and bring to votes in the House a series of proposals long supported by many in the Republican Party, proposals such as a Balanced Budget Amendment, a line-item veto, and term limits for members of Congress. By collectively signing this agreement, the Republican candidates were pledging to run on a set of national issues, not just issues of importance to a particular congressional district. GOP campaign tactics and funding patterns were centrally directed (another form of "nationalization").

The Republicans' Contract also made this pledge:

On the first day of the 104th Congress, the new Republican majority will immediately pass the following major reforms, aimed at restoring the faith and trust of the American people in their government: first, require all laws that apply to the rest of the country also apply equally to the Congress; second, select a major, independent auditing firm to conduct a comprehensive audit of Congress for waste, fraud or abuse; third, cut the number of House committees and cut committee staff by one-third; fourth, limit the terms of all committee chairs; fifth, ban the casting of proxy votes in committee; sixth, require committee meetings to be open to the public; seventh, require a three-fifths majority to pass a tax increase; eighth, guarantee an honest accounting of our federal budget by implementing zero based budgeting. (Federal News Service 1994)

The Contract also called for a balanced budget/tax limitation amendment (not passed within the first 100 days of the 104th Congress) and a legislative line-item veto (passed by House and Senate in different forms and sent to Conference Committee within the 100-day "deadline").

The ten-point Republican plan also included anticrime measures, welfare changes, support for families, tax relief for the middle class and the elderly, small business incentives, increased defense spending, tort reform, and term limits. House Republicans pledged to introduce and vote on bills addressing each of these areas in the first 100 days, and they kept their promise. They did not promise to *pass* all of these reforms within the first 100 days, and they failed to pass term limits in the House. The Contract was very popular with House Republican candidates, less popular with governors and state legislators, and unknown to more than half of the electorate (according to all exit polls the day of the election).

Capitol Hill Aftershocks

The 1994 campaign themes, strategies, and messages helped to bring about a major change in American politics. Campaigns do make a difference for governance, as was clearly seen in the shift of the congressional policy agendas after the election. What impact did the campaign have on the remaking of the structure and organization of Congress?

Despite the evenness of the Republicans' return to power in Congress (roughly 53 percent of the seats in each chamber), the elections by no means had the same effect on the Senate and the House. The immediate impact of the election and the Contract with America was greatest on the House of Representatives and less on the Senate. Republican senators did not sign the Contract, and they were critical (or skeptical) of several of its provisions.

The House: Strengthening the Leadership

As a majoritarian institution, the House changed dramatically. The rules of the 104th Congress, with changes crafted in the Republican Conference and adopted on the floor by a series of lopsided votes, embraced many elements drawn from past complaints of the minority party in Congress. The House of Representatives made major changes in the way it is organized, and the way it is managed (see Leroy N. Rieselbach's Chapter 2 on the history of congressional reform). Speaker Gingrich centralized agenda setting, and he may be the strongest Speaker of the House since Thomas Brackett Reed and Joseph G. Cannon around the turn of the twentieth century.

The changes in the 104th Congress were propelled by two forces: (1) a strong, unified House Republican Party that ran on a common ideology, the Contract, and (2) Newt Gingrich, who effectively consolidated power in the Speakership (see Chapter 6 by Barbara Sinclair on leadership reforms).

The new Speakership actually dates from the 1970s, when majority party reformers fought to counteract the committees' "old bulls." Speaker O'Neill exploited the tools bequeathed by the reformers without alienating policy protagonists. His successor, Texas Democrat Jim Wright, pushed his prerogatives so relentlessly that his enemies, most notably Newt Gingrich, unleashed a successful effort to oust him. The lesson was not lost on the next Speaker, Thomas S. Foley, D-Wash., who pursued a kinder, gentler course. Among many ironies, Speaker Gingrich has followed more in Wright's footsteps than in Foley's.

To the powerful Speakership he inherited, Gingrich added new elements. Using the leverage of his loyal followers, he effectively appointed all of the chairs of House committees, ignoring seniority by sometimes passing over the most senior members. Several chairs felt that they owed their positions to him, including three freshmen who were appointed subcommittee chairs. The Republican Conference also restricted the power of the chairs. It placed term limits of six years on their positions and banned proxy voting by the chairs, thus undermining their ability to act independently of the Speaker. Under the new House rules, the majority leader, not the committee chairs, wields procedural control of limitation amendments ("riders") on funding bills.

Speaker Gingrich and the new House leadership also assigned all freshmen to committees. Putting freshmen on the four most important committees in the House (Rules, Ways and Means, Appropriations, and Commerce) was unprecedented in the history of the modern Congress. This move reinforced their loyalty to the Speaker. Three-fifths of the Republicans were elected to the House in the last two elections; many felt they owed their seats (at least partially) to Gingrich, and in any event they are his natural ideological allies. Gingrich also appointed a new House Administrator, ended funding for the legislative service organizations, and slashed $18 billion from the fiscal year 1995 budget through a special House-generated rescissions bill. All of these actions helped to reinforce the new centralized mode of operating in the House

In addition, Speaker Gingrich appointed the chair of the Republican Congressional Campaign Committee, thus having a direct impact on the flow of campaign funds and political action committee dollars for future elections for Republican members of the House. This was another method of assuring loyalty and consolidation of power by controlling the "mother's milk of politics," campaign funds.

Former Ways and Means Committee chair Dan Rostenkowski summarized the centralization of power under Gingrich best when he wrote: "He's making basic changes that are a virtual guarantee that the House at the turn of the century will be significantly different than it was at the beginning of this decade, irrespective of how long the Republicans retain control. The Democrats won't be able to put Humpty Dumpty back together again. And they shouldn't want to" (Rosenbaum 1994b, 17).

Under the leadership of Republican representative David Dreier of California, vice-chair of the Joint Committee on the Organization of Congress, the House made the greatest changes in the committee system in almost 50 years (since the 1946 Legislative Reorganization Act). Roger H. Davidson describes these changes in his chapter, and C. Lawrence Evans and Walter J. Oleszek discuss the politics behind the Joint Committee on the Organization of Congress that led to the committee reforms. The Republicans eliminated three committees, reduced the number of subcommittees by 20 percent, rearranged several jurisdictional subjects, renamed ten panels, and opened up nearly all committee meetings to the public and television cameras.

The Senate: Decentralization Under Attack

The Senate, an individualistic institution, was less swept by change than the House. For calculating winning coalitions the number 60 (the majority needed to shut off a filibuster) has replaced the number 51 (the normal legislative majority), as discussed by Steven S. Smith and Sarah A. Binder in their chapter on stability and change in the rules of the House and Senate. Thus leaders must seek cross-party alliances in the Senate. The Republicans have fewer seats than the Democrats had in the previous Congress. Despite the conservative coloring of the GOP class of 1994, a core group of moderates (six to eight or more on given issues) has been the object of ardent lobbying from both sides of the aisle as well as from President Clinton.

Recent experience with Senate party turnovers in 1981 and 1987 leads one to expect less than cataclysmic changes. In 1981, regaining power after a 26-year hiatus, GOP leaders instituted innovations to coordinate committee actions and plan Senate business, but the reforms did not endure.

The "new Senate" created in the 1960s and institutionalized in the 1970s survived virtually intact into the 1990s. Senate folkways, including personal assertiveness, committee and subcommittee autonomy, and large staffs, although initially associated with the ascendancy of liberal Democrats, persisted because they seemed to serve the interests of all senators, regardless of party or ideology. After the 1994 elections, senators resisted major procedural reforms or staff cuts. Although they have moved to trim committee spending and limit subcommittees, their most dramatic proposals (eliminating all joint committees and the Office of Technology Assessment) did not come close to the breadth of change in the House.

Another lesson of the 1980s is the Senate's potentially pivotal role in a period of divided government. In 1981 Senate Republican leaders persuaded the Reagan

White House to stress its economic agenda and soft-pedal the so-called social issues. Initially, the Senate spearheaded the president's economic program, pressuring the Democratic House to follow suit. After the first year Senate leaders grasped the initiative from the White House and provided leadership, again forcing the House to respond. In the 104th Congress the Senate found itself in a quite different mediating role—between a Democratic president and a conservative Republican majority in the House.

Putting 1994 into Context

Agitation for changing the way Congress does its business did not materialize overnight as a result of the 1994 elections and the Contract with America. As all of our authors point out, the past decade witnessed mounting tensions on Capitol Hill—between senior leaders and junior members, between appropriators and authorizers, between House and Senate members. Most troubling was the acrimonious and escalating combat in the House between an entrenched, sometimes overbearing, and increasingly desperate Democratic majority and a restless, aggressive, and sometimes reckless Republican minority. Bitter skirmishes erupted over the Democrats' partisan resolution of a 1984 contested election in Indiana's 8th District, their harsh treatment of the minority, especially during Wright's Speakership (1987-1989), and their alleged responsibility for the House "bank" scandal that surfaced in 1991. The partisan battle was fought on many fronts—on the floor, in committees, in public forums, and in election campaigns.

The GOP reform proposals—eight of which were cited in the Contract with America—had been refined and expanded during the 103rd Congress. On January 5, 1993, answering the Democrats' proposed changes in House Rules, Gerald B. H. Solomon of New York, the ranking Rules Committee Republican, offered the party's 43-point "Mandate for Change in the People's House"—detailed proposals for committee and floor procedures, budget process reforms, legislative-executive relations, and housekeeping matters. Later that year the Joint Committee, urged by reform-minded members and reluctantly supported by Democratic leaders, compiled volumes of testimony and hundreds of proposals for reform, including those of the Renewing Congress Project of the Brookings Institution and American Enterprise Institute (see discussion by Norman J. Ornstein and Amy L. Schenkenberg in Chapter 7 and by Thomas E. Mann in Chapter 11). The effort ended in failure, especially frustrating to House Republicans. Joint Committee Vice-Chair Dreier charged that the chairman's markup bill was "neither bipartisan nor comprehensive," noting that it addressed neither committee jurisdictional realignment nor major procedural changes (see Dreier's Foreword to this book). During the acrimonious markups, 33 strengthening amendments were offered by the GOP (see Chapter 5 by Evans and Oleszek). Eight were accepted, but no fewer than 25 failed in 6-6 party line votes—which Dreier denounced as "the attempts of a small but vocal faction of the Democratic caucus to derail this effort" (Davidson 1995, 29).

After these setbacks the Republican Conference was primed to overhaul House structures and procedures, and perhaps even to tackle the contentious and long-overdue task of realigning committee jurisdictions. GOP leaders for the most part showed commendable restraint in dealing with the opposition Democrats. Considering the partisan mistrust in the House and even fiercer animosity between the House and Senate in the 103rd Congress, the reforms of the 104th House were mainly fair and balanced. To give their foes a taste of their own medicine, the Republicans had only to readopt the rules of the Democratic 103rd Congress. Instead, the new rules reaffirmed the minority's right to offer motions to recommit measures to committee—often the only chance to get a vote on the minority's alternative bill.

The postelection reforms centralized power in the House leadership and weakened committee roadblocks to the legislative agenda, as demonstrated by the 104th Congress's swift action on the Contract with America. The House has recast its committee system, imposing the Republican leadership's agenda on committees and subcommittees long accustomed to charting their own course. The zero-sum budgetary game has continued to change, but three-fifths approval of tax increases and the Balanced Budget Amendment failed to win support in the first 100 days of the 104th Congress (see Chapter 8 on the politics of congressional budget reform). The elections of the 1990s seemed to have little impact on campaign finance and lobbying—two long overdue areas of reform, as chapters by Candice J. Nelson and Ronald G. Shaiko explain.

Note

1. The 1994 election landslide for the Republican party followed the Democrats' success in 1992 in recapturing the White House: Bill Clinton won 43 percent of the popular vote in a close three-way race with George Bush and H. Ross Perot. In the 1992 U. S. House of Representatives races, 368 incumbents sought reelection and 325 were successful, bringing 110 new members to the House and a net loss of 10 members for the Democrats. The House bank scandal and redistricting led to high levels of retirements and some defeats, especially in party primaries.

2

CONGRESSIONAL CHANGE:
Historical Perspectives

Leroy N. Rieselbach

When I first came to Washington, people did think we were capable of coming up with solutions. Now we have very little credibility. They don't think we've done anything relevant.

Rep. Robert T. Matsui, D-Calif.

Our concern about upsetting anybody at home is the driving force in Congress. We are afraid to make tough decisions.

Rep. Michael N. Castle, R-Del.

We're dealing with two conflicting impulses. People say "There are problems, do something about it." And then they say, "We don't trust you to do the right thing."

Rep. Philip R. Sharp, D-Ind., retired in 1994

. . . [M]ost Americans are skeptical about the institution of Congress, and I think if we worked toward more openness in the [legislative] process it might help restore confidence.

Rep. Richard J. Durbin, D-Ill.

Americans are congenitally displeased with Congress. They want the institution to change but often doubt whether their elected representatives will "do the right thing." [1]

Contrary to its critics' charges, Congress changes constantly. Change usually comes quietly, noticed only by the closest observers of the legislature: a rules change here, a new precedent there, the gradual erosion of customary ways of conducting business. Thus, Senate rules now permit only 30 hours of postcloture debate, the House Energy and Commerce Committee won jurisdiction over emerging consumer protection issues (King 1994), and the House seems increasingly disinclined to adhere to seniority in selecting its leaders.

Occasionally, however, as the efforts of the newly ensconced Republican majority in the 104th Congress make clear, the legislature undertakes more self-conscious efforts, often labeled reform, to reshape institutional structures and processes. The legislature does so in response to its members' perceptions that their assembly is an ineffective policy maker or that it is at risk of losing the public approbation necessary to sustain its legitimacy. The years 1910-1911, 1970-1977, and 1995 are notable manifestations of the reform impulse. More rarely still, reform is embodied in a major statute, a legislative reorganization act, such as those enacted in 1946 and 1970.

Whatever form it takes, change continually alters Congress. The party-dominated legislature of the early twentieth century gave way to the committee-centered institution of the 1980s. The 1990s spawned proposals for significant change as Congress reeled under the burden of both ineffective policy making and a series of scandals that undermined its popular standing. In the 104th Congress the new Republican majority came to power pledging to reform the way the legislature conducts the nation's business.

Defining Change and Reform

To determine the causes, course, and consequences of congressional change is no easy task. *Reform*—intentional efforts to reshape institutional structures and processes—is only one, and perhaps not the most significant, type of organizational change. *Change,* a broader notion, can affect basic institutional patterns. It can be inadvertent or intended, gradual or abrupt, unobtrusive or dramatic. Of the two, change appears more pervasive and fundamental. Reform is merely one type of change: an explicit attempt to bring about preferable results through specific structural or procedural alterations.

Change may flow from a multiplicity of causes (Rohde and Shepsle 1978). Events outside the legislature may directly affect it. Recession at home or war abroad may highlight Congress's deficiencies. Lawmakers' failure to cope with old issues may goad reformers to restructure the legislature. Such external developments may raise new issues and induce an *agenda change* (Sinclair 1982), which requires new institutional forms. In addition, *membership turnover* brings new people with different backgrounds, experiences, and perspectives to the legislature; newcomers may operate the existing machinery in ways at variance with old routines, or they may try to rebuild the legislative engine to produce more efficient performance. Alternatively, incumbent legislators may be compelled by circumstances to reassess their views, leading to policy change, reform efforts, or both (Asher and Weisberg 1978; Brady and Sinclair 1984; Brady 1988). Events, new issues, and new members, neither planned nor predictable, may contribute to legislative change as much or more than any self-conscious reform movement.

Change flows from pressures inside and outside Congress. *Internal* forces may generate change. Representatives and senators may come to recognize that their institution does not work well, that they have ceded policy-making authority to the executive to the detriment of their own ability to formulate programs or that the legislative process itself has prevented speedy attention to items on the policy agenda. Procedural defects may preclude treating and resolving the issues that the voters in their states and districts sent them to Washington to handle. *External* pressures from the country at large also may induce change. Policy gridlock, the failure to enact workable programs, or ethical transgressions may threaten disaster at the polls, an unhappy prospect for legislators who aspire to long-term careers in Washington. Institutional change may offer the possibility that Congress will get and stay "in touch" with the governed, acting to meet citizen demands and to secure the support of the electorate. Formally, of course, all change is internally driven, since it is the members of Congress who alter their institution. On occasion, and the 104th Congress is the most recent example, the lawmakers seem to feel compelled to respond to popular disapproval of the legislature. In that sense change is a reaction to external pressures. Change has come to Congress pragmatically and incrementally in response to contemporary political pressures.

One strand of change has sought to foster *responsibility*, to make Congress more capable of enacting effective policy with dispatch. A responsible legislature resolves policy problems successfully and efficiently. A second strand of change has emphasized *responsiveness*, the capacity of Congress to consider carefully and act in accordance with the expressed preferences of those whom its actions will affect—namely, citizens, organized groups, local and state governments, presidents, and federal bureaucrats. There is a tension between responsibility and responsiveness: a responsible Congress will act rapidly and decisively; a responsive assembly will move slowly, waiting for those with opinions to voice them and for some basic agreement to emerge. A third focus of change has been *accountability*, the ability of citizens to discover what Congress and its members have done and to hold them to account for what they have, or have not, accomplished. Responsibility, responsiveness, and accountability offer benchmarks against which to assess Congress's performance.[2]

Change to promote responsibility tends to be internally driven; members, recognizing their policy-making shortcomings, undertake to remove structural and procedural impediments to efficient enactment of legislation. Accountability-driven reform, by contrast, is most often a reaction to external forces; the lawmakers act to revive flagging public confidence in Congress's ability and integrity. Change to enhance responsiveness flows from mixed incentives. Some legislators, finding that House and Senate organization and procedure block their ability to influence the substance of policy, seek ways to claim a piece of the policy-making action for themselves. Others, encountering difficulty in serving their constituents, likewise try to create and claim new avenues of authority in the name of representation. Both motives encourage change that forges closer links between the electorate and the elected. The history of congressional change in this century reflects the interplay among these incentives.

Twentieth Century Change and Reform

Reform in the twentieth century has concentrated on the House of Representatives (Galloway and Wise 1976). (Table 2-1 lists some notable landmarks of congressional change.) The larger chamber represents more diverse constituencies than does the Senate; it relies more heavily on a division of labor that uses an

3 Criteria : responsibility , responsiveness , accountability

elaborate system of standing committees, and the personal relationships among its members tend to be less intimate. These circumstances require formal procedures to define an organizational structure that will permit the House to work its will. The rules, when they seem to thwart the purposes of a significant number of members, become the targets for change. The smaller Senate, in sharp contrast, is more open and flexible. Senators represent more heterogeneous constituencies; they have more opportunity to act as generalists, and their personal relationships, while not necessarily intimate, are closer than those among House members. They have less need for strong political parties to impose some central discipline, and they can handle the procedural requisites informally with less recourse to an elaborate set of formal rules. The Senate, in short, has proven more adaptable than the House, and major reform efforts have focused on the latter.

Reform for Responsiveness: The 1910-1911 Revolt Against Cannon

The legislative legacy of the nineteenth century was a House of Representatives more responsible than responsive. The leaders, particularly the Speaker, acting for partisan purposes and with partisan majorities, came to dominate House proceedings. Speaker Thomas B. Reed, a Republican from Maine, established the authority of the majority party. As presiding officer, he dominated floor proceedings, and by controlling the Committee on Rules he defined the terms under which legislation would be considered on the floor. The Democratic minority fumed but was powerless to overcome the Republican majority. The latter enacted its legislative program, or blocked the Democrats', at its pleasure.

Reed's Republican successor, Joseph G. Cannon of Illinois, built on existing precedents to centralize House operations under his, and his party's, aegis. Cannon not only managed floor proceedings with an iron hand, but also controlled the careers of the members. He took charge of the committee assignment process. Members served on panels at the Speaker's discretion. Members opposed so powerful a party leader at their political peril; their careers depended on his good will. The House, for all practical purposes, was Cannon's fiefdom. It could act promptly and efficiently in conformity with the Speaker's wishes, but members, including more moderate elements of his own party, were unable to respond to their own, and their constituents', policy preferences. The House was responsible but unresponsive during this period of "czar rule."

In the process of bending the chamber to his will, Speaker Cannon unwittingly sowed the seeds of reform; a bipartisan majority emerged in 1910 to strip the Speaker of his powers and to undercut the ability of the majority party to have its way. New rules denied the Speaker the authority to appoint members to House committees. Cannon was denied a seat on the Rules Committee, making it difficult for him to control the content of legislation or its movement to the House floor. His power, as presiding officer, was sharply curtailed.

The reformers also set up a Consent Calendar to provide for easy, automatic treatment of routine bills. A discharge petition procedure permitted majorities to extract legislation from recalcitrant committees. The minority won the right to

Table 2-1   Landmarks of Legislative Change and Reform

1910–1911	"Revolt" against Speaker of the House Joseph G. Cannon, R-Ill., stripped the Speaker of ability to manage House affairs through control of powerful political parties; marked the advent of the modern, committee-centered Congress.
1921	Budget and Accounting Act: assigned the president the task of submitting a unified executive budget to Congress; initiated contemporary budget practices.
1946	Legislative Reorganization Act: sought to restructure committee system, create a comprehensive budget process, and provide Congress with improved information resources.
1961	House Rules Committee enlarged.
1970–1977	Major postwar reform era, beginning formally with passage of the Legislative Reorganization Act of 1970: simultaneously de-centralized decision making in the House process (for example, by empowering subcommittees), strengthened the political parties (for example, by enhancing the authority of the Speaker), and opened congressional deliberations to public scrutiny ("sunshine" rules and ethics and campaign finance reforms).
1974	Congressional Budget and Impoundment Control Act: reformed budget process and centralized decisions about spending, taxing, and deficits.
1985	Balanced Budget and Emergency Deficit Control Act (known as the Gramm-Rudman-Hollings bill after its sponsors): revised budget process significantly.
1990	Budget Enforcement Act: major revision of budget process.
1992–1994	Revival of interest in broad congressional reform: Joint Committee on the Organization of Congress considered structural change; renewed interest in reform of lobbying and campaign finance.
1995	Republican majority revised House rules; in particular it opened access to congressional deliberations, strengthened the party leadership, reshaped the committee system, cut congressional staff, and streamlined the administration of the House.

offer a recommittal motion prior to the final vote on the passage of legislation; the dissidents could propose to send the bill back to committee, with instructions to substitute their proposals for those embodied in the committee's version. A year later, in 1911, additional rules changes provided for the election of committee members and leaders. In short, the reformers undermined the ability of a centralized House to act with dispatch. The long-term result of their success was greater freedom for individual members to respond to the interests of their constituents, to exercise authority independently on their own.

Responsible Budgeting: 1921

A responsive Congress, however, made for problems in enacting the federal budget. Budget deficits, particularly the unprecedented spending during World War I, convinced reform-minded progressives that more effective management would curb Congress's tendency to spend large and unnecessary sums for the benefit of special interests (Shuman 1988, 24–31). Consequently, the legislature, in 1921, enacted a Budget and Accounting Act that required the president to submit an annual federal budget. The chief executive was to coordinate the spending requests of the individual departments and agencies of the government and propose a truly national budget. By fixing fiscal responsibility in the White House, reformers expected effective budgeting to follow. Subsequent budgetary politics derive directly from the 1921 act.

Overall, the revolt against Cannon set in train evolutionary change that fundamentally altered the character of Congress. Hierarchical control of the House by a powerful Speaker, with the support of the majority party, gradually gave way to a fragmented, decentralized chamber where independent, individualistic members reached decisions through an intricate politics of negotiation and compromise. The House became "institutionalized" (Polsby 1968); it developed standard operating procedures. Its organizational complexity increased with the emergence of an elaborate committee system. Committees and their chairpersons became the locus of the most important congressional decisions. The political parties became suitors for their own members' affections rather than dispensers of authoritative instructions. Partisan cohesion, when the roll was called, declined over the years.

Congress adopted automatic procedures that served to award and preserve individual members' prerogatives. Seniority (years of consecutive service) defined legislators' standing on their committees; the most senior member of the majority party became panel chair. The rules attempted to spell out the jurisdictions of the burgeoning committees. Norms, unwritten understandings that prescribed and restrained certain behaviors, began to characterize the conduct of congressional business. Lawmakers who failed to observe the folkways—who declined to specialize on a relatively narrow range of policy matters, to act to protect the reputation of the chamber, or to reciprocate favors their colleagues proffered— were denied the respect and influence that membership in the "club" conferred.

By the onset of the Second World War, Congress had become a decentralized institution where individual members shared power widely, if not altogether equally. Parties were weak, acting as brokers in an intricate dance of coalition formation; committees and their chairs were strong, producing Congress's authoritative decisions relatively unchallenged. Although responsive to multiple interests, the legislature was often hard pressed to integrate the views it heard into responsible solutions to policy problems. The lesson seemed to be that a more responsible Congress was needed.

The Legislative Reorganization Act of 1946

Efforts to cope with the Great Depression and the Second World War persuaded many observers that the Congress was ill-equipped to make policy responsibly or to oversee executive branch performance effectively.[3] The message was not lost on Congress, which established in 1945 a Joint Committee on the Organization of Congress. After extensive hearings, the committee weighed in with a proposal advancing some 37 reform recommendations (Davidson 1990). Vested internal interests, mainly those of Democrats holding committee chairs, forced abandonment of many of the committee's most radical ideas. The surviving changes were enacted as the Legislative Reorganization Act of 1946.

The act vastly simplified committee arrangements and wrote them into the House and Senate rules. The 33 Senate committees were reduced to 15, while the 48 House panels were reshuffled into 19; only two House committees and a single Senate committee were actually abolished. A second thrust of the act was to expand legislative expertise. Committee staff resources were enhanced substantially; each committee could hire four specialists. In addition, the Legislative Reference Service of the Library of Congress, a research arm of Congress, was strengthened with a larger, more expert, and better paid staff. The reformers hoped that these new information resources would enable Congress to develop innovative public policy proposals that could compete with those the president initiated. Finally, and boldly, the reorganization act instituted a new budgetary process. Recognizing the incoherence of fiscal policy making in a decentralized legislature, the act established a centralized procedure designed to produce a unified legislative budget that specified the nation's revenues and expenditures.[4]

In operation, there was less to the Legislative Reorganization Act of 1946 than met the eye. Congress subverted the committee restructuring by creating new committees when it so desired, and the proliferation of subcommittees after 1946 enlarged the number of independent work units well beyond the preform total. In the face of opposition from the dominant finance and spending committees, the omnibus legislative budget process was a dead letter by 1950. Enlarged and enhanced staffs endured, but in the hands of independent committees and subcommittees they may have contributed more to the fragmentation of legislative authority than to the creation of an expert Congress poised to challenge a powerful president. The 1946 act recognized the Congress's irresponsibility, but in practice failed to find ways to overcome legislative incapacity and immobilism.

Harnessing the House Rules Committee in the 1960s

During the 1960s, reformers focused on the House Rules Committee, the "traffic cop" that manages the flow of legislation to the House floor. In the previous decade two conservative southern Democrats voted frequently with four conservative Republicans to deadlock the twelve-member committee at 6-6, thus preventing the majority Democrats' policy initiatives from reaching the floor. Following the 1960 election, the liberal bloc in the House narrowly won a difficult fight to enlarge the committee to 15 members, ostensibly giving the majority an 8-7 working margin (Peabody 1963). In the 1970s, the Democrats empowered the Speaker, subject to caucus approval, to nominate Rules members; they set the ratio of members from the majority and minority parties at "2-to-1 plus 1" (9 Democrats and 4 Republicans). Overall, the reformers succeeded in harnessing the sometimes defiant Rules Committee to the party leadership, smoothing the flow of legislation to the House floor (Oppenheimer 1981).

Change and Reform in the 1970s and 1980s

The stimuli for the reforms of the first two-thirds of the century were relatively straightforward. The revolt against Cannon reflected the dissatisfaction of members with the Speaker's autocratic rule. They sought to make Congress more responsive to their preferences and those of their constituents. The 1921 Budget and Accounting Act, the Legislative Reorganization Act of 1946, and the efforts to curb Rules Committee independence were attempts to restore some semblance of the responsibility that the 1910-1911 changes had undercut. In sharp contrast, the decade of the 1970s witnessed wholesale but piecemeal efforts to make Congress simultaneously more responsible, responsive, and accountable. The result was major congressional change that transformed the legislature.[5]

In the 1960s and 1970s, political considerations provided irresistible incentives for reform. Campaign pledges to "improve" a Congress widely seen as ineffective led many newcomers to the legislature to push for change. President Richard Nixon's waning political support gave them the opportunity to do so with minimal political risk. The increasingly large and complex policy agenda often proved intractable. The public, or a newly emerging "public interest" lobbying movement acting on its behalf, made louder and more forceful demands on the legislature and insisted that the lawmakers respond openly. Structural change in the institution of Congress seemed to offer one route to repair policy-making deficiencies and to recapture public esteem. Such alternatives, however, ran up against vested interests in the old ways of doing business; members were disinclined to surrender their established prerogatives.

Reform, when it came, was imposed according to standard congressional operating procedures. It was achieved through the usual bargaining, compromising search for agreements typical of a fragmented, decentralized policy process. Members had neither time nor inclination to pursue some philosophical vision of the ideal Congress; instead they reacted to the difficulties of the moment with a

response to political need

process they found congenial. As a consequence of agitation for change from the Democratic Study Group—an informal caucus of liberal Democrats—and the recommendations of a new Joint Committee on the Organization of Congress, the Legislative Reorganization Act of 1970 inaugurated an unprecedented period of wide-ranging change (Kravitz 1990). In the ensuing years the House Democratic Caucus adopted wholesale changes; bipartisan reform in the Senate was considerably more restrained, although in 1977 the Senate realigned committee jurisdictions and reduced the number of committees and committee assignments (Parris 1979).

Efforts to make Congress more responsible followed two tracks. The first was reclaiming traditional authority ceded unwisely to the president. To resist executive domination, Congress enacted the War Powers Resolution in 1973. Passed over President Nixon's veto, it circumscribed the commander-in-chief's ability to commit the armed forces to combat abroad without congressional approval. Congress could compel the president to withdraw troops within 60 days of deployment if the legislature did not authorize their use. And at any time by concurrent resolution Congress could direct the president to disengage troops involved in an undeclared war.

To regain control over federal expenditures, the legislature enacted the Congressional Budget and Impoundment Control Act of 1974.[6] The law centralized budgetary decision making in Congress and endeavored to produce a coherent, comprehensive budget that compared revenues and expenditures, thus offering a clear picture of the deficit. The act also created new procedures that permitted Congress to curb the president's ability to impound—refuse to spend—duly authorized and appropriated funds. The act did not stem the flow of red ink—members found creative ways to evade its strictures. Congress continued to modify the budget process in 1985 with the Balanced Budget and Emergency Deficit Control Act (the Gramm-Rudman-Hollings bill) and again in 1990 with the Budget Enforcement Act. The former exacted automatic spending cuts if the deficit exceeded prescribed levels; the latter, renewed in 1993, abandoned a focus on the deficit and sought instead to impose spending limits (caps) on domestic, military, and international outlays.

Congress flexed its muscles not only in the domains of foreign policy and domestic budgeting. It also endeavored to strengthen its ability to research and implement new ideas. Building on the precedent of the 1946 reorganization act, Congress gave itself new staff and support agency information resources to enable it to countervail the executive with its own expertise (Weiss 1992).

In all of these ways Congress sought to reclaim authority ceded to the president. The second track Congress followed, in its efforts to become more responsible, was to make the policy-making process less fragmented. To that end, the House Democratic Caucus tried to limit the independence of individual committee chairs. It decreed that seniority would no longer automatically determine who would preside in the committee rooms; it empowered its Steering and Policy Committee to recommend chairs using other criteria, and it retained the right to vote to reject that panel's nominations. The Speaker of the House won new authority to control the Steering and Policy Committee and to nominate, subject to caucus approval, members of the Rules Committee, thus exercising some influence over the conditions under which bills were considered on the House floor. In addition, the Speaker could regulate the flow of legislation to and from committees (through the prerogative to refer bills multiply to several panels), and the Speaker could create ad hoc committees and task forces to facilitate systematic treatment of complex policy issues. These changes, reformers hoped, would give the majority party improved capacity to centralize congressional operations and enact policy more efficiently.

In the Senate the major effort to advance responsibility was a limitation of the minority's ability to filibuster—to use unlimited debate to tie up the chamber and defeat or substantially weaken controversial legislation (such as civil rights bills). Until 1975 a two-thirds majority of those present and voting (67 votes if all senators were in attendance) was required to invoke cloture (end debate). After that year, a three-fifths majority (60 votes) of all members could force Senate action.

The major impetus for these changes was the sense on the part of the members that Congress was irresponsible. In the 1970s, the legislature also put in place significant reforms to improve responsiveness, reflecting dissatisfied lawmakers' desire for greater participation and influence on policy. To facilitate Congress's division of labor and to provide senior members with positions of influence, the number of House subcommittees increased from 97, at the time of the 1946 reorganization act, to 151 by the 94th Congress (1975-1977). In the Senate there were roughly 34 subcommittees in 1946; the number peaked at 140 in the 94th Congress (Ornstein et al. 1994).

New rules reined in the full committee chairs, limited the number of committee and subcommittee chairmanships that any individual could hold, and established procedures that enabled more members to attain desirable subcommittee assignments. A "subcommittee bill of rights" required that subcommittees have fixed jurisdictions and that legislation within their jurisdictions be referred automatically to them; it also authorized subcommittees to meet at the pleasure of their members, to write their own rules, and to manage their own budgets and staffs. In 1975 the Democratic Caucus mandated that all House committees with more than 20 members create a minimum of four subcommittees. These changes in the 1970s democratized the House. More members occupied positions from which they could influence the legislative agenda. At the same time responsible decision making became increasingly problematic: more players made forging coalitions to enact meaningful legislation more difficult.

A third route to reorganization and reform led toward increased accountability. To restore its popular standing, damaged by policy failure and highly publicized scandals, the legislature enacted a set of reforms designed to expose its operations to citizens' scrutiny. Members were to conduct the public's business in public; committees were to meet in open session; and votes in committee and on the floor were to be recorded. In addition, proceedings were made available for live television coverage on the C-SPAN network. Both the House and Senate adopted codes of ethics, including financial disclosure provisions, intended to deter or expose conflicts of interest. The Federal Election Campaign Act (1971, amended 1974), as interpreted by the Supreme Court in *Buckley v. Valeo* (1976), set up an election finance system that limited contributors' donations but not candidates' expenditures. More importantly, candidates must report in detail the sources—individuals and political action committees (PACs)—of their funds and the uses to which they put the money; the Federal Election Commission, which administers the campaign act, publishes these data. Both the ethics codes and the campaign statute should help concerned citizens to discover to whom, if anyone, senators and representatives are financially beholden and to assess whether members' personal or political interests impinge on matters about which they must vote or otherwise act. Dissatisfied voters can exact retribution at the ballot box.

In the short term congressional change in the 1970s and 1980s favored responsiveness (fragmentation) over responsibility (centralization). It simultaneously enlarged the potential for (if not the reality of) accountability. On balance, Congress neither reclaimed authority from the executive nor imposed its programmatic judgments on the executive with any regularity or success. In particular, the War Powers Resolution has not enabled the legislature to impose its will systematically on the president. The 1974 budget act, the Gramm-Rudman-Hollings experiment with automatic spending cuts in 1985, and efforts in 1990 to cap spending did not reduce outlays and only began, perhaps temporarily, to slow the growth of the deficit. Even enlarged legislative expertise produced mixed results. Although Congress does have greater access to data with which to craft legislative alternatives to executive initiatives, politically motivated lawmakers often have little time or incentive to use it.

Nor did the House majority party's new authority—control over committee chairs, the Speaker's enhanced influence over committee assignments and the Rules Committee, and the multiple referral power—consistently produce cohesive partisan majorities. To be sure, a curious concatenation of events at the end of the 1980s—increased party polarization stemming from divided government and greater ideological homogeneity among the Democrats coupled with Speaker Jim Wright's aggressive use of the full panoply of leadership powers—led to somewhat greater party cohesion. Members came to recognize the need to pull together to enact party programs (Davidson 1988; Rohde 1991; Sinclair 1992). Such centralization and its attendant party discipline, it seems, reflect members' acquiescence more than party leaders' ability to compel recalcitrant followers to toe the party line.[7]

Significantly, legislative change made Congress more responsive. The breach of the seniority tradition, the allocation of leadership positions among a wider array of junior members, the devolution of authority to independent subcommittees at the expense of full committee chairs, and the provision of greater staff and analytic resources, especially in the House, afforded more members responding to wider interests a piece of the policy-making action. Enhanced responsiveness, however, was not costless. Responsibility—in other words, policy-making efficiency—suffered. Specialization and expertise declined; fewer members could formulate coherent and effective policies on any given subject. With more participants possessing influence, assembling coalitions at the multiple stages of the law-making process became increasingly difficult, requiring painstaking negotiation and compromise and reducing the possibilities for truly innovative programs.

By the end of the 1980s Congress was more accountable, a mixed blessing. In principle, the campaign and financial disclosure rules made the public better able to ferret out members' potential ethical and economic conflicts of interest; in reality, there is little evidence that citizens actually did so. There was no diminution in charges of ethical and campaign malfeasance, but incumbents continued to win reelection in overwhelming numbers, though their electoral margins decreased appreciably. Moreover, the necessity of acting openly, in public, forced members to protect their political flanks; with lobbyists, journalists, and administrative officials monitoring their behavior, they seemed reluctant to take the political risks that responsible policy-making entails. Indeed, hypersensitivity to public opinion, regularly aroused by modern mass media, may have accounted for legislative policy-making inadequacy rather than the "gridlock" attributed to divided government (Mayhew 1991).

Change and Reform in the 1990s

Conspicuous reform sentiment flagged after 1977. The changes of the 1970s played out unobtrusively during the next decade, but they failed to revive Congress's sagging reputation. A series of new revelations further undercut public support for the legislature: charges of ethical improprieties led to the resignations in 1989 of House Speaker Jim Wright, D-Texas, and Majority Leader Tony Coelho, D-Calif.; more than 300 members wrote overdrafts on the House bank; five senators were chastised for ethically dubious relations with a savings and loan executive; and the public became aware of members' perquisites—for example, subsidized meals and beauty services and free ("franked") mail—and regarded the lawmakers as a pampered elite. Further reforms ensued in 1991 and 1992. As a quid pro quo for a sizable salary increase, the House and Senate gave up honoraria that various interests paid members for speeches and articles. The House bank was shut down, the franking privilege limited, and other perquisites eliminated or reduced; professional administrators, particularly a director of nonlegislative and financial services, assumed responsibility for day-to-day House operations. Again the intent of these changes was to demonstrate that Congress acts openly and above board, and thus to rekindle public confidence in the legislature.

The 103rd Congress: The Democrats

These changes were not enough. Poll after poll revealed that the public had low esteem for Congress; barely one-fifth of the electorate believed the legislature was performing well.[8] In 1992, 43 House and 5 Senate incumbents lost their seats.

Divided party government and the power of interest groups appeared to hamstring creative policy making (Thurber 1991). When the 103rd Congress convened in January 1993, its members confronted a citizenry clearly concerned about congressional ethics and performance. As it had before enacting the reorganization acts of 1946 and 1970, the legislature created another Joint Committee on the Organization of Congress to study and assess reform proposals and to recommend appropriate revisions in the legislative process. With the aid of an extensive analysis and review of reform options (Congressional Research Service 1992), the Joint Committee held voluminous hearings and produced a detailed report on congressional organization (JCOC 1993f, vol. 1). In the end, however, the House and Senate members could not agree on a set of recommendations and each delegation offered its own modest reform bill (JCOC 1993f, vols. 2 and 3).

In contrast to earlier episodes, the main impetus for change was external. Critics of Congress excoriated the institution and virtually compelled its members to confront reform issues. Outside pressure regularly highlighted deficiencies in accountability, and throughout the 103rd Congress the lawmakers (especially the junior members, many of whom had campaigned on a reform platform) struggled to recapture the public's respect, trust, and confidence.[9]

The agenda of reforms to enhance accountability was broad and deep. Finding the sunshine illuminating congressional operations not bright enough, they discussed measures to expose more of legislative activity, in committee and on the floor, to public scrutiny. The House experimented with televised "Oxford style" floor debates—one on health care, another on welfare reform—in which teams from the parties debated these major issues. The minority Republicans proposed to put their policy alternatives before the country by limiting the ability of the Rules Committee to restrict floor consideration of GOP amendments. The Joint Committee on the Organization of Congress suggested a campaign to "enhance public understanding" of the institution.

The major thrust of change to improve accountability was to make members "Caesar's wives"—in other words, persons beyond suspicion of conflict of interest and unethical behavior. To that end, reform-minded members introduced legislation to stiffen the out-of-date and ineffective regulation of lobbyists and to tighten controls over campaign finance. With respect to the former, proposals included tougher registration requirements for group representatives, stricter limits on permissible contributions to legislators, and fuller disclosure of legitimate gifts. With regard to campaign finance, discussion revolved around efforts to impose overall spending ceilings, to equalize incumbent and challenger resources, and to limit the direct contributions of political action committees to individual candidates and large donors' gifts (of "soft money") to the political parties. Here, too, the proposed changes sought increased disclosure as well as limits on suspect behavior.[10] The Senate reassessed its procedures for handling charges of ethical improprieties by members, and both chambers talked about applying to themselves various statutes from which they (and the executive and judicial branches) were exempt (for example, the Americans with Disabilities Act and the Occupational Safety and

Health Act). These ideas, and others, aimed to convince a skeptical public that a Congress devoted to the public good—acting "in the sunshine," unbeholden to "fat cat" contributors, and free of ethical taint—merited citizens' confidence.

The critics' complaints about irresponsible congressional policy making, which many members found justified, put on the reform agenda changes to overcome policy incapacity. The most significant and controversial ideas sought ways to centralize legislative operations to permit the majority to enact its programs with dispatch. One possibility was to reduce the ability of independent committees and subcommittees to thwart floor majorities. To that end, a streamlined committee system—with sharply defined jurisdictions and limits on the number of subcommittee assignments any member could hold—might help. The result, proponents asserted, would be smaller committees with more policy-making expertise. Similarly, stronger political parties, with stronger leaders making more effective use of the powers available to them, might harness the committees to partisan purposes.

Procedures to promote more responsible budgeting also attracted considerable attention. A balanced budget amendment to the Constitution won substantial support in both chambers but fell a handful of votes short of the two-thirds majority needed for passage. Granting the president a line-item veto—to reject single items in appropriations bills—appealed to many members despite the ceding of authority to the executive. The rationale is that Congress cannot be trusted to put aside parochial, "pork-barrel" concerns in the name of broader national interests and must empower the president to prevent legislative profligacy. A less extreme version of the line-item veto, "expedited rescission," passed in the House; the president proposes to rescind a spending item, and Congress must vote on the proposal, but the rescission takes effect only if simple majorities in both houses approve. Less sweeping changes were also considered. One called for replacing annual budgeting with a two-year cycle; authorization and appropriations decisions would come in the first year and Congress would oversee the results in the second. Another proposal to control the federal deficit concerned "sunset" provisions mandating periodic reexamination and reauthorization of all federal programs. All of these ideas sought to make the budget process simpler, more coherent, and thus more likely to represent a clear statement of Congress's budgetary priorities.

Other ways to improve congressional responsibility also surfaced. Limits on lawmakers' terms of office—from six to twelve years for House members and two terms for senators—won support from voters in 22 states. These voters believed that if members were freer from the long-term reelection incentive to curry favor from pressure groups, campaign contributors, or special interests, they would be more likely to "bite the bullet" and pass effective programs even in the face of concerted opposition.[11] Rules changes, such as relaxation (if not elimination, as some House members proposed) of the Senate filibuster rule, might facilitate the flow of innovative legislation. Improved information resources, using modern computer technology, could augment policy analysis and lead to the formulation of more creative programs.

Because the bulk of the criticism focused on Congress's lack of accountability, responsiveness was not high on the reform agenda. Nonetheless, some of the ideas discussed had potential, though indirect, implications for responsiveness. If campaign finance changes permit challengers to unseat incumbents, the former may bring to Congress policy preferences more in tune with the electorates in their states and districts. Similarly, limits on PAC contributions may decrease PACs' access to, and possible influence on, lawmakers, allowing the members to pay closer attention to the views of ordinary citizens. Responsiveness also offers a second rationale for term limits: without a need to concentrate on securing their long-term careers, members will respond less to special interests and more to citizens' sentiments.

In addition, House Democrats and Republicans were concerned with empowering rank-and-file party members. The Democrats enlarged their whip organization and established a Speaker's Working Group to advise on policy matters. The minority Republicans proposed changes that would enable their party to act more forcefully and with greater impact as the opposition. For example, they favored committee membership ratios commensurate with the party balance in the House and a guarantee of the opportunity to offer a motion to recommit with instructions, detailing their policy alternatives, as a matter of course. Such changes promised to make the House more responsive to minority party concerns.

These items—to facilitate accountability, responsibility, and responsiveness—were "on the table" during the Democratic 103rd Congress. Junior members and minority Republicans were forceful proponents of reform, but they could not forge a coalition to impose basic changes. Senior Democrats, including the party leaders, were unenthusiastic about reform; they preferred to protect their vested interests in the status quo. As their election prospects improved, the Republicans concluded that it was preferable to defer reform to the next Congress. In the end, after much debate, none of the major changes passed both houses.[12]

The 104th Congress: Republican Reform

Reclaiming majority status in the 104th Congress, the triumphant Republicans advanced their own reform agenda, especially in the House. (The Senate seemed more inclined toward "business as usual.") In keeping with their "Contract with America," the campaign document to which they attributed their electoral success, House Republicans simultaneously adopted changes with implications for accountability, responsibility, and responsiveness.

They assigned high priority to assuaging the public's discontent with Congress—that is, to making the legislature more accountable—and they took numerous steps to mollify their external constituency. The House Republicans quickly enacted a Congressional Accountability Act, discussed in the previous Congress, to ensure compliance with laws imposed on the private sector but not on the legislature. They undertook a "comprehensive audit" to ferret out waste and abuse in congressional operations, and they reshaped the chamber's organizational structure to promote efficient management of the institution. They cut committee staffs by one-third as a tangible step toward reducing congressional profligacy. To keep citizens informed about the legislative process, House Republicans promised to hold more committee and subcommittee meetings in public, to publish more comprehensive committee records, to make the *Congressional Record* an accurate transcript of floor proceedings, and to transmit a host of government documents through the Internet (the "information superhighway").

More effective policy making—that is, a more responsible Congress—would enable the new majority both to demonstrate that the legislature can address the nation's problems and to promote prompt passage of the party's 10-point policy program. The Republican leaders, to meet an internal need, moved rapidly to impose some centralization on the chamber. Most significantly, they restrained committee autonomy in three ways. First, they abolished three minor committees, eliminated 25 subcommittees, and cut back on the number of available subcommittee assignments. Second, they took control of the committee assignment process and appointed party loyalists to chair the most important panels, ignoring seniority in three instances. Third, they constricted the chairs' power by imposing six-year term limits on their service and by eliminating their ability to cast proxy votes on behalf of absent members.[13]

In addition, House leaders sought to cement the support of the 73 newly elected freshmen Republicans by giving record numbers of them choice committee assignments. Freshmen were appointed to the Rules, Ways and Means, Appropriations, and Commerce committees, the four most important panels in the House. New rules also altered the Speaker's bill referral authority. Now the Speaker must send a bill to a single committee, where presumably it will get favorable treatment, though sequential and partial referral remain within the Speaker's province. In addition, the House will no longer consider commemorative bills (for example, establishing National Mushroom Week), which increasingly have clogged the legislative calendar at the expense of more serious matters. Finally, the chamber will no longer subsidize 28 legislative service organizations (caucuses) that (like the Congressional Black Caucus) offered alternative perspectives to those of the parties. By making these changes, Republicans endeavored to create a less fragmented decision-making process and thus facilitate rapid enactment of their policy initiatives.

Reforms to promote accountability and responsibility address short-term imperatives: to regain public trust and to shape public policy. Additional changes, to enhance responsiveness, seem likely to be important over the longer haul. To reassure a public that seems to demand fiscal prudence, House Republicans enacted a balanced budget amendment and a line-item veto that will enable the president to control pork-barrel spending; they also passed a requirement that only a three-fifths majority can enact tax increases (which cannot be retroactive). Republicans proposed a 12-year limit on service in the House. Term limits, advocates argued, would lessen members' need to court special interests for reelection purposes and increase attention to broad national concerns. Too controversial, the measure was defeated.

To satisfy junior legislators eager to plunge into legislative politics, the GOP succeeded in limiting members to service on no more than two full committees and four subcommittees. Full committee chairs cannot also chair a subcommittee. Coupled with term limits on chairs and the ban on proxy voting, these changes should enable newcomers to involve themselves quickly in House business. In addition, Republicans in the 104th Congress vowed to open floor proceedings by reducing the use of restrictive Rules Committee resolutions blocking amendments to pending bills and by guaranteeing the minority the right to offer a motion to recommit a bill with instructions to incorporate its preferred provisions. Overall, these reforms, if implemented in full, should permit more opinions to find their way into congressional deliberations.

Over the long haul such increased responsiveness may undercut efforts to centralize House operations, as members increasingly assert their own prerogatives. More importantly perhaps, reforms may alter the balance of political power in favor of the president. Some combination of term limits on service and leadership, staff cuts, a balanced budget amendment, and presidential line-item veto authority may have this effect. Can a more amateur, inexperienced, and inexpert Congress pose alternatives to those of the White House and make them stick? The answer is, probably not.

The Lessons of History

This narrative of twentieth century change and reform in Congress teaches several lessons, some obvious, some less so. First, change comes constantly, quietly, mostly with whimpers, punctuated only occasionally by a big bang of systematic reform (1910-1911, the 1970s, perhaps the 1990s). Change occurs when events or new agenda items convince members that it is necessary (1910-1911, 1921, 1961) or when change cannot be resisted (the 1970s, 1993-1995). It flows from forces internal to Congress (1910-1911, 1961, budget changes of 1974, 1985, and 1990), from external pressures (1993-1994), or from some combination of the two (1946, the 1970s, the 104th Congress). Seldom reflecting broad philosophical visions of an ideal legislature, change arrives piecemeal, sometimes stressing efforts to make Congress a more responsible policymaker (1921, 1946, budget reform), more responsive to a wider range of member and citizen concerns (1910-1911, the 1970s), or more accountable to the electorate (1993-1994). Needless to say, reform most commonly seeks some improvement in all three regards. The historical trend, though variable, has been toward promoting responsibility and accountability, and increasingly in reaction to outside influences.

Second, less obtrusive change may be more significant in the long run than the highly dramatic reform episodes. The revolt against Speaker Cannon set in motion the evolution of the modern Congress. Over two generations, it led to a fragmented, decentralized legislature, with influence widely dispersed among individualistic members, that makes incremental policy changes through a painstaking process of negotiation and compromise. Congress has become more responsive, less responsible. Changing Senate Rule 22 to reduce the number of votes needed to invoke cloture and force a vote is perhaps less important than the breakdown of the custom of reserving extended debate for matters of major substantive import. Frequent filibusters on trivial issues surely contributed to the public's perception of an irresponsible Senate. Party discipline may come when leaders use the powers available (Jim Wright did, Tom Foley allegedly didn't) rather than from giving leaders new authority (which goes unused). A heavy influx of new members (as in 1964, 1974, 1992, and 1994) with new outlooks may alter legislative performance far more than explicit reform. The latter may merely codify changes that more ubiquitous but less visible forces have unleashed (King 1994).

Third, change may fail to produce its proponents' intended consequences or, worse still, may lead to unanticipated and undesirable results. Neither the Congressional Budget and Impoundment Control Act of 1974 nor the Gramm-Rudman-Hollings budget act of 1985 stanched the flow of governmental red ink. To date, the post-1990 focus on spending limits has at best slowed the growth of the federal deficit. The 1946 consolidation of full committees spawned a proliferation of subcommittees that increased the number of independent, and often uncoordinated, congressional work units, making responsible policy making more difficult. The sunshine reforms were well-intentioned efforts to enhance accountability. (Who can quarrel with the concept of open covenants openly arrived at?) But they may have heightened Congress's sensitivity to the outside influences of groups and citizens. This sensitivity, critics argue, cripples congressional capacity to make responsible public policy. The potential impact of the changes enacted and debated in the 104th Congress is certain to animate future debate on these matters. To be sure, reformers have won some notable victories—the House Rules Committee is a much more reliable agent of the leadership—but the moral remains clear: change and reform are risky and uncertain ventures. Indeed, this may be the ultimate lesson history teaches: change *will* come, and observers may identify and explain it, but to predict when, why, and with what results events, issues, and members will change Congress remains an enterprise fraught with peril.

Notes

1. The quotations in the epigraph of Representatives Matsui, Castle, and Sharp can be found in Hook (1994a) on pages 785, 831, and 789, respectively. Representative Durbin is quoted in Cooper (1993c) on page A29.

2. For additional discussion of these standards for assessing Congress, and citations of the relevant literature, see Rieselbach (1994, 14-20).

3. These external criticisms were codified in a report of the American Political Science Association's Committee on Congress. The academic analysis suggested some fundamental reforms designed to help the legislature reassert its policy-making influence vis-à-vis the executive.

4. The 1946 statute (Title III) contained a Federal Regulation of Lobbying Act that required lobbyists to register and to file reports disclosing their activities. Judicial interpretation, however, undercut enforcement of the law, leaving it "more loophole than law" (Congressional Quarterly 1987, 35-36).

5. For fuller treatment of the reforms of the 1970s, see Davidson and Oleszek (1977), Sheppard (1985), Center for Responsive Politics (1986), and Rieselbach (1994). During the 1970s and 1980s, congressional introspection grew. The House established three separate reform panels: the (Bolling) Select Committee on Committees in 1973-1974; the (Obey) Commission on Administrative Review in 1977; and the (Patterson) Select Committee on Committees in 1979. In addition, since 1974, the House Democratic Caucus has used a Committee on Organization, Study, and Review to assess proposals and recommend reforms to the Caucus. Not to be outdone, the Senate launched the (Hughes) Commission on the Operation of the Senate in 1975, the (Stevenson) Temporary Select Committee to Study the Senate Committee System in 1976, the (Culver) Commission on the Operation of the Senate in 1979, and the (Quayle) Temporary Select Committee to Study the Senate Commit-tee System in 1984. From these committees an impressive welter of ideas emerged. Some were adopted, but many were not because of members' reluctance to surrender existing bases of influence.

6. The literature on budget reform is voluminous. See, inter alia, Shuman (1992), White and Wildavsky (1989), Schick (1990), Thurber (1992), and Thurber and Durst (1993).

7. David Price, a political scientist and close observer of Congress who became a member of the House (1987-1994) puts it succinctly. He notes "an unmistakable fragility to leadership strength, which is now based less on 'strong parties external to the Congress' and more on the acquiescence of freewheeling individual members" (Price 1992, 78-79).

8. This finding is from "Congress: Election Prospects," *Public Perspective* 5 (July-August 1994): 84-85.

9. Prior to the 1970s, reform regularly flowed from internal imperatives, though out-side observers pushed for the 1946 Reorganization Act and President John F. Kennedy lent his support to the House Democrats' 1961 move to tame the Rules Committee. The changes in the 1970s reflected a complex mix of external and internal pressures—and motives—to promote responsibility, responsiveness, and accountability. Current reform ef-forts seem more externally driven and more focused on accountability than earlier attempts to alter Congress.

10. By mid-summer 1994, each house had enacted both lobby and campaign reform legislation, but wide and deeply held differences blocked conference committee resolution of the interchamber disagreements.

11. A federal court in Washington State and the Arkansas and Nebraska Supreme Courts have found state-enacted term limits impermissible additions to the constitutional requirements—age, citizenship, and residence—for legislative service. The Supreme Court concurred in a 1995 decision based on the Arkansas case. On the term limits issue, see Ben-jamin and Malbin (1992).

12. The House did write into its rules a requirement that it comply with 10 statutes from which it had been exempt.

13. The chairs did reclaim the formal authority to appoint subcommittee chairs and to hire committee staff; presumably, party loyalist chairs and less independent subcommittees will foster committee approval of Republican programs.

3

CONGRESSIONAL COMMITTEES IN THE NEW REFORM ERA:
From Combat to the Contract

Roger H. Davidson

Congressional government may or may not be committee government, as Woodrow Wilson held. But the work that takes place in the committee and subcommittee rooms of Capitol Hill is critical to the productivity and effectiveness of Congress. These work groups are the institution's nerve ends—gatherers of information, sifters of alternatives, drafters and refiners of legislation. By the 1990s, evidence was mounting that the congressional committee system was acutely ailing—beset by mounting workloads, duplication and jurisdictional battles, and conflicts between program and funding panels. Already their monopoly over important portions of the legislative workload was threatened, especially when controversial and broad-gauged legislation was at stake. "Today, committees are often irrelevant or, worse yet, obstacles," wrote journalist Richard E. Cohen, who termed the phenomenon "crumbling committees" (Cohen 1990). Consider the following developments:

- Committee boundaries, codified one or two generations ago, now compete or overlap on hundreds of policy questions, especially such "mega-issues" as health care, foreign trade, crime, financial institutions, energy, and the environment. According to a recent study of "jurisdictional spread" in 10 major issue areas, from 7 to 14 House committees held hearings on each of these issues every year from 1980 through 1991 (Baumgartner et al 1994, 9).

- Increasing numbers of bills and resolutions have been referred not just to a single committee but to two or more committees. In recent Congresses up to one in five House bills and joint resolutions and up to one in ten Senate measures were multiply referred; the figures for major measures were even higher (Davidson, Oleszek, and Kephart 1988; Davidson 1989; JCOC 1993c, 812; Sinclair 1994b).

- In many instances committees are bypassed altogether in the shaping of major legislation. Examining major issues over the 1987-1990 period, Barbara Sinclair discovered that House committees were bypassed in 19 percent of the cases and Senate committees in 16 percent of the cases (1994b, 3).

- Before they can be passed by one or both chambers, measures reported by committees frequently undergo major alterations—most often in negotiating processes supervised by majority party leaders. In the 1987-1990 period such postcommittee adjustments (in cases where the committee was not formally bypassed) marked 38 percent of major House bills and 29 percent of major Senate measures (Sinclair 1994b, 4). In the case of health care reform, four congressional panels reported out no fewer than five separate omnibus bills in 1994, not one of which could have passed the two chambers. Subsequently, Senate and House leadership-sponsored measures also foundered. Health care is an example—albeit extreme—of the mounting incapacity of individual committees to broker agreements among all the contending parties involved in mega-issues.

• The wall that separates authorization and appropriation jurisdictions is frequently breached. Appropriations panels often fund programs in advance of authorizations, pinch-hit for deadlocked authorizing committees through the vehicle of continuing resolutions, or insert legislative provisions in funding bills—despite rules in both chambers proscribing such provisions. By the same token, authorizing committees have devised ways of preempting the appropriations panels' authority or bypassing them altogether. According to one recent estimate, the House Appropriations Committee determines only 63 percent of annual outlays from the general fund; the Senate Appropriations Committee handles 69 percent (Cogan 1994). Thus spending decisions, like program decisions, are scattered among a multitude of committees.

• Senators and representatives themselves profess to be dissatisfied with the committees and their operations. Eighty-four percent of the members surveyed in 1993 by the Joint Committee on the Organization of Congress claimed that committee structure and membership assignments should be examined. Asked to rank the five top reorganization priorities, more members (32 percent) ranked committee reform first than any other reform category; budget and floor procedures were runners-up (JCOC 1993f, 247-257).

In light of such disquieting indicators, it was inevitable that the committee system would loom large in the reform politics of the 1990s. By the 103rd Congress, questions of committee organization were on the formal agendas of several House and Senate work groups. From the early organization caucuses (December 1992) to *sine die* adjournment (October 1994), myriad reform proposals both major and minor were debated on the floor, in party caucuses and standing committees, and by the temporary Joint Committee on the Organization of Congress, the third such body in modern times. As the Congress neared adjournment, frustrated Republican leaders in the House trumpeted congressional reform as part of the "Contract with America," their unprecedented national platform for the 1994 elections. With the GOP's stunning takeover of both houses for the first time in forty years, congressional reform moved into the public spotlight. The new House majority quickly implemented significant reforms; Senate Republicans, unwilling to be left behind, made more modest changes.

Committee membership, structures, and procedures figured prominently in all these discussions of reform, especially in the House of Representatives and in the Joint Committee. Although the 103rd Congress, with its reform-minded new members, made several nontrivial adjustments in committee structures and procedures, Democratic leaders resisted major changes. It was left to the Republican 104th Congress to implement key items on the reform agenda. The GOP reformers, while offered a unique opportunity, were by no means immune to the forces of inertia that stymied reformers in the past. The "laws" of reform politics remained intact.

Outside and Inside Pressures for Change

Institutional changes are driven by the need to respond to *external demands* and *internal stresses* (Davidson 1981). These outside and inside pressures for structural and procedural innovation, operating alone or in tandem, can force Congress to reassess its traditional ways of doing things. Most of these alterations are unplanned, piecemeal adjustments; a few are effected by reorganization plans drawn up by leadership groups or by panels created especially for that purpose.

External pressures, most typically emanating from the societal problems the institution is expected to resolve, bear down on Congress and its committees. As the volume and scope of public issues have expanded, so has work group complexity on Capitol Hill, manifested not only in committees and subcommittees but also in task forces, informal caucuses, and other entities. Historical events and shifting public agendas lead to the creation (and sometimes abolition) of committees, to scrambles for jurisdiction among existing committees, and, increasingly, to bypassing the committees in whole or in part.

Another external pressure emanates from public demands and levels of trust in government. Hovering over Congress like a vast storm cloud in the 1990s was an unprecedented level of public discontent and even anger—what one member of Congress called a "civic temper tantrum." It reflected not only generalized distrust of politicians and outrage at widely reported scandals, but also a feeling that government was not working well and that the nation itself had strayed off course (Asher and Barr 1994). Although the public's policy message remained indistinct, the overarching distrust in government and desire for change were undeniable. This sour mood found concrete expression in the 1992 and 1994 elections, which reconfigured membership and party control at both ends of Pennsylvania Avenue.

Pressures for innovation also come from within Congress, primarily from the goals and careers of individual members. Legislators harbor a variety of personal goals—reelection to be sure but beyond that a chance to contribute, to shape public policy, to see their ideas come to fruition, to gain respect for their work. Hence, legislators make a variety of claims upon the institution, shaping its structures and procedures to serve their own needs as well as the demands of the outside environment.

Internal stresses and strains are no novelty in Congress, whose members are increasingly independent entrepreneurs possessing relatively equal formal power and representing diverse viewpoints and constituencies. Often the effects of external demands ricochet and create interpersonal stresses—as when a ballooning workload (external demand) produces personal or committee scrambles for jurisdiction (internal stress), or when voter unrest (external) yields high membership turnover (internal). Other tensions flow from institutional rivalries (for example, House versus Senate, authorizers versus appropriators) or shifts in personnel, factional balances, or members' attitudes or norms. Such conflicts surface in recurrent bickering over perquisites, committee jurisdictions, rules, scheduling, seniority, and budget-making processes.

In the early 1990s, partisanship and seniority caused Congress's deepest internal fissures. Members and outsiders alike were distressed over the acrimonious and escalating warfare between cohesive and militant congressional parties on both sides of Capitol Hill. The partisan warfare was fought on a thousand different battlegrounds—on the floor, in committees, in public forums, in local and national campaigns. Majority prerogatives clashed with minority rights, especially in the House, where an entrenched, sometimes overbearing, and ever more desperate Democratic majority faced a restless, aggressive, and sometimes reckless Republican minority. After 1994 the tables were turned, but the partisan strife continued unabated.

Seniority tensions also surfaced in both chambers. Junior members, with less power to lose and less attachment to traditional procedures, are a potent clientele for innovation. By contrast, senior members tend to be hostile to many substantive changes, especially those that threaten their formal leadership positions or zones of influence. The 1992 elections produced the largest incoming class in two generations—110 new House members (87 of whom returned in 1995) and 14 new senators. The 1994 contests added 86 new representatives and 11 senators. Many of these newcomers owed their seats to retirements prompted by redistricting, the House "bank" affair and other scandals; most of them vowed they would shake up the way Washington worked.

The Prereform 103rd: Rearguard Actions and Stalemate

In the years before the Republican takeover, criticism of the congressional committee system increased among members and outside critics. During the 1993 hearings of the Joint Committee on the Organization of Congress, 34 representatives, 8 senators, and outside witnesses spanning the spectrum from academic observers to H. Ross Perot endorsed the goal of rationalizing jurisdictions. Testimony came from a wide range of members, from Ronald V. Dellums (D-Calif.) to Larry Combest (R-Texas); some of the most thoughtful lawmakers cited cases of overlap that had hampered policy making (JCOC 1993a, 814-816). Witnesses endorsed a variety of other committee innovations: 41 representatives and 14 senators urged cutting the numbers of committees, subcommittees, or both; 15

representatives and 2 senators pressed for cutting committee and subcommittee sizes.

Member and staff surveys conducted in 1993 also revealed widespread support for committee reform. "Committee structure and membership assignments" ranked very high on the reorganization agendas of the 161 members responding to the Joint Committee's survey.[1] Sentiment for change was especially strong in the House. More than half the respondents claimed they would support "comprehensive" committee alignment and another 30 percent wanted more modest consolidation of selected committees. Only 14 percent preferred few changes or none at all (JCOC 1993f, vol. 2, 261).

Even congressional staff aides professed to support committee reorganization in principle. Four out of the five reform proposals most often cited by staff members dealt with the committee system. Reducing jurisdictional overlap, endorsed by 87 percent, was the most popular of 29 proposals on which staff members were quizzed. Other favored reforms were limiting senators' assignments (80 percent), limiting representatives' assignments (77 percent), and adopting parallel jurisdictions (76 percent).[2] Reducing committee and subcommittee sizes also received overwhelming support (JCOC 1993f, 327).

The 1992 elections were expected to bring about major changes, with most Democratic and GOP freshmen voicing urgency about institutional reform. Yet despite its initial promise, the 103rd Congress ended in frustration and stalemate—not only over committee reforms, but ethics rules, campaign funding, and lobby reform as well.

Virtually all the action took place in the House of Representatives. Initial committee system alterations originated with Democratic Caucus groups and were brokered by the leadership. But in two instances, leaders were confounded by a bipartisan coalition of reform-minded members and forced to accept changes against their will (see Table 3-1).

Partisan Reform Agendas

Even before the newly elected lawmakers arrived in the nation's Capital, Rep. Louise M. Slaughter, D-NY, had prepared a package of proposed changes in House or party caucus rules for consideration by the Democrats' Committee on Oversight, Study, and Review (OSR), which she chaired. As adopted, the OSR package included provisions dealing with committee assignments, chairmen's powers, and authorizations-appropriations disputes. The Democratic Study Group (DSG) had its own package of proposals, some of which were merged with the OSR list. Eventually the Democratic Caucus debated the proposals, accepting some and modifying others. Meanwhile, the Republican Conference was refining its rules proposals. Its 43-point plan, "Mandate for Change in the People's House," embraced numerous changes in committee operations, including reductions in subcommittees and subcommittee assignments, abolition of select committees, a ban on proxy voting, cuts in committee staffs, and party ratios more favorable to the minority.

Table 3-1   House Committee System Changes, 103rd and 104th
Congresses

103rd Congress (1993–1994)	104th Congress (1995–1996)
Four select committees eliminated	Three standing committees eliminated; jurisdictions shifted
Major committees (except for Appropriations, Foreign Affairs) limited to six subcommittees; minor committees to five	Committees (except for Appropriations; Governmental Reform and Oversight; and Transportation and Infrastructure) limited to five subcommittees
"Rolling quorums" authorized	"Rolling quorums" prohibited
	Proxy voting in committees prohibited
Members restricted to five subcommittee assignments	Members' assignments limited to two committees, four subcommittees
Democratic Steering and Policy Committee given added controls over selection of committee chairs	Majority party leaders dominate selection of committee chairs
Discharge petition signers may be made public	Committee, subcommittee chairs limited to three two-year terms; Speaker limited to four terms
Authorizing committees allowed preferential motions to disagree with Senate legislative provisions in funding bills	Joint referrals prohibited; Speaker granted enhanced powers over other multiple referrals (to designate "lead" committees, set deadlines for all involved committees)
	Verbatim transcripts of hearings and meetings
	Members' votes published in committee reports
	Committee chairs hire subcommittee staffs
	Committee staffs reduced by at least one third; caps set by House Oversight Committee

Source: Schneider (1995) and Donovan (1992, 3777–3780).

Although the GOP's bold plan was scuttled virtually without debate, changes were adopted that (1) reduced the number of subcommittees; (2) limited committee chairmen's powers; (3) protected authorizing committees from Senate amendments; and (4) permitted "rolling quorums" in committees.

Members' assignments were squeezed when the Democratic Caucus voted to limit the number of subcommittees on major committees to six and on nonmajor committees to five. Members would be restricted to five subcommittees overall. This change would have eliminated 16 subcommittees of 11 full committees. Because of retirements, downsizing was achieved with limited upheaval. The only exception occurred in the Foreign Affairs Committee, where the Congressional Black Caucus (CBC) fought for, and won, an exception for the Africa Subcommittee, which otherwise would have been merged with Latin America (Simpson 1993).

The House made further changes in committee operations. First, steps were taken to increase the accountability of committee chairmen. New Democratic Caucus rules expedited open caucus votes for selecting chairmen, subjected acting chairmanships to caucus approval, and gave the Steering and Policy Committee authority to declare a committee or subcommittee chairmanship open at any time, thus sending the matter to the full caucus. The Republican Conference adopted a rule limiting its members to a single ranking minority post on a committee or subcommittee. (A similar rule for Democrats, proposed by freshmen reformers, was turned down by OSR.) Term limits for committee and subcommittee chairmen were advocated by GOP freshmen and by some Democrats. And junior Democrats talked about punishing committee leaders who deserted the party on key votes—especially the eleven subcommittee chairs who voted against President Bill Clinton's budget in 1993.

Finally, House rules were altered, over Republicans' objections, to permit "rolling quorums" in committees (establishing a quorum for conducting business or voting over a period of time rather than requiring the quorum to be physically present all at once), and to stiffen the requirement for points of order that a committee quorum was not present.

Backbench Reformers' Revolts

Democratic leaders may have been in command of the initial House rules changes in the 103rd Congress, but they—and, to a lesser extent, their GOP counterparts—were overrun by two "backbench" revolts later that year.

Killing "The Selects". The more startling of the incidents was the House's surprise elimination of four of its five select committees: Aging; Children, Youth and Families; Hunger; and Narcotics Abuse and Control. (The fifth, Select Intelligence, is a legislative committee that was never at issue.) Temporary panels charged with investigating specific policy topics, "the selects" lacked the authority to report legislation and faced reauthorization with each new Congress. But all four had vocal supporters and clienteles both inside and outside the House, and they had taken on an aura of permanency (Aging dated from 1972, the others from 1983). Rejecting a motion to stop funding the panels altogether, the Democratic Caucus agreed to squeeze them by bringing them under each member's five-subcommittee limit (Foerstel 1992). But an alliance of Republicans and freshmen reformers of both parties pressed for a floor test. The Rules Committee countered by reporting out separate authorizing resolutions, hoping to discourage a "reform vote" and force members to vote on the four panels' individual merits. Neither party's leaders, according to reports, bothered to whip their members in advance. Thus, when the first floor vote was taken, they were caught off-guard when 83 Democrats (including 18 freshmen) joined most Republicans in voting, 237 to 180, to end authorization for the Narcotics panel (Jacoby 1993; Cooper 1993a). The remaining three panels would surely have met the same fate.

The negative vote signaled that rank-and-file members were eager to strike a blow for reform. Leaders of both parties were befuddled. Majority Leader Richard A. Gephardt, D-Mo., canceled votes on the other three panels, and there ensued frantic negotiations between party leaders and senior members of the four panels. Minority Leader Robert H. Michel, R-Ill., refloated the proposal to reauthorize all four panels through 1993 but was denounced angrily within GOP ranks.

In the end the four select committees were simply allowed to expire at the end of March (Cooper 1993b). The doomed committees' members, staff, and outside allies fought to reverse the decision but to no avail. Once rank-and-file members had drawn first blood, the leadership found it convenient to let the victims succumb.[3]

Not all supporters of the move were junior or reform-minded members. Senior committee leaders, who claimed jurisdictional ownership over the topics covered by the selects, quickly realized that money saved by abolishing them would relieve pressure for cutting their own standing committees' spending requests. Annual committee staff authorizations and appropriations had turned into battlegrounds where Republicans attacked Democratic management of the House and demanded deep cuts in committee funding. For 1993 Republicans had called for 25 percent cuts in House committee budgets. The committee funding bill that was eventually passed (over unanimous GOP opposition) represented a 5 percent cut from the previous year—nearly all of which came from dismantling the four select committees (Krauss 1993).

The Discharge Petition Dispute. A more ominous challenge to the Democratically controlled committee system came in the summer of 1993, when four-term Representative James M. Inhof, R-Okla., masterminded a drive to open up the committee discharge process. Dating from the 1910 "revolt" against the Speaker's agenda control, this procedure (Rule 27, clause 3) requires a petition signed by 218 members followed by a motion on the floor to "discharge" the committee from further consideration of a measure (Beth 1990). From the 1930s, it was held that petitioners' names would be publicly disclosed only when the required signatures were achieved—ostensibly to protect the petitioners against pressures, either from their leaders or from outside interests. Although rarely invoked, the device serves as one of several safety valves to promote accountability of committees and their leaders.

Discharge petitions were filed in 1993 against several measures bottled up in committees—the balanced budget amendment, the line-item veto, and term limits—all touchstone conservative issues. Although the petitions fell far short of the required signatures, Inhofe hit upon a way to speed up the process. First he filed a petition to discharge the Rules Committee from considering his own proposal (H. Res. 134) to open up the petitions. Then he worked to verify his list of signers and announced that he would release the names of those who had not signed. His ploy gained the support of H. Ross Perot, numerous talk-show hosts, and editorialists on the *Wall Street Journal*, who published Inhofe's list on August 17. In the face of what posed as a populist attack on "secret rules," most of Inhofe's opponents had fled the field by September 14, when the Rules Committee held its hearing on his proposal (House Committee on Rules 1993). When the Inhofe resolution reached the House floor, only 40 members voted against it.

The death of "the selects" and the discharge petition imbroglio were embarrassing defeats for the House's Democratic leaders (and, to a degree, their Republican counterparts). The two events demonstrated the breadth of reformist sentiment and the possibility of mobilizing outside support for given innovations. But despite these warning bells, the leadership pursued its policy of containment. The Joint Committee on the Organization of Congress was the chief case in point.

The Joint Committee's Modest Proposals

A new Joint Committee on the Organization of Congress, proposed in 1991 but initially resisted by House Democratic leaders, was established in 1992 to "make a full and complete study" of Congress's organization and operation, including "the structure of, and the relationships between, the various standing, special, and select committees of Congress" (H. Con. Res. 192). Leading the inquiry would be its prime cosponsors: Oklahoma Democrat David L. Boren (who announced his retirement from the Senate in April 1994); Sen. Pete V. Domenici, R-N.M.; Rep. Lee H. Hamilton, D-Ind.; and Rep. Bill Gradison, R-Ohio, who resigned from the House and was replaced on the Joint Committee by Rep. David Dreier, R-Calif. However, these leaders confronted formidable obstacles.

First, joint committees, although useful mechanisms for resolving issues between the two chambers, are ill suited for considering rules or procedures that apply primarily to one house or the other—and that includes most aspects of committee structure and procedures. The two chambers regard their internal arrangements as separate domains: committee structures vary between House and Senate, and even among individual committees. The 1946 Legislative Reorganization Act, to be sure, applied an overall scheme to both chambers; but the act's neat design soon unraveled as new committees were created, subcommittees proliferated, committee sizes ballooned, and professionalized staffing took hold unevenly. Subsequent alterations to committees were mostly single-chamber efforts.[4]

Second, the Joint Committee faced a daunting timetable. Its delayed authorization meant that it could not begin work until the 103rd Congress convened in January 1993, and it had to finish its work by December. Between January 26 and July 1, 1993, the Joint Committee held 36 public hearings comprising more than 114 hours of testimony from 243 witnesses. This crowded schedule left scant time for members to deliberate or staff to do research. Instead, numerous studies by the Congressional Research Service were commissioned; outside groups were consulted; and roundtable discussions held to gather ideas from current and former staff members, scholars, and other observers. Member and staff surveys gathered suggestions and gauged reactions to specific proposals. Time constraints virtually precluded detailed consideration of jurisdictional realignment, a complicated issue requiring sustained attention on the part of members as well as staff.

Third, even if time had been available, the Joint Committee's members by no means concurred on the need for major alterations in the organization and operation of Congress. Party leaders, who served *ex officio* on the panel, carefully chose the other members to reflect their party's views. Some reform-minded members were selected, but not among the House Democratic contingent. Having controlled their chamber for forty years, House Democrats had the most to lose in a major reorganization; their party leaders would strive to protect their procedural prerogatives, while committee chairmen would guard their jurisdictional domains.

Finally, even if members had been disposed to consider broad-gauged committee reorganization, the mixed record of past efforts dampened their enthusiasm. The House had proved especially hostile toward jurisdictional reorganization: it scuttled a far-reaching 1974 plan in favor of marginal adjustments, and a 1980 effort came to naught. The Senate had realigned its committees in 1976; but a new round of proposals would surely confront resistance, buttressed by the chamber's requirement of a two-thirds vote to change the rules.

The Committee: Taking the "Joint" Out

As hearings drew to a close, behind-the-scenes negotiations among the Joint Committee's four principals and their staff aides cast about for proposals that could be reported to the two chambers. A two-day retreat at the U.S. Naval Academy in June covered a wide range of proposals but yielded few agreements. Eventually the Senate leaders, Boren and Domenici, settled on a fairly ambitious list of proposals. But the chasm that separated House Democrats and Republicans was too wide to be breached by Hamilton, who had to contend with unbending Democratic leaders, and Dreier, who pursued the GOP's reformist agenda. As a result, the Joint Committee's Senate and House members resorted to separate markup sessions—something that neither the 1945 nor the 1965 joint committees had been forced to do.

The Senate members held their day-long markup session on November 10, 1993. The Boren-Domenici package included, among other items, biennial budgeting, committee assignment limitations, abolition of joint committees, and committee oversight agendas. The bulk of the session was taken up with statements and procedural maneuvers by senators who objected to one or more of the draft measure's provisions (JCOC 1993b, 10-16, 42-44). The unanimous vote to report out the final product (with minor changes) was mainly symbolic; many senators clearly opposed key portions and hoped to modify or eliminate them in the Rules and Administration Committee or on the Senate floor. Sen. Ted Stevens of Alaska, Rules's ranking Republican, complained at length about the proposed assignment limitations but moved to report the measure "so the bill could be referred to the Rules Committee and we can strip out the portion we can do by rule" (JCOC 1993b 8). "You'll pick up the hood, and look under it, and all the rest of it," Boren observed. "I just kick the tires," replied Stevens (JCOC 1993b, 68). Rules chairman Wendell H. Ford, D-Ky., held his fire, but it was obvious that he too had quarrels with the Boren-Domenici document.

Not even polite acquiescence surrounded the House members' markup, which convened November 16 and did not adjourn until the 22nd, as Congress itself recessed for the year. Hamilton's markup draft included only items agreed upon by the majority of House members—notably subcommittee cuts, committee and subcommittee assignment limits, and oversight planning. "By design," the chairman explained, "the most controversial reforms mentioned during our six months of hearings are not included in the markup draft." He promoted his draft as "the first step in a longer process. . . . At this point we should primarily focus on keeping the reform process moving" (JCOC 1993b, 75-76).

Vice-Chairman Dreier countered that "this bill is neither bipartisan nor comprehensive. . . . The culmination of seven months of hearings and two months of negotiations is a document that on most pressing issues recommends more studies and nonbinding sense of the House resolutions." He complained that the report sidestepped essential issues (committee jurisdictional realignment and major procedural changes such as eliminating proxy voting in committees) and was too timid in cutting committees and staffs. Other Republicans heaped scorn on the chairman's draft. Rep. Gerald B. H. Solomon of New York called it "a 'minimalist approach' to tinkering." Pennsylvania representative Robert S. Walker said that "it should have been a strong document," and "if in fact the leadership had problems with it, then the leadership should have been in here asking for items to be removed from it because of its unacceptable nature" (JCOC 1993b, 78, 80, 82).

The markup itself was an acrimonious affair during which 35 amendments were presented and voted upon. Eight GOP amendments were accepted, but 25 amendments failed in 6-6 party-line votes—which Dreier denounced as "the attempts of a small but vocal faction of the Democratic caucus to derail this effort" (JCOC 1993b, 500). Among the Republicans' failed amendments were those that would have banned or curbed proxy voting in committees, tightened quorum requirements, assured the minority party one-third of committee staffs, and made deeper cuts in legislative branch funding.

Also killed was Dreier's committee realignment plan, which would have reduced standing committees from 22 to 16 and subcommittees from 118 to 96. The brief debate over Dreier's amendment was virtually the only time that the Joint Committee's members exchanged views on jurisdictional issues. Democrat Al Swift of Washington warned that any substantial reorganization plan would be defeated on the floor. Anyway, he said, jurisdictional problems would be resolved by curbing joint referrals—a point disputed by the GOP's Walker (JCOC 1993b, 193-194).

The most heated objection came from David R. Obey, D-Wis., who argued on the one hand that Dreier's scheme did not go far enough and on the other that it wasn't a serious proposal because it hadn't been fully discussed by the Joint Committee (JCOC 1993b, 196-197). "If it is so important to realign committees," he charged, "then why should we pass a proposal which avoids the most serious committee problem of all, which is the total dysfunction of the Ways and Means/

Appropriation/Budget Committee process?" (JCOC 1993b, 200). And he maintained that major jurisdictional realignment would need extended discussion within the Joint Committee and throughout the House:

> With all due respect, I was around here during [the 1974 reform battle], and I saw what a serious effort was. A serious effort meant that people talked to each other every day on the floor, anywhere you could grab people, walking people through different options like this. (JCOC 1993b, 198)

Dreier countered that he had not chosen to delay the markups to the end of the 1993 session, and his colleague Solomon asserted (rather unconvincingly) that realignment plans had indeed been considered in the Joint Committee's hearings, during which "every day these old bulls who were about my age—John Dingell and all the rest—would come down and they would look at these charts, we would discuss them, we would debate them, and we spent months doing this" (JCOC 1993b, 199). The skirmish reflected the partisan division that defeated the Dreier plan by a 6-6 vote.

Finally, the members voted 8 to 4 to report Chairman Hamilton's package as amended. All Democrats voted to report, along with two Republicans—Dreier and Bill Emerson of Missouri—who vowed to "keep the process moving forward" and to present amendments on the House floor, where members might fear to oppose bolder reforms.

The House and Senate members of the Joint Committee settled for a backdoor approach to committee reorganization. Rather than grappling directly with committee numbers, sizes, and jurisdictions, they proposed to make the committees (and subcommittees) compete for membership by imposing further limits on individual members' assignments, thus forcing members to choose which assignments to drop. House members would be limited to no more than two standing committees and four subcommittees. A more elaborate rule for senators would establish limits among four categories of committees. Procedural barriers would be erected to discourage violations of these limits. Moreover, if any standing committee dropped to fewer than half of its 103rd Congress membership level, the committee would risk being eliminated (the so-called *de minimis* rule).

Even this minimalist approach proved too drastic for the 103rd Congress. The second session had hardly convened when the Congressional Black Caucus weighed in against House assignment limits, which they claimed would hinder their members from rising to leadership positions. As Joint Committee member Eleanor Holmes Norton (Delegate, D-D.C.) put it, proposed limits would have "a disproportional racial effect" by reducing the number of committee leadership posts just as black members were gaining enough seniority to fill them (Jacoby 1994a, 31).

The Leaders: Delay and Attrition

Throughout 1994 the House and Senate reorganization measures were taken up respectively by the House Rules and Senate Rules and Administration committees. House and Senate leaders who dominated these panels sensed that the reports might eventually reach the floor but were in no hurry to send them there—hoping they could further dilute the recommendations before a public debate occurred. House Rules Committee Democrats loosened the reorganization measure's limits on committees and subcommittees and weakened other provisions. Dreier charged that "cynicism" and "irresponsibility" on the part of Democratic leaders and Rules Committee members had left the 103rd Congress "gliding into complete gridlock" (Sammon 1994b, 2660). Meanwhile, Senator Ford's Rules and Administration Committee killed the Joint Committee's recommendations for shrinking the number of committees through attrition, eliminating four joint committees, and banning proxy voting in Senate committees (Carney 1994). Eventually, the Rules Committee approved a watered-down version of the Joint Committee package but was in no hurry to take it to the floor.

The reformers, for their part, struggled to keep the issue alive and to bring public and media pressures to bear on leaders and members. However, theirs was a losing struggle. Leaders of both parties were solidly opposed to structural changes, and the public and the press seemed uninterested. "Every single member of this institution knows that the committee system is in desperate need of repair," protested Rep. John A. Boehner, R-Ohio. "But the leadership isn't willing to address this issue because politically, it's very, very explosive" (Carney 1994, 1736).

At the close of the 103rd Congress, Boren and Domenici offered the full package of Joint Committee proposals as an amendment to the District of Columbia appropriations bill. However, the 58-41 margin for their amendment fell short of the Senate's now-common requirement of 60 votes to forestall a filibuster. "Our approval rating is down to 14 points," Boren commented. "Are we going to wait to do something until not a single soul in America trusts us?" (Seelye 1994).

The House experience was similarly frustrating. In vain Hamilton and Dreier urged House leaders to report the total package—coupling the controversial procedural features with the more popular provision for congressional compliance with workplace laws. With tensions mounting and adjournment only days away, the Rules Committee finally scheduled a vote on the package. To counter Dreier's expected jurisdictional realignment amendment, Rep. Anthony C. Beilenson, D-Calif., floated two realignment proposals of his own. Confusion erupted in the Democratic ranks, and the Rules sessions were abruptly suspended. Last-minute efforts to revive the reform package were unavailing.

The Insurgents: Building a Record

In congressional politics no issue is ever finally settled, no proposal entirely beyond resurrection. Although the 103rd Congress floundered on the reform issue, it brought forth detailed blueprints for future action. The Joint Committee, whose timid efforts irritated Democratic leaders (and some Republicans) and languished in House and Senate committees, documented widespread discontent and support for change, especially among junior members. More importantly, it assembled an extraordinary set of historical, statistical, and analytical materials covering every phase of congressional operations, including the committees.

Late in the summer of 1994, as the Joint Committee's reports were breathing their last, House Republicans were dredging them (and other documents as well) for a reformist platform that could be sold to an angry, restless electorate. Three Joint Committee Republicans—Dreier, Solomon, and freshman Jennifer Dunn of Washington—drafted a wide-ranging list of reforms as part of a package to be known as the "Contract with America." Unveiled in a Capitol-West-front ceremony on September 27, the Contract was something unprecedented in American politics: a congressional party platform signed by virtually all its candidates, incumbents and challengers alike, and touted as its proposed agenda. "On the first day of the 104th Congress," the Contract's mastermind, Republican leader Newt Gingrich of Georgia, told the crowd, "the new Republican majority will immediately pass . . . major reforms aimed at restoring the faith and trust of the American people in their government" (Federal News Service 1994, 11). He promised his party would: (1) apply workplace laws to Congress; (2) launch an independent House audit; (3) cut House committees and committee staffs by one third; (4) limit terms of committee chairs; (5) ban proxy voting in committees; (6) open committee meetings to the public; (7) require three-fifths majorities for tax increases; and (8) implement baseline budgeting.

The Republicans Take Over

The elections on November 8, 1994, transformed the politics of congressional structures and procedures. The Republicans' long-standing complaints and campaign promises now comprised the program of a new majority party. The dramatic takeover of both houses of Congress afforded Republicans a rare opportunity to change not only the nation's policy agenda but also the procedures that would promote or retard their policies. Yet the reversal of fortunes confronted the victors with a novel and ironic problem: Now that we are the majority party, how many of the reforms we advocated as a minority can we live with?

Continuity in the Senate

The 1994 elections did not eradicate bicameral differences, despite the deceptive evenness of the Republicans' return to power (53 percent of the seats in each chamber). As an individualistic institution, the Senate is insulated against radical shifts. Although its Class of '94 was very conservative, a core group of moderates (six to eight or more on given issues) still held the balance of power on a host of important issues.

Recent experience with Senate party turnovers in 1981 and 1987 further leads one to expect less than cataclysmic changes. The 1981 Republican takeover brought far fewer changes than might have been expected after 26 years in the minority (Davidson and Oleszek 1984). To expedite President Ronald Reagan's agenda, GOP leaders initially instituted innovations to coordinate committee

Table 3-2 House Committee Sizes and Seats, 102nd–104th Congresses (1991–1996)

Committee[a]	102nd Congress (1991–92)			103rd Congress (1993–94)			104th Congress (1995–96)		
	Members	Sub-committees	Total Seats[b]	Members	Sub-committees	Total Seats[b]	Members	Sub-committees	Total Seats[b]
Agriculture	45	8	174	45	6	166	49	5	139
Appropriations	59	13	194	60	13	208	56	13	196
Banking and Financial Services (Banking, Finance, and Urban Affairs)	51	8	210	51	6	191	50	5	144
Budget	37	6	112	43	0	43	42	0	42
Commerce (Energy and Commerce)	43	6	149	44	6	150	46	5	149
Economic and Educational Opportunities (Education and Labor)	37	8	147	39	6	144	43	5	121
Governmental Reform and Oversight (Government Operations)	40	7	105	42	6	98	50	7	135
House Oversight (House Administration)	24	7	77	25	6	66	12	0	12
International Relations (Foreign Affairs)	43	9	142	44	7	128	41	5	107
Judiciary	34	6	103	35	6	107	35	5	98
National Security (Armed Services)	54	7	181	55	6	171	55	5	161

Resources (Interior and Insular Affairs until 1993; National Resources until 1995)	42	6	143	43	5	127	45	5	129
Rules	13	2	27	13	2	27	13	2	27
Science (Science, Space, and Technology)	51	6	149	55	5	149	50	4	136
Select Intelligence	19	3	49	19	3	49	16	2	36
Small Business	44	6	105	45	4	108	41	4	99
Standards of Official Conduct	14	0	14	14	0	14	10	0	10
Transportation and Infrastructure (Public Works and Transportation)	55	6	216	62	6	226	61	6	183
Veterans Affairs	34	5	91	35	5	93	33	3	72
Ways and Means	36	6	102	38	6	104	36	5	99
District of Columbia	11	3	35	11	3	31			
Merchant Marine and Fisheries	45	6	136	46	5	131			
Post Office & Civil Service	22	7	57	23	5	48			
Select Aging	68	6	190						
Select Hunger	33	2	62						
Select Narcotics Abuse and Control	34	0	34						
Select Children, Youth, and Families	36	0	36						
Totals	1,024	149	3,040	887	117	2,579	784	86	2,095
Members' Averages	2.4	4.6	7.0	2.0	3.9	5.9	1.8	3.0	4.8

Sources: Congressional Quarterly Weekly Report 49 (May 4, 1991); 51 (May 1, 1993); 53 (March 25, 1995); *Roll Call* (Jan. 23, 1995), B19–B29; and author's inquiries.

a The names of committees before 1995 change are given in parentheses.

b Includes members' seats on committees and subcommittees added together.

actions and plan Senate business, but these faded in subsequent years. Turnover of the partisan committee staffs was the most destabilizing feature of the 1981 transition, but even that underscored the degree to which the Senate's staff apparatus had become institutionalized. Continuity also marked committee procedures and folkways: one or two of the new chairmen tried to centralize committee operations but were effectively blocked.

The underlying lesson of recent Senate transition is that the "new Senate" created in the 1960s and institutionalized in the 1970s has survived virtually intact in the 1980s and 1990s. Its folkways—personal assertiveness, committee and subcommittee autonomy, and large staffs—although initially associated with the ascendancy of liberal Democrats, persisted because they seemed to serve the interests of all senators, regardless of party or ideological bent. Thus senators continue to resist major procedural reforms or staff cuts: although they moved to trim committee spending and limit subcommittees, their most drastic proposals were aimed outside the chamber—for example, eliminating all joint committees and the Office of Technology Assessment.

The House's Strong Speakership

As a majoritarian institution, the House of Representatives changed swiftly and dramatically with the 1994 election results. The Republican Conference was fully primed to overhaul House structures and procedures. The GOP-drafted rules bore the imprint of the party's 43-point package of two years earlier, and especially of Dreier's failed amendments from the Joint Committee markups. Dreier estimated that at least 90 percent of his amendments were included in the new House rules (Kahn 1995, A44).

Easy targets for elimination (actually, the work was transferred to other panels) were committees closely linked to Democrats' clienteles—District of Columbia (mostly Democratic voters), Post Office and Civil Service (postal and public employee unions), and Merchant Marine and Fisheries (environmentalists, maritime unions, and seaport cities). A few jurisdictions were rearranged—most notably financial institutions, transportation, and nonmilitary nuclear issues. Aside from the three dropped panels, promised cuts in member's assignments and committee sizes were modest. Too many members, including newcomers, clamored for choice assignments (see Table 3-2). In the end 31 subcommittees and 484 member seats were deleted (of those, 13 subcommittees and 210 seats came from the three dropped panels).

The new rules were designed to encourage members to focus on their committee duties by requiring them to be present for votes (no more proxies or "rolling quorums"), by publishing votes on committee reports, and by further discouraging committee meetings while the House is in session.

Joint referrals of measures to committees were prohibited, but not split or sequential referrals. Indeed, the Speaker now asserted a novel multiple-referral procedure, sending measures to a "lead committee" and other committees (dubbed "additional initial referrals") with the option of imposing deadlines upon any or all of the involved committees.

GOP leaders for the most part showed commendable restraint in dealing with the opposition. To give their foes a taste of their own medicine, the Republicans could simply have readopted the rules of the Democratic 103rd Congress. Instead, the new rules reaffirmed the minority's right to offer motions to recommit measures to committee, often the only chance to obtain a vote on the minority's alternative bill.

On the other hand, the new regime acted to marginalize if not eliminate 28 important noncommittee member groups. These were the issue-oriented caucuses called legislative service organizations (or LSOs), which had occupied House office space and procured staff and supplies with funds pooled from members' allowances. Notable examples were the Democratic Study Group (DSG) and the Congressional Black Caucus (CBC).

The GOP-crafted rules for the 104th Congress were adopted on the floor by wide margins; many Democrats conceded the innovations were long overdue. The changes rivaled in magnitude the great institutional turning points of the past—the "Reed rules" of 1890, the revolt against Speaker Joseph G. Cannon in 1909-1910, the Legislative Reorganization Act of 1946, and the "reform era" of the 1970s.

The vehicle for these changes was a cohesive majority party powered by a centralized leadership of a type not seen on Capitol Hill since Speaker Cannon's reign. The revitalized Speakership has its roots in the 1970s, when majority party reformers fought to counteract the committees' "old bulls" not only with caucus restrictions but also with enhanced powers for elective leaders (Sinclair 1983). Democratic Speakers exploited their new prerogatives in varying degrees and with mixed success.

To the powerful Speakership he inherited, Gingrich added new elements that threatened the power of the committees and their chairmen. Using the leverage of his loyal followers, he named committee leaders (departing from seniority in four instances). He also consolidated leadership control of committee assignments and housekeeping matters. Chairmen can now serve no more than six years. Their staffs were capped at a level one-third lower than during the 103rd Congress and placed under the discretion of the leadership-dominated House Oversight panel; allocation of 30 "statutory" staff members per committee would no longer be automatic (Nyhan 1995). Chairmen no longer enjoyed the scheduling support afforded by proxy votes or rolling quorums. To keep their policy promises, Republican committee managers would have to defend their bills against unpredictable amendments allowed by open (or at least liberalized) rules on the House floor. And under the new House rules, the leadership, not the committee chairmen, would wield procedural control over limitation amendments ("riders") on funding bills. In short, stronger party leaders and weakened committees would characterize the Republican regime.

Basic Principles of Turf Politics

The reformist surge of the early 1990s was hardly the first instance of congressional self-examination and structural innovation. Despite its unflattering public image as a fusty and unresponsive body, Congress since World War II has sponsored no fewer than three House-Senate reorganization committees, four chamber-wide studies of the committee system, and three wide-ranging administrative commissions, not to mention numerous *ad hoc* study panels. Some of these efforts produced major innovations; others ratified and codified arrangements that had gradually taken hold on their own; still others resulted in reports that were ignored or rejected.

Piecemeal responses to perceived problems add up to equally significant changes. Few Congresses convene without adopting at least a few structural or procedural alterations. The pace of change speeded up in the 1970s and the 1990s; in the interim, marginal adjustments continued to alter the way Congress and its committees operated (Davidson 1992, Rieselbach 1994). Out of this complex history, several generalizations can be made about the politics of committee innovation.

Although the outcomes have varied, the "laws" of reform politics have not. The GOP reformers of 1994-1995 were by no means immune to the forces of inertia that stymied reformers in the past.

• *Generalized support for "reform" quickly fades when specific proposals are put forward.*

Reorganization principles inevitably suffer when they surface as concrete proposals that promise to benefit some members, harm others, and raise the uncertainty levels for all. As members weigh these matters, their generalized endorsement of reform fades. This happened in the 103rd Congress and again into the 104th. In the Joint Committee's member survey, 85 percent of the representatives "voted" to limit committee assignments to four (two committees and two subcommittees of each), and 76 percent of the senators supported a limit of six (counting standing committees and subcommittees). But fewer than half the members said they would willingly give up one of their standing committee assignments (JCOC 1993f, Report II, vol. 2, 263).

Proposed shifts in committee jurisdictions face their fiercest resistance from affected members, staff aides, and allied outside interests. As Ways and Means chairman Dan Rostenkowski reminded the Joint Committee, ". . . there are potentially no more explosive issues relating to the reform of the operations of Congress than committee jurisdiction" (JCOC 1993c, 90). Nonetheless, there was no shortage of realignment plans floated during the 103rd Congress. None of these plans was discussed in any detail, either in the Joint Committee or in the House or Senate rules panels. Only one of them, the Dreier plan, was formally acted upon: it was rejected by a party-line vote during the House markup (JCOC 1993b, 166-201, 423-424).

With the GOP takeover, the prospects brightened for a major overhaul of committee jurisdictions. But although the new majority could move farther along this road than the old majority could, they faced similar roadblocks. It was easy enough to think of eliminating the three committees with declining and predominantly Democratic clienteles, but beyond that, the terrain grew rougher.

Again, there was no shortage of proposals. Of the four plans seriously debated by Republican leaders, the leading contender was drawn up by Dreier and two Joint Committee colleagues—based largely on Dreier's earlier scheme. In addition to dropping the three targeted panels (District of Columbia, Merchant Marine and Fisheries, and Post Office and Civil Service), the 17-committee plan would have rebuilt several others: Empowerment (education, labor, nutrition, housing, welfare), Ways and Means (revenues; minus welfare and health care), Public Infrastructure (public works, railroads, environment), and Ethics and Administration (combining House Administration, Standards of Official Conduct). Needless to say, the Dreier plan touched off frenzied debate within the party (Hosansky 1994).

After intense negotiations, Speaker-designate Gingrich and his close advisors decided against extensive committee realignment (Kahn 1995, A44-A45). "We have a committee structure that . . . is a very efficient structure," explained incoming majority leader Dick Armey of Texas. Although no doubt achievable, major jurisdictional shifts would set off bruising competition among newly named committee leaders and would jeopardize fragile working relationships between senior moderates and junior firebrands. Perhaps most important, realignment would divert energies from the substantive goal of implementing the Contract with America. There were other considerations as well. The Small Business and Veterans Affairs committees, often mentioned as candidates for phaseout, both had powerful constituencies and close Republican ties. Besides, Jan Meyers, R-Kan., in line to chair Small Business, was the only woman in the leadership ranks. So that committee realignment would not be wholly forgotten, the GOP Conference authorized a task force to address jurisdictional entanglements and to "further reduce the number of committees . . . and clarify questions of multi-committee jurisdiction."

Thus, even within the Republican ranks, support for realigning committees quickly faded once specific proposals were on the table. Support for smaller committees also weakened. Republicans' ambitious goals for downsizing committees took a back seat to their cravings for attractive committee assignments, their desire to compensate members of the dropped panels, and their need to accommodate Democrats trapped by shifting partisan ratios. As a result, the 20 remaining committees shrank in size by less than 3 percent.

• *Influential lawmakers, aided by outside clientele groups, stand ready to mount counteroffensives to preserve their committee domains.*

Although congressional reorganization is regarded as strictly an insider's game, outside groups oftentimes do more than kibitz. Like the members and staff they deal with, these groups have a stake in maintaining a given committee or upholding a particular procedural arrangement. A few groups propound ideological solutions to structural or political problems as they perceive them. Still others—among them the so-called public interest groups—profess a dedication to the generalized goal of more efficient or effective government.

From the evidence of the Joint Committee's 1993 hearings, groups bent on protecting the status quo are far more numerous and seemingly better mobilized than proreform groups—the latter either expecting tangible benefits from proposed changes or simply claiming to work for "good government." Environmentalists, fisheries associations, and public employees lobbied the Joint Committee to save the Merchant Marine and Post Office and Civil Service committees. Members and groups that might benefit from changes in committee jurisdictions were notable by their absence. Perhaps such interests regarded the potential changes as unlikely; perhaps they feared that such changes, even if beneficial in the long run, would impose costs by forcing them to establish new political contacts or access points. This might be called a "Replacing-your-Rolodex" phobia.

Members and their lobbyist allies defend established arrangements even when their cause appears to be lost. Interest group networks associated with the four "selects" mounted frantic efforts to preserve them in 1993; groups allied with the three doomed committees and 28 Legislative Service Organizations reacted similarly in 1994.

• *Those who stand to lose power are invariably more vocal than those who stand to gain; assets in jeopardy always seem more tangible than expected benefits.*

Leaders and members who suspected that their committees might be targets for elimination or jurisdictional trimming were on hand to state their case before the Joint Committee. Most conspicuously, the House Ways and Means Committee's vast territory alienated rival committees and seemed ripe for redefinition. (Indeed, it had been especially targeted 20 years earlier.) Rostenkowski's admonition was uncharacteristically gentle but nonetheless unmistakable (JCOC 1993c, 90):

My advice to you in this area is go slow. . . . I would urge you not to make recommendations simply because the current committee jurisdictional lines do not conform to some intellectually elegant model. The standard of proof that there is a real problem in this area has to be very high. I would hate to see the valuable work that this committee will do in all areas of a broad mandate fail solely as a result of proposed changes in committee jurisdiction.

When asked about proposals to transfer portions of his own panel's taxing jurisdiction to other panels, Rostenkowski in effect rejected them (JCOC 1993c, 92).

Other chairmen and ranking members, often appearing in tandem, denounced the proposed jurisdictional schemes and upheld their committees' interests before the Joint Committee. The chairmen and ranking minority members of House Small Business, Merchant Marine and Fisheries, and Post Office and Civil Service appeared, as did those from Senate Veterans' Affairs and Select Aging. G. V. "Sonny" Montgomery, D-Miss., of House Veterans' Affairs testified, as did Senate Small Business head Dale Bumpers, D-Ark., and Senate Indian Affairs' senior Republican, John McCain of Arizona. Rep. Don Young, R-Alaska, went so far as to say that he would sooner eliminate Natural Resources than Merchant Marine and Fisheries—although, as senior Republican on both panels, he had chosen to become ranking minority member (and later chairman) of the former rather than the latter (JCOC 1993c, 400). Members of the House and Senate Intelligence panels attacked proposals for a joint body.

After the 1994 elections Republican would-be chairmen were as quick to defend existing jurisdictions as Democrats had been at the Joint Committee hearings. Protecting committee turf is a bipartisan trait. For the 104th Congress the Commerce Committee was chaired not by blustery John Dingell but by mild-demeanored Thomas J. Bliley, Jr., R-Va. Yet Bliley fought skillfully to preserve his newfound patrimony. The initial realignment plan would have dismantled large chunks of the panel's turf (securities regulation, health care, transportation, energy, and environmental regulation). Bliley's arguments and horse trading left his committee largely intact—ceding only railroads (to Transportation), some securities (to Banking), energy research (to Science), and the Alaska pipeline (to Resources). "My goal was to hold on to as much jurisdiction as I could," he said, "And I think I did a pretty good job of it" (Andrews 1994, D11).

• *Where you stand depends on where you sit—as true of reform politics as any other.*

Under Democratic rule, committee leaders stubbornly fought against any incursions upon their jurisdictional domains. Yet many of them, like Dingell (D-Mich.), Rostenkowski (D-Ill.), and Montgomery, pleaded for cutting committee and subcommittee sizes, in order to relieve vexing problems of committee scheduling and management. Describing his 51-member Banking Committee as "one half of the U.S. Senate plus one," Texas Democrat Henry B. Gonzalez noted in 1993 that five of its subcommittees were too large to use the two available subcommittee rooms, making scheduling of their meetings difficult (JCOC 1993c, 222).

Senior committee leaders backed assignment limits for the same reasons they favored smaller sized committees. Sen. Robert C. Byrd, D-W. Va., declared that the Senate's root problem was members' "fractured attention" (JCOC 1993e, 4). With fewer assignments, it was reasoned, lawmakers would focus on legislative matters. Rostenkowski held that "the House is worse off as its members are spread thinner and each member spends less time on the critical issues he or she faces in committee" (JCOC 1993c, 89).

In the 104th Congress such newly named committee chairmen as Bill Archer, R-Texas, of Ways and Means, voiced the same concerns in arguing for smaller committees. But GOP leaders—like their Democratic predecessors—needed committee slots to hand out to the huge freshman class and favored senior colleagues (Hook and Cloud 1994).

For Republicans, the 1994 elections were a kind of epiphany: what appeals to a minority party bent on amending or halting action is likely to impede a majority party charged with scheduling and passing legislation. The more partisan of the 43 reform points urged by Republicans in the 103rd Congress were quickly forgotten in the 104th Congress. No one pressed, for instance, for a bipartisan House Oversight Committee or a minority controlled Government Reform and Oversight Committee. Fair committee ratios are fine for the minority, but majority parties need firm control of Rules and other key panels. (The GOP had no qualms about keeping the majority's 9-4 margin on Rules.)

• *Party leaders tend to be brokers rather than barnburners.*

Where do congressional leaders sit? The answer is, inescapably, somewhere at the center. Leaders are "middle people" who swim in their party's mainstream and are acceptable to most of the party's factions. Although they are key players in the politics of reform, they rarely introduce their own proposals but more typically manage or broker proposals made by others, mediating between insurgent factions and those members defending the status quo (Davidson 1994). Some leaders, like former Speaker Thomas S. Foley, begin their careers as reformers but end up resisting change, siding with senior colleagues against junior movers and shakers. Others, like Speaker Gingrich, build their careers as insurgents, only to end up at the center of their party and subject to its internal crosscurrents.

Occasionally, leaders do serve as sponsors or advocates of structural changes. This happens when they perceive that changes are needed if they are to fulfill their goals. Thus Speaker Sam Rayburn, D-Texas, fought in 1961 to "pack" the Rules Committee in order to process the activist agenda he expected from the Kennedy White House. In 1994 Gingrich moved quickly to enlarge his influence over committee personnel and procedures. Yet he carefully chose his battlegrounds: all but four of his committee chairmen were the most senior Republicans on their panels. (Their average seniority was no less than 9.65 terms.) In the process he accepted several chairs with distinctly "moderate" voting records (having been assured, however, that they would bring Contract bills quickly to the floor). And he declined to wage war over large-scale jurisdictional realignment, deferring to the committee chairmen whose loyalty would be required to implement his party's program.

• *Successful reformers are bound to be disappointed: many reforms outlive their usefulness, and all of them have unexpected results.*

New arrangements don't always work out the way they are supposed to. Invariably they have consequences that are wholly unanticipated, or even antithetical to their purposes. The 1946 Reorganization Act slashed committees but hastened subcommittee proliferation. Committee reforms of the 1970s made seniority leaders more responsive but inhibited bargaining across party lines. The 1995 reforms cannot escape a similar fate.

In pushing their ambitious agenda through committees and onto the floor, the new Republican majority was soon ensnared by the very reforms they had championed while in the minority. First, the ban on proxy voting impeded action, especially in committees like Judiciary or Government Reform that bore the brunt of the Contract's agenda. Second, limits on committee sessions during House floor sessions, while admirable in theory, further complicated scheduling of committee business.

Third, the very pressures of the 100-day schedule overwhelmed several affected committees and stood the lawmaking process on its head: rather than devoting months to hearings and deliberations, panels were rushed into action by the leadership in order to bring bills to the floor on time. "It was chaos," admitted William F. Clinger, whose Government Reform and Oversight Committee handled five separate Contract items. At the first organizational meeting, Clinger moved immediately from adopting committee rules to marking up the unfunded mandates bill, on which no hearings had been held. "We just got off on the wrong foot," Clinger said of the partisan furor that ensued. Of the 100-day deadline he said; "God knows why we ever agreed to that" (Kahn 1995b, 3). In the past central management had often been thwarted by committee obduracy; now efficient central scheduling was achieved at the cost of committee deliberation.

Finally, the promise of "open" rules for floor debate simply could not prevail over the desire to gain action within 100 days on the ten elements of the Contract, while maintaining party discipline and fending off minority challenges (Ornstein 1995). Compromises had to be reached, and inevitably political necessity trumped political principles. Once again, reforms had turned out to carry costs and liabilities.

Conclusions

The committee system remains at the heart of the beleaguered Congress, facing renewed challenges from within and without in response to pressures at once personal, partisan, and public. Numerous changes were implemented by the 103rd Congress—in some cases with considerable controversy. With partisan and member turnover and fresh leadership, the 104th Congress was able to effect more dramatic reorganization, albeit under severe pressures of time and an ambitious substantive agenda. Three concluding thoughts emerge from the reforms of 1995.

First, broad-scale reorganization of the committee system requires more detailed and more extended deliberation than was devoted to it during the 103rd Congress (even by the Joint Committee) or in the frenzied negotiations that preceded the 104th Congress. As Obey observed, "[such a reorganization] would have been scouted around with members . . . and we would have talked about it in a great variety of meetings until we could work out what we felt to be the kind of structure that we would want to take to the House by way of a reform structure" (JCOC 1993b, 196). Unfortunately, limits of time, staff resources, and politics militate against such an investment.

Second, external demands are mismatched with internal needs. Although external forces generate many of the institution's most acute organizational needs, they seldom address the means of meeting those needs. Public pressures for change are largely nonspecific, in the tradition of "Don't just stand there, do something!" To the extent that reform-oriented outside groups are interested at all in specific proposals they focus on high-profile items such as campaign finance laws, lobbying and ethics rules, congressional compliance with workplace statutes, term limits, and (briefly) the discharge petition issue.

Less glamorous but nonetheless acute organizational problems rarely excite widespread interest. "I don't think that the public much cares whether surface transportation, for example, is in the Commerce Committee or in Public Works," Representative Obey explained. "I don't think they care whether the Merchant Marine Committee exists or not" (JCOC 1993b, 196). The glaring exception to this rule—the 1993 controversy over House discharge petitions—was portrayed by advocates and media alike as a battle between openness and secrecy—a good versus evil scenario that ignored the issue's subtle aspects. As always, what is needed is congressional leaders who are skilled at managing institutional change, who are shrewd enough to think about harnessing generalized public unrest to the cause of specific institutional innovations. Such leadership, absent in the Democratic 103rd Congress, was a prominent feature of the Republican 104th.

Finally, Congress's organizational problems, if unattended, are bound to worsen. The lesson of the 1960s and 1970s was repeated in the early 1990s: if leaders fail to accommodate planned and modulated changes, they may very well be confronted by more extreme and unplanned upheavals—with institutional consequences that are far more acute and unpredictable.

Notes

1. The survey had a 30 percent response rate: 136 representatives and 25 senators. Although Senate respondents were relatively representative in party and seniority, the House sample was skewed somewhat toward Republicans and first-termers. See JCOC 1993f, 293-294.

2. There were 1,422 respondents in the general staff survey and 252 in the survey of administrative assistants and staff directors, for response rates of 41 percent and 53 percent respectively. The sample seemed representative of the various categories of staff that were identified. See JCOC 1993f, 323, 344-345.

3. The Senate, on the other hand, rejected a move to drop two of its select committees—Aging and Indian Affairs. Sen. Daniel K. Inouye, D-Hawaii, who chaired Indian Affairs, even persuaded his colleagues to remove the word "Select" from his committee's title. His amendment to the committee funding bill, which he described as "technical" (Indian Affairs has limited legislative jurisdiction), was passed by voice vote (*Congressional Record*, February 24, 1993, S1977-S1978).

4. The second (1965-1966) Joint Committee was barred from proposing jurisdictional changes; its recommendations regarding committees, most notably the "committee bill of rights," were softened by the Senate and almost scuttled by the House (which approved a watered-down version almost four years later). Indeed, the most searching inquiries into committee structures and procedures were single-chamber undertakings: the House's Bolling-Martin Committee (1973-1974) and the Senate's Stevenson-Brock Committee (1976-1977) conducted extensive research and hearings and issued thoughtful reports, many elements of which were adopted.

4

ACQUIRED PROCEDURAL TENDENCIES AND CONGRESSIONAL REFORM

Sarah A. Binder and Steven S. Smith

At the opening of the 104th Congress in January 1995, the newly elected Republican majority in the House enacted a full slate of procedural reforms promised to voters during the 1994 midterm congressional elections. The new rules—coupled with promises of free-flowing debate and amending activity on the majority of legislation—had been heralded by Speaker Newt Gingrich, R-Ga., as a sign that the House would be "far more open, far more participatory" than Democratic-controlled chambers of the previous decades (Cooper 1994). Across the Capitol in the Senate, no such sweeping change occurred. Senators of both political parties resoundingly rejected new limits on their right of nearly unlimited debate. "I think the Senate has acted wisely," commented Sen. Robert C. Byrd, D-W. Va., "in retaining the rule that has governed our proceedings since 1806."[1]

Such efforts at reform in the 104th Congress came, of course, on the heels of failed reform in the preceding Congress. How can we account for the record of reformers before and after the midterm elections? In this chapter, we present a perspective on procedural change that relates parties' choices over procedural rules to their underlying policy and electoral goals.

By the late 1980s, after more than two decades of remarkable change, floor activity in the House and Senate had settled into new patterns. In the House nearly all major legislation was considered under special rules that restricted amendments in some way. The special rules were written by the Democrats of the Rules Committee, always under the guidance and sometimes under the direction of the Speaker. The Senate, in contrast, continued to allow largely unrestricted amending activity, with the exception of limited but important classes of budget and trade legislation. For most Senate floor action, amendments could be limited only by unanimous consent; in effect, any senator could offer amendments on any subject to nearly any bill. But in both chambers, a limited agenda and leaders' procedural adjustments yielded a lower volume of amending activity than in the 1970s.

The apparent stability in the character of House and Senate floor activity masked frustration with how the chambers conducted business on the floor. Some frustration, of course, can be found in all large legislative bodies, particularly those representing a diversity of interests and bearing heavy work loads. Legislators cannot possibly master all of the policy issues on which they are asked to record public votes. Only a few can take an active part in the debate on most issues. Even the winners of legislative battles often express disappointment with the content of the legislation that is adopted.

In 1993 and 1994 frustrations beyond the usual frustrations of legislative service were aired before the Joint Committee on the Organization of Congress (JCOC). In the House, Republicans complained, as they had for more than a decade, about restrictions on their freedom to offer amendments to bills drafted in committees dominated by Democrats. Even some conservative Democrats evidenced unhappiness with the constraints under which they were forced to maneuver to influence policy choices. In the Senate, unlimited amending activity and unpredictable floor scheduling were a source of frustration for nearly all members. But Senate Democrats, or more particularly their leaders, exhibited exhaustion as well as frustration about the ability of the minority party Republicans to hold up Senate action on their legislation. And tensions arising from differences in House and Senate rules, particularly with respect to procedure on budget measures, exacerbated the usual tensions between the two houses.

The responses of the House and Senate to demands for change in legislative procedure in the 103rd Congress were consistent with historical patterns. The majority party of the House, in the absence of sustained public interest or a serious threat from a crossparty coalition, had little incentive to reinforce minority rights in their chamber. The minority party in the Senate, with its remarkable cohesiveness in the 103rd Congress, had sufficient strength to prevent action on proposals to streamline Senate floor activity that would help Senate majorities bring issues to a vote. Only with the appearance of the Republican majority in the 104th Congress were significant procedural reforms made in the House—as Republicans adopted rules changes both to serve their policy goals and to avoid reneging on past commitments to reform.

A Perspective on Procedural Change in Congress

Rules of procedure—required in most formal legislative bodies to give some order to the consideration of policy alternatives—allocate rights to participate in decision making. Some rules specify a sequence to the decision-making process and so limit either what can be done or who can do it at the various stages of the process. Other rules specify who is allowed to offer motions or propose certain actions. Still others set a standard for making decisions—a ruling of the presiding officer, a simple majority, a supermajority, unanimous consent, concurrence of subgroups of legislators, and so on.

Rules of procedure can influence policy outcomes. The degree and direction of the bias of rules depend on the circumstances, including the division of opinion among legislators and the character of the issue. Unfortunately, political science has not yet developed a general theory of legislative rules, so we cannot fully predict when and in what direction rules will change. Scholars have identified, however, numerous factors that influence institutional change: the size of the

House and Senate, demands placed on the institution from its environment, the size and complexity of the legislative work load, legislators' needs for information, and so on. For example, there is little doubt that chamber size is one reason why the House limits debate and amendments more than does the Senate.

Our focus is on two explicitly political sources of institutional change: partisan advantage and electoral calculation. The primary dynamic is partisan: when legislators of a party or policy coalition believe that changes in the rules are likely to have an effect on policy outcomes, they have an incentive to modify the rules. The incentive increases with the number and importance of the issues at stake. Specific conditions under which partisan advantage produces procedural change are the subjects of recent research (see Binder forthcoming a; Dion 1991; Fink and Humes 1992). But it also appears that electoral motivations come into play in shaping members' choices over rules. Constrained by prior public commitment to reform or seeking to avoid political embarrassment, legislators at times find themselves bound to procedural reforms that potentially run counter to their policy interests.

Policy Goals and Procedural Choice

The key to the relationship between partisanship and procedure appears to be the strength (size and cohesiveness) of the parties or coalitions. This strength shapes both the motivation and the ability of a party or coalition to change rules of procedure. A sufficiently large, cohesive majority party generally has enough votes from within its own ranks to enact its policy agenda without worrying about the rules. But success for the majority depends on two factors. First, it depends on the size and cohesiveness of the minority party. A sizable and highly cohesive minority party increases the strength required of the majority for the majority to succeed. Second, the required size and cohesiveness for a majority to have its way on legislation depend on existing rules. If the rules make it impossible for a simple majority to bring a matter to a vote, a highly cohesive but small majority may not have the necessary strength to ensure victories for its policy positions.

A party will seek to change procedural rules when the combination of rules and party strength make it likely that a change in the rules will improve its chances of legislative success. At times, the majority party may be strong enough to change the rules without the cooperation of any minority party members. In contrast, the minority party cannot win adoption of favorable rules without some support from the majority. This perspective on procedural change seems to account for much of the history of House minority rights (see Binder forthcoming b). Facing minority obstructionism that prevents them from pursuing their policy goals, strong majority parties have suppressed minority rights: reducing the opportunities of the minority party to delay action by debating, offering amendments and other motions, or refusing to be counted for a quorum. Crossparty coalitions composed of the minority party and at least a few majority party members have created new minority rights when weakened majority parties confronted a relatively large and cohesive minority party.

The development of House rules of procedure has been contingent on the ability of a simple majority to cut off debate and bring a matter to a vote. This is accomplished through a motion on the previous question, a privileged motion dating back to 1811. When adopted, a motion on the previous question precludes additional amendments and debate. Depending on the circumstances, the failure of the majority party to gain sufficient support for a previous question motion enables the opposition to extend the debate or offer amendments. Generally, the previous question rule has allowed majority parties to force action on rules changes that work to their advantage. As a result, the House has acquired a distinctive procedural tendency—accumulating numerous rules and practices that formalize the role of party in structuring the agenda, allocating time for debate, and shaping the amending process. When crossparty coalitions have gained sufficient strength to reassert minority rights, the tendency has been to further recognize party as the basis for organizing the legislative process.

Senate rules of procedure have evolved very differently. The Senate never adopted a previous question motion similar to the modern House rule, and it eliminated the weak rule that it did have in 1806. Consequently, a minority of senators can extend debate or offer an unending series of amendments to obstruct final action on a measure. Indeed, during most of the nineteenth century, Senate rules provided no way to stop a member from talking or yielding the floor to a friendly colleague to continue the debate. As a result, a determined group of senators could act as a tag team and prevent Senate action on legislation, including measures that would change Senate rules.

Not until 1917 did the Senate adopt its first cloture (debate ending) rule. After several revisions Rule 22 now permits three-fifths of the Senate (60 of 100 members or a supermajority) to shut off debate on substantive issues. Once cloture is invoked, there still remain 30 hours of debate time on the pending matter before the final vote. Thus, it is possible to stretch out the 30 hours for several days, producing what senators refer to as postcloture filibusters (Davidson and Oleszek 1990, 347).

To this day, a minority of just one more than one-third of the Senate can prevent adoption of a rule change, since a higher threshold is required to overcome a filibuster on such a matter. Plainly, the barrier to procedural change is higher in the Senate than in the House. In only two Congresses since World War II have the members of one party comprised more than two-thirds of the Senate. Only on budget issues has the Senate been determined to adopt time limitations and amendment restrictions. A 60-vote supermajority is needed to waive budget rules. This requirement has been applied only to a limited set of particularly salient measures—generally to enforce delicate deals within fragile coalitions.[2]

In practice, therefore, Senate procedural change occurs when it benefits the vast majority of all senators—members of both parties. Not surprisingly, its modern rules do not allocate rights by party, as House rules do in several ways. Even Senate practices are far less structured by party. Instead, Senate procedure has remained far more protective of the individual rights of senators, irrespective of party. And, notably, Senate rules are less than one-third of the length of House rules.

Electoral Goals and Procedural Choice

A caveat is in order. Procedural change is not always driven by the policy or legislative objectives of the members. Members may simply want to avoid blame for blocking procedural and policy change. At the start of World War I, Republican senators who had filibustered a bill to authorize American merchant ships to arm themselves against German attack were bullied by President Woodrow Wilson into approving the creation of Rule 22. More recently, minority party House Republicans in 1993 used a well-orchestrated, public campaign to embarrass the Democratic majority into accepting a rule change to reveal signatures on confidential committee discharge petitions.

In other words, political motivations and electoral calculation can lead members to support procedural reforms otherwise at odds with their party's policy interests. Electoral goals also can cause a party to back off from a reform it favors. House Democrats in 1994, for example, considered but decided against abolishing the committee discharge rule. Such a move, many argued, might provide Republicans with an effective campaign issue. "The last thing they [the Democrats] wanted to do was [to] put the discharge petition back in the news," one Democratic aide noted at the time (Jacoby 1994e).

But the public generally pays little attention to congressional procedure. Former House minority leader Robert Michel, R-Ill., once observed: "Nothing is so boring to the layman as a litany of complaints over the more obscure provisions of House procedures. It is all 'inside baseball.' Even among the media, none but the brave seek to attend to the howls of dismay from Republicans over such esoterica as the kinds of rules under which we are forced to debate" (Michel 1987, A14). Only rarely, when the connection between a rule of procedure and an unpopular policy outcome becomes especially obvious or when members' campaign obligations constrain their choices over rules, can we expect members to support procedural change to avoid political embarrassment or blame.

In sum, the two chambers have acquired distinctive procedural tendencies that shape the motivation and the ability of parties and coalitions to change rules of procedure. Those tendencies yield a set of expectations for developments in the 103rd and 104th Congresses. In the House a simple majority—either the majority party or a crossparty coalition—must see a procedural or political advantage to be gained or a disadvantage to be eliminated before rules of procedure are changed. In the Senate an extraordinary majority—necessarily a crossparty majority in the 103rd and 104th—must support a rules change for it to be adopted.

Procedural Reforms Proposed in the 103rd Congress

Members of both chambers challenged the existing array of parliamentary rights in the 103rd Congress. And in both political parties, members expressed frustration with the balance between majority rule and minority rights. No single reform agenda, however, characterized the wide-ranging proposals that would have affected members' rights in committee and on the floor.

House Proposals

Separate challenges to the highly majoritarian character of the House were offered in the 103rd Congress by two coalitions: the House Republican Conference and the Fair Rules and Openness Group (FROG), a coalition of moderate and conservative Democrats. Despite differences in the two groups' scope of reforms, both groups sought changes in Democratic leaders' reliance on restrictive special rules to structure floor consideration of chamber bills. Republican and Democratic freshman classes also proposed several changes, although they failed to endorse a single slate of procedural reforms.

House Republicans. Before the Joint Committee on the Organization of Congress in 1993, Minority Leader Michel called for more open debate. "The minority's views are noted, recorded, and then thrown into the memory hole, never to be heard from again," he lamented. "The Majority does what it wants, satisfied that it has played its role in the ritual" (JCOC 1993e, 32). His party challenged the way the majority structured floor debate, waived existing House rules, and permitted voting by proxy in committee. Table 4-1 lists the major proposals enhancing minority procedural rights that were endorsed by House Republicans before the Joint Committee.

An increasingly common practice of the Rules Committee was to report special rules that denied the minority the right to offer amendatory instructions in a motion to recommit (the last motion before final passage of a bill).[3] Republicans advocated a rule that would guarantee the absolute right to offer such a motion "with instructions." Republicans also advocated new rules to liberalize the majority party's use of restrictive rules governing floor debate and amending activity. Under their proposals the minority party would be guaranteed the right to offer an alternative to any restrictive rule reported by the Rules Committee, and supermajorities would be required to approve special rules waiving points of order against legislation. According to the Republicans, such proposals would not radically alter the majority party's ability to control the floor agenda; instead, they would offer the minority a chance to play a constructive role in making policy. Republicans lambasted the majority's practice of limiting amendments and placing minority amendments in a disadvantageous sequence as politically motivated moves to shelter members from casting controversial votes (JCOC 1993b, 267).

Republicans also targeted committees for reform. They wanted to ban proxy voting, publish committee voting and attendance records, make committee party ratios reflect the partisan division in the full House, and guarantee one-third of committee investigatory staff for the minority party. Supporters of a proxy voting ban, for example, argued that the casting of proxy votes gave the majority undue influence over committee outcomes. By prohibiting committee chairs from casting votes for absent members, Republicans also claimed that the ban would increase committee attendance and participation rates. Witnesses before the Joint Com-

Table 4-1   House Proposals Affecting Procedural Rights, By Sponsor, 103rd Congress

House Republican Conference	Freshman Class[a] of 1992	Democratic Leadership
Protect all recommittal rights	Ban proxy voting	Extend recommittal rights
Ban proxy voting	Publish committee attendance	Oxford-style debates
Publish committee votes		
Publish committee attendance		
Make committee party ratios equitable		
Guarantee minority party staff		
Amend committee quorum rules		
Guarantee amendments on closed rules		
Limit special rules		
Limit budgetary waivers		
Limit "suspension" procedure		
Boost minority party oversight control		

[a] Proposals received some bipartisan support.

mittee testifying in favor of a proxy ban were predominantly Republican, but some Democrats voiced support for a ban—perhaps not surprising since a handful of House committees already banned the casting of proxy votes (JCOC 1993f, 27).

Fair Rules and Openness Group (FROG). Under the leadership of Representatives Charles W. Stenholm, D-Texas, and Timothy J. Penny, D-Minn., more than a dozen conservative and moderate Democrats formed the Fair Rules and Openness Group in March 1994. The purpose of the group was to fight restrictive rules that barred floor consideration of amendments it supported. Citing growing dissatisfaction with closed and restrictive rules crafted by the Rules Committee—and sensing the potential clout of the 75 to 100 Democrats voting occasionally against special rules—FROG met each week to discuss whether anticipated rules were fair to members with conservative and moderate views. They also decided which Democratic or bipartisan amendments they would support. The group vowed to oppose any rule that failed to make FROG-backed amendments in order. The two amendments to the 1994 crime bill were made in order, FROG claimed, only after the group threatened to vote against any rule that excluded it (Jacoby 1994c).

FROG was not organized at the time the Joint Committee held hearings in 1993, but future members testified about restrictive special rules and other subjects. The decision to organize in 1994 suggests the emergence of a fracture line among Democrats on how to allocate parliamentary rights in the House. As

Representative Penny noted, conservative Democrats "feel resentful of not being allowed to offer serious policy alternatives on the floor. . . . The only way to put them [the leadership] on notice is to have a formal group to put them in motion."[4] From Stenholm's perspective, the paucity of conservative Democratic representation on the Rules Committee necessitated FROG's formation.[5] Neither Stenholm nor Penny opposed restrictive rules in principle. To the contrary, both argued that the majority had a legitimate need to structure floor debate in some fashion. But, they said, special rules had been used too often to advance the dominant ideological perspective within the majority party.

Freshman Class of 1992. After the 1992 elections it appeared that the freshmen of both parties would push hard for changes in the way Congress conducted its business. Most had campaigned on a platform of congressional reform, and the size of the group (110) indicated that sheer numbers made substantial reform likely. However, the class of 1992 failed to agree to a joint slate of congressional reforms. Instead, the 63 Democratic and 47 Republican first-termers presented separate reform agendas early in 1993 (Donovan 1993a, 1993b). Only two recommendations appeared on both lists—the application of workplace employment laws to Congress (known as "congressional compliance" legislation) and cuts in spending on staff for former Speakers.

For the most part the freshmen viewed rules of procedure from predictably partisan perspectives. On the Democratic side, the freshmen offered two proposals targeting minority obstruction—one setting limits on motions to adjourn and one ending the daily recorded votes on the *House Journal.* They did make one concession to Republicans, however, by proposing longer debates on measures subject to closed rules. On the Republican side, the freshmen advocated their party leaders' agenda (for example, supermajority votes to approve restrictive rules). Only in one area—forcing attendance at committee meetings and banning proxy voting in full committee—did at least some bipartisan agreement among freshmen emerge by late 1993 (see Table 4-1).

House Democrats. House Democrats proposed relatively few reforms addressing the balance of parliamentary rights in the chamber. Rules Committee Chairman Joe Moakley, D-Mass., did show some sympathy for the Republicans' procedural predicament when he expressed willingness to make concessions on the motion to recommit.[6] Instead of looser rules during floor consideration of legislation as advocated by the minority, Majority Leader Richard A. Gephardt, D-Mo., indicated majority party support for "Oxford-style" debates as an after-hours addition to regular debate time on major issues. To address another source of frustration among members of both parties, other members suggested that the House adopt the Senate's schedule of three weeks in Washington followed by one week in the district.

Much of the testimony before the Joint Committee from leading Democrats reflected their opposition to Republican proposals on rules of procedure. From the majority's perspective, tightly structured special rules enabled the House to act efficiently on a heavy legislative load and to avoid politically motivated and purely obstructive motions offered by the minority. Speaker Thomas S. Foley, D-Wash., argued, for example, that "it is not always true . . . that we serve the interests of the House best by having unlimited debate, unlimited amendments" (JCOC 1993e, 16). Foley noted later that even minority members were complaining about the time it took to debate and consider amendments under an open rule on an education bill (Jacoby 1994b). Several committee chairs also expressed opposition to minority party reforms, in particular proposals to bar proxy voting.[7]

Senate Proposals

Major proposals offered in the Senate that would affect the distribution of procedural rights focused primarily on changes to Rule 22 (see Table 4-2). Such recommendations offered by Democratic senators sought to reduce minority and individual obstruction, shifting greater parliamentary control to the majority party. In the Senate, unlike the House, Republicans did not propose extending further protections to minority party members. In fact, some Republicans on the Joint Committee expressed support for majority efforts to limit floor obstructionism.

Citing dramatic increases in the number of filibusters and threatened filibusters—and arguing that many were initiated for trivial reasons—then majority leader George Mitchell, D-Maine., proposed limiting the opportunities available for filibustering on the Senate floor. For example, Mitchell advocated banning extended debate on the motion to proceed to legislative business. Other Democratic senators proposed ratcheting down the number of votes needed to invoke cloture and limiting the informal practice of placing holds on measures.

Senators' reactions to such proposals split largely along partisan lines. Support for Mitchell's proposals came primarily from fellow Democrats, who paid most attention to his call to eliminate the filibuster on motions to proceed. Opposition stemmed from the minority party, whose leader, Kansan Robert Dole, quickly opposed changes in Rule 22. Dole emphasized the value of the filibuster to both majority and minority party senators. Pete V. Domenici, R-N.M., the Senate vice-chair of the Joint Committee, indicated support for limiting debate on the motion to proceed, but other Republicans did not join him.

Bicameral Issues

Disputes over the allocation of procedural rights were not confined to the separate chambers: several issues sparked bicameral tussles as well. In particular, proposals to reaffirm Senate commitment to the Byrd Rule and to link changes in House and Senate minority rights flamed intense interchamber disputes.

The Byrd Rule. The Senate's Byrd Rule—named after its author, Robert C. Byrd, D-W.Va.—excludes from budget reconciliation bills any extraneous items that have no direct impact on reducing the deficit. Sixty votes are required to waive the rule. The Senate's Joint Committee panel recommended amending the

Table 4-2   Senate Proposals Affecting Procedural Rights,
                103rd Congress

Proposals Sponsored by Democrats

Ban filibuster on the motion to proceed[a]

Reduce other opportunities to filibuster

Adopt "sliding scale" for cloture

Amend postcloture quorum rules

Require three-fifths vote to overturn chair postcloture

Limit the use of legislative "holds"

Permit imposition of germaneness requirement

Permit dispensing with reading of conference report

Extend and codify Byrd Rule

Limit proxy voting[a]

Publish committee votes[a]

Publish committee attendance[a]

---

[a]Proposal received some Republican support.

Congressional Budget and Impoundment Control Act of 1974 to clarify the permanence of the Byrd Rule.[8] In recent years the rule has forced House committees to strip numerous House-passed provisions from deficit reduction bills. (On the politics of the Byrd Rule, see Cohen 1993b; Foerstel 1994a, 1994c.) Senators argued that the rule was essential for ensuring fiscal discipline. Many Democratic chairs of House committees disliked the Byrd Rule, however. They maintained it gave the Senate undue influence in House-Senate budget deficit conferences. From their perspective, the rule exacerbated interchamber conflict and perpetuated gridlock. Because any changes to the Budget Act require Senate and presidential approval, there was little House Democrats could do to alter the Byrd Rule. Indeed, introducing a bill to strike the Byrd Rule from the Budget Act, House Budget Chair Martin O. Sabo, D-Minn., conceded as much: "We just keep hoping to educate them" (Jacoby 1994d, 12).

Linking House and Senate Minority Rights. The other bicameral dispute was a proposal by several House liberals and the House Democratic Study Group (DSG) to make extension of minority rights in the House contingent on major changes to the Senate filibuster. House Republicans cried foul, arguing that the linkage proposal was a thinly disguised move to kill reform. Numerous Republican senators also resented the House's meddling with Senate rules; House Democrats simply wanted to derail reform, they claimed. Some Senate Democrats, however, were said to favor the DSG reform.

Summary

Pressure for procedural reform in the 103rd Congress came primarily from the House minority party and Senate majority party. House Republicans complained about the way in which their opportunities to offer alternatives to legislation were limited by the rules and practices imposed by the majority party Democrats. Senate Democrats complained about the way in which the rights to debate and offer amendments were used for dilatory purposes by the minority party Republicans. In both chambers the groups most dissatisfied with chamber procedure fit our expectations about the partisan sources of pressure for procedural reform.

Failure of Reform in the 103rd Congress

The partisan or electoral motivations necessary for significant procedural change failed to emerge in the 103rd Congress. The House majority party was not interested in weakening its procedural advantages, and no crossparty coalition of Republicans and conservative Democrats seemed strong enough to gain a majority in the face of opposition from the majority party leadership. The Senate minority party clearly opposed, and was large and cohesive enough to block, any reforms that would reduce its opportunities to debate or offer amendments. And in both chambers, partisanship continued to run high on substantive policy questions. Democratic majorities in neither the House nor the Senate seemed electorally motivated to push hard for reform in the 103rd Congress. Thus, although the pressure for reform came from predictable sources, the conditions were not ripe for the enactment of significant procedural change.

Committee Action

The Joint Committee reported a package of House reforms in November 1993, with a majority of Republicans voting against the package (Table 4-3). Only two of many Republican proposals on rules of procedure were included in the bill: a motion to recommit with instructions was guaranteed for the minority leader, and committee attendance and voting records were to be made public in the *Congressional Record* (a requirement that Republicans believed would compel Democrats to attend meetings, reduce the use of proxy voting, and increase Republican opportunities to appeal to Democrats for support). Twenty-five amendments offered by House Republicans were defeated on a party-line vote of 6-6.[9]

In contrast, the Senate package was unanimously reported from the Joint Committee (Table 4-3). It limited to two hours debate on a motion to proceed, required a three-fifths vote to overturn rulings of the chair after cloture, and counted quorum call time against the member calling for the quorum. The Senate package also banned proxy voting when it would affect the outcome of a committee vote. Although there was no opposition or discussion of these reforms during markup of the bill, senators on the Joint Committee seemed to recognize that Republican objections to debate limits probably doomed their recommendations in that respect.

Table 4-3   Significant Procedural Reforms, By Chamber,
103rd and 104th Congresses

	Rules Changes	
Chamber	Recommended by the Joint Committee on the Organization of Congress but Never Adopted in the 103rd Congress	Adopted in the 104th Congress
House	Guarantee recommittal rights	Guarantee recommittal rights
	Publish committee attendance	Publish committee attendance
	Publish committee votes	Publish committee votes
		Ban proxy voting
		Ban "rolling" committee quorums
		Require three-fifths majority for tax rate increases
		Motion to rise reserved to majority leader on appropriations bills
Senate	Ban filibuster on motion to proceed	No changes adopted
	Require three-fifths majority to overturn chair postcloture	
	Amend postcloture quorum rules[a]	
	Limit proxy voting[a]	
	Publish committee attendance	
	Publish committee votes	
	Extend and codify Byrd Rule	
	Limit Sense of Senate resolutions[a]	
	Permit dispensing with reading of conference report	

[a] Dropped by Senate Rules Committee, 103rd Congress.

The JCOC issued reports to the House and Senate in late 1993, but would both chambers make room on already crowded floor agendas to consider them? The answer depended on whether the issue of reform was sufficiently salient, or could be made sufficiently salient, to the public. In the House both majority and minority members recognized that the only portion of the JCOC recommendations with sufficient popular appeal concerned congressional compliance with laws governing the private sector.

Therefore, Democratic leaders chose to split the package into two and force separate consideration of congressional compliance: "There's no one element except compliance that would resonate beyond the beltway," noted one minority party staff member of House Rules.[10] Democratic representative Lee H. Hamilton of Indiana, one of the co-chairs of the Joint Committee, argued that the compliance provisions served as a "valuable sweetener for reforms that are less popular" (Foerstel 1994e, 18). Despite leadership promises to Hamilton to bring the rest of the reforms to the floor before the end of the 103rd Congress, the House Rules Committee abandoned its markup of the JCOC recommendations in late 1994.

Some of the impetus for Senate action seemed to dissipate when Sen. David Boren, chair of the Senate's contingent of the Joint Committee, announced his retirement and appeared to stop pushing reform. The Senate Rules Committee did report a package of procedural reforms in 1994, but the panel proved to be a far tougher arena for supporters of limiting minority and individual rights (Table 4-3). Although the committee retained the provision eliminating extended debate on the motion to proceed, both Democratic senator Byrd and Republican senator Ted Stevens of Alaska argued against efforts to dilute minority rights, and several Republicans vowed to kill the provision on the floor. On bicameral issues as well, the Senate continued to antagonize House Democratic committee chairs by approving an amendment that would allow the Senate, under the Byrd Rule, to strike House-passed nongermane provisions in appropriations bills.

Causes of Failure

In both the House and the Senate the distribution of procedural rights did not change in the 103rd Congress. How well then do the acquired procedural tendencies of each chamber explain the failure of reform? If the extension of significant minority rights in the House is contingent on the emergence of a crossparty coalition, then we would expect the lack of meaningful reform to reflect partisan conditions antithetical to such a coalition. In the Senate we would expect minority rights to be retracted when large bipartisan coalitions form in support of such change. But no such voting alignments prevailed in the 103rd Congress. Neither did public pressures for reform mount sufficiently to bully members into action.

The House. Observers of the House in recent years have widely noted the partisan strife dominating chamber politics. Indeed, during debate over creation of a reform panel, Rep. David R. Obey, D-Wis., noted the "poisonous atmosphere in Congress today that makes this a peculiarly bad time to proceed with this effort" (Hook 1992, 1580). Measures of House partisanship capture that bitterness in chamber relations. Table 4-4 shows levels of party unity votes in the House from 1974 to 1994, as well as Democratic and Republican party unity scores over the same 20-year period.[11] Not only did the level of party voting continue to rise in the 1990s, but it reached a two decade high in the first session of the 103rd Congress. In light of such sharp partisan differences, it is unlikely that any Democrats would see their policy or political interests furthered by joining Republicans in a coalition for procedural change. Despite the potential for crossparty coalitions between Democratic FROG members and House Republicans or between term Democratic and Republican freshmen, no such coalitions emerged. Both of these potential alliances deserve a closer look.

As noted earlier, both Republicans and FROG Democrats expressed opposition to Democratic leaders' reliance on overly restrictive special rules. Despite overtures from House Republicans, FROG leaders refused to endorse Republican amendments unless they had bipartisan support. Citing the GOP's tendency to offer dilatory amendments just as often as constructive ones, Stenholm argued that the minority should fight its own battles.[12] In short, conservative and moderate Democrats seemed to have little sympathy for House Republicans. By virtue of having a guaranteed motion to recommit, "Republicans have more rights in this process than we do," contended FROG leader Penny.[13] A FROG-GOP alliance, in other words, showed little likelihood of forming in the 103rd.

Freshmen members also could have formed a crossparty coalition. But Democrats and Republicans offered separate reform proposals, and freshmen found few areas of bipartisan agreement on procedural grounds. Those procedural disagreements reflected significant policy differences in the two party delegations. Both Democratic and Republican first-term members were more likely to vote with their respective party majorities than were returning party members (Donovan with Moore 1994). For example, freshmen Democrats averaged a 92 percent party unity score compared with 88 percent for more senior members. Only on several votes to kill federal spending for big science projects did the freshmen contingents join with House Republicans. In contrast, freshmen votes on budget issues and social policy reflected strong partisan cleavages. Such partisan policy differences suggest that first-termers would gain little from joining Republicans in support of significant extensions of minority rights.[14]

Finally, the Joint Committee's proposals earned few adherents within the Democratic Caucus.[15] Reforming arcane chamber rules clearly was perceived to have little resonance with the public. Unlike the Republicans' highly public drive in 1993 to reveal discharge petition signatures, the committee, budget, and ethics reforms were largely seen as "inside baseball stuff" that would not improve Congress's image.[16] With more politically popular congressional compliance and lobbying and gift reform at the top of the reform agenda, few Democrats pushed for procedural reform. Even a Republican aide close to the reform process conceded that few minority party members were focused on such procedural matters.

Outright opposition to the reforms, as well as Democratic indifference, plagued the reform effort. Those opposed to the JCOC package included Congressional Black Caucus members who resisted limits on their committee assignments, senior Democrats opposed to streamlining committees, and Democrats opposed to conceding rights to the minority.[17] Had there been a larger core of support within the Democratic Caucus for the panel's recommendations, Democrats might have had a greater incentive to extend new minority rights to Republicans as a sweetener to build a crossparty coalition for reform. But, with House Democrats

Table 4-4 House Partisanship, 1974–1994

Year	Party Unity Votes[a]	Party Unity Scores of Democrats[b]
1974	29	72
1975	48	75
1976	36	75
1977	42	74
1978	33	71
1979	47	75
1980	38	78
1981	37	75
1982	36	77
1983	56	82
1984	47	81
1985	61	86
1986	57	86
1987	64	88
1988	47	88
1989	55	86
1990	49	86
1991	55	86
1992	64	86
1993	67	85
1994	62	83

[a]Percentage of all recorded votes on which a majority of voting Democrats opposed a majority of voting Republicans.
[b]Percentage of Democrats voting with a majority of their party on party unity votes.

Sources: Ornstein, Mann, and Malbin (1994); Congressional Quarterly Weekly Report, December 31, 1994, 3624–3625.

either largely indifferent or strenuously opposed to the reforms, there was little incentive for Democrats to concede new rights to the Republican minority.

The Senate. The priorities of health care, campaign finance, and gift ban reforms pushed procedural reform off the Senate's summer agenda in 1994.[18] "The climate is getting worse," noted Senator Domenici. "A lot of lesser reforms are getting all the attention" (Hook 1994b, 1274). Moreover, when the JCOC provisions came before the Senate Rules Committee, Ted Stevens, R-Alaska, made clear his intent to filibuster any changes to Rule 22. More opposition to the JCOC bill was aroused by the addition of a Rules Committee amendment that would have imposed a germaneness requirement on amendments to appropriations bills. In short, the combination of indifference and minority opposition prevented the large bipartisan support necessary to alter parliamentary rights in the Senate in the 103rd Congress.

Procedural Reform in the 104th Congress

The surprise outcome of the 1994 elections produced Republican majorities in both chambers. The simultaneous party change in the House and Senate serves as a contemporary natural experiment. Would the House, in response to the needs of the new majority, show greater procedural change than the Senate? Would the Senate exhibit little or no change because of the continuing ability of a few senators to block action?

As expected, the Senate adopted no new rules of floor procedure. In fact, an amendment offered by Sen. Tom Harkin, D-Iowa, to allow a simple majority to invoke cloture on a filibuster was tabled 76-19, with both Democrats and Republicans opposed to the rule change. Supporters of the proposed rule were primarily liberal Democrats. The Democratic leadership said that the time was not ripe for the Democrats to make a stand on reforming a rule that enhanced their influence over Senate proceedings. Senate Republicans' unified opposition to reforming the rule likely stemmed from their desire not to let procedural matters derail consideration of the "Contract with America" agenda.

In contrast, House Republicans proposed, and the House approved, several reforms of House rules (see Table 4-3). For example, a three-fifths vote is now required for a measure that raises income tax rates. On its surface the new rule reduces the ability of a chamber majority to act, so it may not appear consistent with the thesis that the majority sets chamber rules to serve its policy interests. In this case House Republicans opposed tax increases and therefore wanted to make them harder to enact. The rule, of course, can be changed or waived by a simple majority in the future.

Another new rule granted the majority leader the exclusive authority to offer a motion to rise (to finish action in the Committee of the Whole) on appropriations measures.[19] This change enhances the power of the majority leadership over floor consideration of spending bills. At issue is the opportunity of members to offer "limitation amendments" to appropriations bills in the Committee of the Whole. Limitation amendments prohibit the use of federal funds for certain purposes. As such, they are a means of changing federal policy through a spending bill rather than through the more typical route of an authorizing bill.

In 1983 Democrats had amended House rules governing limitation amendments: they could be considered only after other amendments to an appropriations bill had been considered in the Committee of the Whole and after a motion to rise had been offered (if any member chose to make such a motion). The rule greatly limited the number of amendments to the Democrats' appropriations bills because the Appropriations Committee bill manager usually offered and gained majority support for a motion to rise. By amending the 1983 rule to allow only the majority leader to make the motion to rise, Republicans have reduced the opportunities of any member, Democrat or Republican, to offer a limitation amendment without the approval of the majority leader, unless, of course, a majority can be mustered to defeat a motion to rise.

In addition, the 104th Congress guaranteed a motion to recommit with instructions, banned proxy voting in committee, revised committee quorum rules, published committee voting and attendance records, and promised more open rules. These developments are curious because they appear to run counter to the policy interests of majority party Republicans. Only by allowing for party motives beyond the achievement of policy goals can the apparent generosity of the Republicans be explained. In fact, the Republicans themselves gave some clues.

The new rule on the motion to recommit guarantees the minority party's right to include amendatory language or "instructions" in a motion to recommit. For years Republicans had complained that restrictive special rules written by Democrats had taken away their traditional last opportunity to amend a bill, at least as the Republicans interpreted House precedents. Many speculated that majority status would lead Republicans to change their view of the motion to recommit with instructions. But Republicans included the provision in the rules package that was adopted by the House. Republicans also followed through on their previous commitments to revising chamber rules regarding committee procedures—reforms favored by past Republican minorities to enhance minority party influence in committee. Beyond the changes in the standing rules affecting floor procedure, House Republicans also vowed to end the practice of severely limiting floor amendments on major bills through special rules written by the Rules Committee (Jacoby 1994f).

What accounts for these apparently voluntary concessions to the minority? Two factors seem to have been at work. The first is the goal of retaining majority status. The Republicans' "Contract with America" promising an "open" Congress, as well as many years of complaints about unfair treatment under the rules imposed by the Democrats, may have compelled Republicans to follow through on reforms they supported when they were in the minority. They feared criticism for changing their tune once in power. Eager to claim credit for changing the House, Republicans likely did not want headlines that "politics as usual" was still alive in Washington.[20]

Republicans' self-confidence in the aftermath of the election also seems to have played a role. For example, while discussing his prediction that three-fourths of special rules would be open, Rules Committee Chairman Gerald B. H. Solomon said, "We don't have a fractionalized situation, as they do in the Democratic party. I can afford to be even more fair than you would be under normal circumstances" (Towell 1994, 3320). Many Republicans believe that their inability to build a coalition with conservative Democrats in the recent past was due to special rules, designed by Democratic leaders, that barred amendments that would divide the Democrats. By opening up amending activity, many Republicans seem to think, the true weakness of the support among Democrats for liberal policy will become transparent.

It's hard to interest the public in the internal problems of the House. In fact, although the Senate cloture rule has attracted public attention from time to time, House procedure has very seldom been subject to public discussion. Former minority leader Michel once observed:

> What is more important to a democracy than the method by which its laws are created? We Republicans are all too aware that when we laboriously compile data to demonstrate the abuse of legislative power by the Democrats, we are met by reporters and the public with that familiar symptom best summarized in the acronym "MEGO"—my eyes glaze over. We can't help it if the battles of Capitol Hill are won or lost before the issues get to the floor by the placement of an amendment or the timing of a vote. We have a voice and a vote to fight the disgraceful manipulation of the rules by the Democrats, and we make use of both. All we need now is media attention, properly directed to those boring, but all-important, House procedures. (Michel 1987, A14)

Ironically, acquisition of majority party status made Republicans demonstrate their credibility by supporting rules that reduced their control over the floor. We expect the Republican majority to tighten its control over the floor when media attention to House procedures fades or when intraparty divisions force Republican leaders to use the rules to avoid embarrassing defeats on important questions of public policy.

Conclusion

Procedural change in Congress is the product of two factors: the self-interested behavior of parties or crossparty coalitions and the inherited rules governing changes in the rules. In most circumstances, policy goals drive procedural change; congressional procedures seldom become directly relevant to electoral goals. They become relevant only when one party persuades a large segment of the electorate that it is greatly disadvantaged in the legislative process under current rules.

The record of the 1993-1994 reform effort is consistent with this perspective.[21] House Democratic leaders in the 103rd Congress failed to bring a reform package to the floor because they viewed procedural reform as electorally unimportant and thought that there was little to be gained and much to be lost by fighting over and adopting the reforms. Certainly the Democrats had little incentive to enhance minority rights under those circumstances.

The developments in the 104th Congress were out of the ordinary for procedural change. The House majority party, without the threat of a crossparty coalition, supported procedural changes that enhanced minority rights. To be sure, the majority party strengthened its grip over House proceedings in some ways. Nonetheless, the party kept true to its promise to reinforce the minority's right to a motion to recommit with instructions and to ban proxy voting in committee. A desire to avoid blame with the electorate motivated actions seemingly contrary to the majority party's short-term policy interests. The Senate, in contrast, continued to resist change. The need for a supermajority—a bipartisan majority, in most circumstances—made the adoption of more majoritarian procedures impossible. The Senate majority of the 104th Congress was left to struggle with the same rules that have limited the ability of other recent Senate majorities to overcome filibusters by a cohesive minority party.

Thus, both houses acted in a manner consistent with their acquired procedural tendencies. The House remains strongly majoritarian, and the Senate remains individualistic. This observation does not imply that the chambers are unchanging, of course. Rather, the frequency, timing, and direction of procedural change in the two houses reflect the inherited rules and practices that have accumulated over two centuries.

Notes

1. *Congressional Record,* January 5, 1995, S349.

2. In fact, on budget issues the Senate has been more successful than the House in protecting budget agreements from individual and partisan challenge. As a continuing body, the Senate does not adopt a new set of rules every two years. The permanence of Senate rules makes it difficult to alter budget rules and enhances the credibility of the enforcement procedures. In the House, any change in budget procedures would be open to challenge every two years during adoption of chamber rules. Without the practice of special rules, the Senate is unable by simple majority vote to waive budget rules. In contrast, a simple partisan majority in the House can always use special rules to waive budget rules with ease.

3. The motion to recommit is a privileged motion guaranteed in House rules. It gives opponents of a bill a chance to return a bill to committee prior to final passage. Simple recommittal motions, if successful, kill the bill. Motions "with instructions" offer the minority a chance to obtain a recorded vote on its preferred policy alternative. The question of whether recommittal motions with instructions can be denied in a special rule is a matter of partisan dispute within the House (see House Committee on Rules 1992).

4. Interview with authors, July 13, 1994. After more than 10 years of service, Penny retired from the House later that year.

5. Ibid.

6. Moakley proposed that whenever a special rule precluded minority amendments, the minority leader would be guaranteed a motion to recommit with instructions (see JCOC 1993c, *Floor Deliberations,* 60).

7. Authors' interview with Rep. Lee Hamilton, D-Ind., June 14, 1994. See also Foerstel (1994b).

8. The Joint Committee also recommended several technical changes to the Byrd Rule that, according to Senate Budget Chair Jim Sasser, D-Tenn., extended the reach of the Byrd Rule. See Sasser's statement opposing such changes in JCOC (1993f).

9. Those amendments included efforts to ban proxy voting in committee, to increase minority party representation on committees and committee staffs, to require supermajority votes on certain rules, and to give the minority party control of the Government Operations panel when the presidency was held by the majority party.

10. Authors' interview with Donald Wolfensberger, July 12, 1994.

11. The level of party unity votes is the percentage of all recorded votes on which a majority of voting Democrats opposed a majority of voting Republicans. Party unity scores show the percentage of party members voting with a majority of their party on party unity votes.

12. Interview with authors, July 13, 1994.

13. Ibid.

14. The creation of FROG likely had an effect on first-termers' unwillingness to join the GOP in supporting procedural reform. Of the 17 members of FROG's steering committee, 6 were freshmen Democrats. By creating a forum for first-term Democrats, FROG arguably provided an outlet for conservative and moderate freshmen who otherwise might have found appealing a procedural alliance with the minority party.

15. Authors' interviews with several JCOC and leadership aides as well as Rep. Barney Frank, D-Mass.

16. Steny Hoyer, D-Md., as quoted in Sammon (1994a, 1856).

17. Authors' interviews with Democratic aides on the House Rules Committee who wish to remain anonymous, and with Rep. Hamilton.

18. Authors' interviews with Sen. Harry Reid, D-Nev., on July 14, 1994, and with Sen. Wendell Ford, D-Ky., on July 3, 1994.

19. To expedite business, the House resolves itself into the Committee of the Whole to consider amendments to most major bills. The Speaker is supplanted with a "chairman" who presides over debate and voting on amendments. When work on a measure is complete, the Committee "rises," the Speaker returns to the chair, and the full House then votes on passage of the legislation.

20. But not every procedural reform advocated by Republicans in the 103rd Congress was included in the Contract with America. Republicans declined to endorse equitable party ratios on committees or to guarantee one-third of funding for minority party committee staff—rules changes unsuccessfully sought by the new Democratic minority at the start of the 104th Congress.

21. For a similar perspective on procedure and political goals, see Sinclair (1994a).

5

THE POLITICS OF CONGRESSIONAL REFORM: The Joint Committee on the Organization of Congress

C. Lawrence Evans and Walter J. Oleszek

Amid widespread public distrust of the national legislature, Congress in August of 1992 voted overwhelmingly to establish a bipartisan and bicameral committee to explore how the internal operations of the legislative branch should be reformed. Expectations for the Joint Committee on the Organization of Congress were high and were reinforced in November 1992 by the election of a large class of reform-minded freshmen legislators. According to Rep. David Price of North Carolina, a well-known scholar of the legislative process, the work of the Joint Committee would "enable the Congress to improve its operations and address the nation's needs more effectively."[1]

One year later—after six months of hearings and as many months of private meetings, caucuses, and informal discussions—the Senate and House members of the Joint Committee reported their recommendations to their respective chambers. The panel then formally disbanded on December 31, 1993. The following month the House and Senate reform packages were introduced in their respective chambers as the Legislative Reorganization Act of 1994. Hearings on each bill were conducted by the main committees of jurisdiction—the Senate Rules and Administration Committee and the House Rules and House Administration committees. After dividing and dropping certain sections of the Senate package, the Senate Rules Committee reported three reform bills to the floor in June. After three months of inaction, the Senate reform plan was offered as an amendment to an appropriations measure, but it failed to secure the necessary 60 votes, and the Senate reorganization effort died for the 103rd Congress. The House committees of jurisdiction also divided the House reform plan, choosing to consider separately from the rest of the package the highly salient issue of applying laws to Congress. A proposal applying laws to Congress was passed by an overwhelming margin on the House floor in August. On October 7, 1994, with action on compliance stymied in the Senate, the House adopted a resolution applying 10 workplace safety laws to its employees. The Rules and House Administration committees failed to complete markup of the rest of the package, and the 103rd Congress ended without floor consideration of the remaining reform proposals.

On January 4, 1995, with new Republican majorities in place in both chambers, the House began the 104th Congress by passing the most sweeping reforms of its internal operations in many decades. Among the changes were reforms recommended by the Joint Committee, including the application of laws to Congress, as well as additional reforms that had been considered but not accepted by the panel. Within weeks the Senate also passed legislation applying laws to Congress. Shortly thereafter a Senate Republican working group co-chaired by former Joint Committee leader Pete V. Domenici and Connie Mack of Florida proposed additional reforms, mostly based on the Senate recommendations of the Joint Committee on the Organization of Congress.

Clearly, the outcome of the Joint Committee effort was complex. This chapter reports on a broader study of congressional reform by exploring what happened to the Joint Committee on the Organization of Congress; it describes how the Joint Committee approached the difficult work of congressional reform, and how the House and Senate responded to its proposals. In particular, we address the following questions: What were the key challenges confronted by the Joint Committee? How were the wide-ranging proposals winnowed down into concrete recommendations? Why did public support for congressional reform not result in the passage of a comprehensive reform package in 1994? How did the work of the Joint Committee help shape the reforms of the 104th Congress? And what lessons can we learn from the work of the Joint Committee for future reform efforts?

Origins

Resolutions to create the Joint Committee (H. Con. Res. 192 and S. Con. Res. 57) were first introduced in August 1991 by Democrat David L. Boren and Republican Pete Domenici in the Senate, and by Democrat Lee H. Hamilton and Republican Bill Gradison in the House. The temporary Joint Committee proposed by the four legislators was patterned on the two other bipartisan, bicameral reorganization committees created by Congress. In 1945 Congress established the first Joint Committee on the Organization of Congress to conduct a comprehensive review of the legislative branch. It was created as World War II was winding down and in a period of expanded presidential authority and widespread interest in legislative reorganization. The first Joint Committee's recommendations were eventually enacted in the Legislative Reorganization Act of 1946. The Act reduced the number of standing committees, provided for permanent professional and clerical staff for House and Senate committees, and established a legislative budget.

Renewed calls for major reform in the mid-1950s and early 1960s led to the establishment in 1965 of the second Joint Committee on the Organization of Congress. Despite the improvements made by the 1946 Legislative Reorganization Act, more reforms were needed. Congress faced new conditions, such as the addition of two states to the Union, the dawning of the space age, a national population that had increased sharply and shifted geographically, and at least a doubling of the daily workload of lawmakers. Much of the work of this Joint Committee was eventually adopted in the Legislative Reorganization Act of 1970, which enhanced analytical support for Congress, opened the institution to greater public visibility, and clarified the rights of majority and minority party members.

In the fall of 1991, reform-minded members, academics, and other observers believed that a third Joint Committee on the Organization of Congress was needed to modernize the internal operations of the House and Senate. The four key reform leaders—Boren, Domenici, Hamilton, and Gradison—argued that times had changed since the last reorganization effort. Procedural inefficiencies in both chambers were promoting legislative gridlock. The three-layered congressional budget process was overly complicated. The number of staff had grown markedly. Congress seemed bogged down with short-term concerns and increasingly unable to confront the longer term challenges of the post-cold war world. "Congress needs to stand back, and take stock of itself from time to time," the reformers argued. Now was the "time for another comprehensive look at the operations of Congress."[2]

The resolutions introduced by the four reformers to create a third Joint Committee quickly gathered support, particularly among Republicans and junior Democrats. Senior Democrats in both chambers, however, were less enthusiastic. In particular, a number of Democrats were concerned about the proposed panel's bipartisan, bicameral structure. Rep. David R. Obey, D-Wis., argued that Senate procedures were the main reform problem. "I don't think you ought to approve this resolution at this time," he said, "unless you really do believe that all four caucuses [House and Senate Democrats and Republicans] are willing . . . to use this as a device to improve the Institution, rather than . . . transfer power to different groups of people." Rep. John Dingell, D-Mich., chairman of the powerful Energy and Commerce Committee, believed the proposal did not "adequately recognize that the responsibility for running Congress and for moving legislation lies with whichever party is in the majority."[3]

After the Senate Rules Committee held a hearing about the proposal in November 1991, attention focused on building support for it in the House. Hamilton and Gradison recognized that no previous House reform effort had succeeded without strong support from key party leaders. Indeed, without the Speaker's endorsement, it was unlikely that hearings on the resolution would be scheduled before the leadership-dominated Rules Committee, which had jurisdiction over reorganization issues. As a result, Hamilton and Gradison stepped up their meetings with party leaders, committee chairmen, ranking minority members, and other influential members. The two reformers avoided mentioning specific proposals, recognizing that generalized support for reform in the abstract begins to break down when detailed recommendations are discussed. The reception received by Hamilton and Gradison in these meetings was mostly friendly but often noncommittal.

Then the climate for reform improved. Unforeseen events gave Hamilton and Gradison a hand. On March 13, 1992, the House voted 426-0 to release the names of all members who had bounced checks in the so-called House bank. But the House bank scandal was not the only incentive for members to support reform publicly. The post office scandal, the savings and loan scandal, and the Anita Hill-Clarence Thomas hearings contributed to the public's poor image of Congress. During the spring of 1992, public confidence in Congress plunged to record lows. Members as well as their constituents were increasingly dissatisfied with the way Congress was working. The times were propitious for a shakeup of the legislative branch of government.

At a press conference on March 25, Speaker Thomas S. Foley endorsed the creation of the Joint Committee, effectively ensuring that the reform panel would be established. Hearings and a markup were conducted before the House Rules Committee in May, and the authorizing resolution passed the House in June. Senate action followed during the summer, and the House accepted the Senate version of the resolution creating the Joint Committee in August 1992.

Under the terms of its authorizing resolution, the Joint Committee was to "make a full and complete study of the organization and operation of the Congress" and recommend improvements with a view toward "strengthening the effectiveness of Congress, simplifying its operations, improving its relationships with and oversight [of the other branches of government and] improving the orderly consideration of legislation." The 28 members of the Joint Committee were to be equally divided between the chambers and the two political parties. The majority and minority leaders of each chamber were included on the panel as ex-officio, voting members. Appointments to the Joint Committee (in high demand) were made by the appropriate party leaders. As expected, the four chief sponsors of the authorizing resolution were asked to lead the panel. Boren was appointed co-chairman for the Senate, Hamilton was appointed House co-chairman. Domenici was named vice-chairman for the Senate, and Gradison became his House Republican counterpart.

The four leaders, as well as the other members appointed to the Joint Committee by their respective leaderships, are listed in Table 5-1, along with each member's 1993 party support score and conservative coalition support scores. Key aspects of the panel's coalitional structure are apparent from the table. First, the composition of the Joint Committee meant that the House contingent would be substantially more polarized than the Senate contingent. The Senate appointments included key moderates from both parties. Co-Chairman Boren, for example, was well known for his bipartisan approach to legislating. Senate Republicans on the panel included Nancy Kassebaum of Kansas and William Cohen of Maine, two party moderates. In contrast, with the important exception of Gradison, partisan House Republicans were appointed to the Joint Committee by House Minority Leader Robert Michel. When Gradison resigned from the House in February 1992, he was replaced as vice-chairman by David Dreier of California, a leader among House Republicans from his position on the Rules Committee.[4] On the Democratic side, Foley's appointments included two moderate

Table 5-1   Joint Committee Partisanship and Ideology, 1993

	Democrats			Republicans	
Committee Member	Party Unity Score[a]	Conservative Coalition Support Score[b]	Committee Member	Party Unity Score[a]	Conservative Coalition Support Score[b]
Senate					
Boren	80	63	Domenici	86	88
Sasser	87	68	Kassebaum	77	88
Ford	86	80	Lott	96	100
Reid	86	50	Stevens	82	92
Sarbanes	98	12	Cohen	69	58
Pryor	91	49	Lugar	88	90
House					
Hamilton	83	68	Dreier	97	93
Obey	95	30	Walker	98	91
Swift	94	30	Solomon	96	93
Gejdenson	98	18	Emerson	89	86
Spratt	86	82	Allard	93	73
Norton	100	3	Dunn	90	91

Source: Congressional Quarterly Weekly Report, December 18, 1993, 3480–3488.

Note: Data for the majority and minority leaders of each chamber are not included because, by agreement, they did not participate formally as committee members in the decision-making process. The average House party unity score in 1993 for Democrats was 85 percent; for Republicans, 84 percent. The average Senate party unity scores in 1993 for Democrats and Republicans were identical to those in the House.

[a] Based on **party unity votes**, recorded votes in the Senate or the House that split the parties, with a majority of voting Democrats opposing a majority of voting Republicans. **Party unity support** is the percentage of party unity votes on which members voted "yea" or "nay" *in agreement* with a majority of their party. Failures to vote lowered scores for chambers and parties.

[b] The "conservative coalition" means a voting alliance of Republicans and southern Democrats against the northern Democrats in Congress. This meaning, rather than any philosophic definition of the "conservative coalition" position, provides the basis for CQ's selection of coalition votes. A **conservative coalition vote** is any vote in the Senate or the House on which a majority of voting southern Democrats and a majority of voting Republicans opposed the stand taken by a majority of voting northern Democrats. Votes on which there was an even division within the ranks of voting northern Democrats, southern Democrats, or Republicans are not included. The **conservative coalition support score** is the percentage of conservative coalition votes on which a member voted "yea" or "nay" *in agreement* with the position of the conservative coalition. Failures to vote, even if a member announced a stand, lower the score.

Democrats—Co-Chairman Hamilton and John Spratt of South Carolina. But the remaining four House Democrats appointed to the panel were strong party loyalists.

At the Joint Committee's organizational meeting on January 6, 1993, the four leaders described the reform priorities: the ethics process; the application of laws to Congress; the budget process; the committee system; floor deliberations and scheduling; congressional staffing; relationships between the chambers, the branches, and the parties; public understanding of Congress; and communications and information technology in Congress. Deliberately excluded from the Joint Committee's agenda were campaign finance and lobbying reform—issues already moving on other legislative tracks.

In short, the origins and structure of the third Joint Committee on the Organization of Congress revealed the key challenges that the panel would have to confront throughout the reform process. Five are especially noteworthy, for they shaped the context and character of decision making by the Joint Committee.

First, substantial dissonance existed between the nature of the public demand for reform and the details of the reform agenda on Capitol Hill. The public was primarily concerned with perks, privileges, pork, and perceived ethical lapses in Congress, rather than the important but less salient details of congressional procedure and structure that constituted the bulk of the Joint Committee's formal mandate. The "outside" agenda for reform, in brief, failed to correspond in many particulars with the "inside" agenda advocated by change-oriented lawmakers.

Second, the Joint Committee was created because of broad support among members for reform in the abstract. There was little evident congressional backing for particular reform proposals. Unlike some previous reform efforts, where the scope and direction of change were clearer, little agreement existed about the proper course for congressional reform. And the election of Bill Clinton as president in November 1992 potentially diminished a major impetus for reform—the legislative frustrations associated with divided government.[5]

Third, as with previous congressional reform efforts, success depended on sustained support from party leaders in both chambers. But as the panel began its work, the nature of the commitment to reform among party and committee leaders in both chambers remained unclear. Some party leaders worried that the Joint Committee might address politically explosive and divisive reform issues; others wondered whether any set of reforms could satisfy the demands of so-called "populist" reformers such as H. Ross Perot.

Fourth, a key source of legitimacy for the Joint Committee was the credibility of its four leaders. To be effective, lawmakers must work together in an atmosphere of trust to achieve collective goals. Relatedly, they must submerge to a reasonable level their personal autonomy to accommodate the views and win the support of their colleagues. Maintaining trust and collegiality—and holding the four chairmen and vice-chairmen together on key reform questions—would be critical to the panel's success.

Fifth, the structure of the panel meant that a proposal required some bipartisan and bicameral support to be accepted as a recommendation. A reform proposal that received the support of just House Democrats, for example, or just Senate Republicans would fail on a tie committee vote. Every proposal for change required some Democratic and some Republican support to be adopted as a Joint Committee recommendation.

Preliminary Action

From January 26 to July 1, 1993, the Joint Committee conducted 36 hearings about the issues on its agenda. The purposes of the hearings were to explore the broad landscape of reform alternatives, to enable many members of Congress to participate early on in the reform process, to publicize reform issues throughout the country, and to begin narrowing the range of proposals under consideration. The Cable Satellite Public Affairs Network (C-SPAN) televised nationally all of the hearings. Testimony was provided by 243 witnesses, including 133 representatives and 37 senators, who proposed more than 500 recommendations for reforming Congress. The House Speaker and the majority and minority leaders of each chamber appeared at the panel's first hearing—the first time in congressional history that the leaders of both chambers appeared at a single hearing. Other witnesses included H. Ross Perot, former vice-president Walter Mondale, and Robert C. Byrd of West Virginia, the Senate president pro tempore.

In addition to conducting hearings, the Joint Committee initiated, commissioned, or utilized numerous other information-gathering and analytical studies of Congress. Included were surveys of members and staff, studies by the Congressional Research Service and the Congressional Budget Office, roundtable discussions with current and former congressional staff aides, consultations with scores of knowledgeable individuals, as well as reports by various think tanks such as the Carnegie Commission's study about information technologies in Congress. Particularly useful was the Renewing Congress Project of the American Enterprise Institute (AEI) and the Brookings Institution, which enlisted the expertise of a number of congressional scholars and other informed observers (see Chapters 7 and 11). Coordinated by Thomas Mann of Brookings and Norman Ornstein of AEI with the able assistance of Matt Pinkus, the Renewing Congress Project provided an analytical framework for evaluating reform needs and alternatives, as well as a degree of political cover to reform-minded members in controversial areas such as committee jurisdictional realignment.

Deliberations within the Joint Committee did not occur in a political vacuum. In the House, change-oriented lawmakers expected the huge class of freshmen, many of whom campaigned on the need to revamp Congress, to form a key constituency for comprehensive reorganization. But after three months of effort, the Democratic freshmen were unable to translate their general support for reform into concrete proposals that drew broad bipartisan backing. Instead, the Democratic freshmen's reform package contained proposals that were often narrow in focus (such as a ban on private use of frequent flier miles) or lacking precise language. Freshman Republicans united behind a more substantial reform plan, but their proposals were perceived as highly partisan and unlikely to secure a majority, either in the Joint Committee or in the House.[6] The disunity of the freshmen's reform effort was an indicator of the difficulties to be confronted by the Joint Committee.

While the freshmen grappled with reform, partisan tensions in the House over minority party rights reached new heights. In early 1993 the Rules Committee reported a succession of restrictive rules limiting the opportunities to amend bills on the floor. Strongly opposed to this infringement on their rights, House Republican leaders appointed Gerald Solomon of New York to head a task force on "restrictive rules strategy." In addition to Solomon, other Joint Committee members appointed to the task force included Vice-Chairman Dreier and Robert Walker of Pennsylvania, the official Republican "objector" in his role as chief deputy whip. Solomon criticized Democrats for "systematically silencing not just Republicans, but also conservative Democrats. . . . Members are being denied their constitutional right to represent their constituents by offering amendments" (Foerstel 1993, 22). Although Speaker Foley promised greater openness on the floor, Republicans' concerns about restrictive floor procedures increased just as the Joint Committee turned its attention to such matters.

The broader political context in the Senate also influenced the prospects of the Joint Committee. By the summer of 1993, Senator Boren had alienated many congressional Democrats because of his outspoken opposition to the Clinton economic program. Boren argued that he was simply representing his constituents and other moderate Democrats by attempting to stop his party from veering to the left. When asked about Boren's criticism of Clinton, one Senate leader commented, "We plead with our Members that if you can't say anything good, don't say anything at all. . . . Not all Senators have got that message" (Cohen 1993a, 1308). The response to Boren's maverick role among many House Democrats was strongly negative, with some threatening that reforms associated with Boren would be dead-on-arrival in the House. According to one insightful observer, "[m]ore than a few Democrats are salivating to extract a pound of his flesh" (Cohen 1993a, 1308). Boren further alienated House Democrats by publicly endorsing a Republican-led effort to open up the discharge petition process.

The deliberations of the Joint Committee also were influenced by bicameral tensions that increased during 1993. As Democratic representative Al Swift said, "Republicans are the opposition, but the Senate is the enemy." Actual or threatened filibusters in the Senate endangered a range of measures, from gun control to grazing fees. Senators also used one of their budget procedures—the so-called Byrd Rule—to strip House-passed items off the year's reconciliation bill, generating angry protests from many House members. Renewed efforts in the House to publicize perceived obstructionism in the Senate were resented by Senate Republicans and many Senate Democrats. Some House Democrats actively supported formation of an outside lobbying organization—"Action, Not Gridlock"— aimed at generating a national grassroots movement to change the Senate's filibuster practices.

The Joint Committee's hearings and other activities did much to publicize reform issues and provide members of Congress and outside observers with opportunities to participate and articulate their views about reform. But into the summer no clear consensus developed about the specific direction that reform ought to take. Some witnesses urged the Joint Committee to go slow and recommend incremental changes; others urged the panel to take a bold, comprehensive approach to reform.

In late June a private, two-day retreat was conducted by committee members at the U.S. Naval Academy in Annapolis. The objectives of the retreat were to review reform suggestions and to assess where there might be areas of consensus. Although the four leaders of the Joint Committee stated at a June 28 press conference following the retreat that they had made progress, these sessions were not without tension. Most important, some House Democrats expressed concern about the Senate's use of the filibuster and its lack of germaneness rules for floor amendments. "Without [changing] those, anything else is marginal," stated Representative Obey after the retreat. "But the indication from the Senate side is, it's not willing to deal with either one of those items. If we don't deal with those items, we don't deal with the need for reform." Senate Vice-Chairman Domenici expressed his hope that the filibuster dispute was not being raised "to prevent real reform" in streamlining the budget process, reducing members' committee assignments, and cutting back on the number of panels.[7]

In early August, the Joint Committee agreed to recommend to the House and Senate more than a broad reform platform; it also agreed to include in the final report a draft legislative reorganization bill. The four chairmen and vice-chairmen said they would construct a "mark," or draft bill, which would be open to amendment during formal markup sessions. As attention turned to the mark, there was a degree of optimism, even camaraderie, among the more active members of the Joint Committee. Both co-chairmen had developed constructive working relationships with their minority counterparts.[8] And the staff hoped their own efforts would help produce something positive.

The Chairmen's Mark

Because of the rules and membership of the Joint Committee, the chairmen's mark was critical—much more than a simple first draft of reform. Committee rules prohibited proxy voting, which meant accommodating lawmakers by "stacking" (back-to-back) votes and ensuring everyone's attendance through other scheduling efforts. Further, the panel's authorizing resolution stipulated that "no recommendation of the Joint Committee shall be made by the Committee except upon a majority vote of the members representing each House, respectively." These two requirements, combined with practical political realities, effectively mandated bipartisan majorities on every recommendation.

All additions and deletions to the mark needed the support of both a majority of House members on the panel and a majority of senators on the panel. Thus, once a reform proposal was included in the chairman's mark, one of the four party contingents on the Joint Committee acting alone could not vote to drop the proposal from the bill because the panel's membership was equally divided by party and by chamber. For example, if an item opposed by all House Democrats on the Joint Committee were included in the draft bill brought into markup, an amendment to strike the language could not pass without the vote of at least one House Republican.[9] Once a reform proposal was included in the mark, it would be extremely difficult to drop the proposal from the package without voting to kill the entire bill.

The Joint Committee leaders began preparing a draft mark in August 1993. They worked off a master list of reform proposals presented to the panel during the hearings and other information-gathering activities. Proposals opposed by most or all of the four committee leaders, such as abolishing the appropriations committees, were clearly off the table. Other proposals, such as applying private sector workplace laws to Congress and clamping down on excessive committee assignments, were supported by all four committee leaders. These items were likely candidates for inclusion in the mark. Issues such as staff reductions and House minority party rights were more problematic, but they needed to be addressed in some way. At the end of the month, the four leaders agreed to consult with other influential members of their party and chamber contingents, particularly about this last category of reform proposals.

For a number of reasons, Senators Boren and Domenici appeared to face fewer and more manageable political hurdles than did their House counterparts during this vital stage of the reform process. On a range of issues, Boren had demonstrated his willingness to break with Senate Democratic leaders. The Senate is generally more individualistic and less partisan than the House, facilitating the development of a bipartisan mark. The Senate side of the Joint Committee was less polarized than the House contingent. Also there was an expectation in the Senate that whatever was produced by the Joint Committee would be carefully reviewed by the leadership-influenced Rules and Administration Committee, headed by Majority Whip Wendell A. Ford, D-Ky. (a Joint Committee member). And the preferences of Boren and Domenici were similar on many key reform issues. More generally, the work of the Joint Committee drew less attention from senators (on and off the panel) than it did from House members. By most accounts, the majority and minority leaders in the Senate were less involved in the reform process than were top party leaders in the other chamber. The most significant challenges to forging consensus were in the House.

Representatives Hamilton and Dreier had decided early on to work closely with their respective party leaders. As Co-Chairman Hamilton stated repeatedly, House reform was unlikely to succeed without the active involvement and support of the majority party leadership, and his goal was to produce reform recommendations that could pass. During the panel's organizational meeting in January, Hamilton said:

> In the end, we have to have a bipartisan vote of support for all of . . . [our] recommendations. [We] . . . have to be thinking . . . not just of some idealized conception of how we would like this institution to work, but what kind of proposals can we get through the institution on the basis of the authority that we are operating under. We have to keep our eye on that or we will stray very far off the reservation.

Hamilton personally favored bold reforms, but he believed that reform proposals opposed by key Democratic leaders and large portions of the Democratic Caucus simply could not pass. An "ideal" reorganization plan likely would be dismissed as being politically impractical and unachievable. For example, top Democratic leaders early and often stressed that committee realignment was "off the table" for two fundamental reasons. First, it would tear the party apart just as it did in 1974 when a major committee realignment plan was turned down by the House. Second, Democrats needed to focus on passing their new president's program, especially after 12 consecutive years of GOP control of the White House, and not on an internally divisive committee modernization plan. As a result, House Co-Chairman Hamilton focused on proposals that might be acceptable to top Democratic leaders and a majority of House Democrats.

Throughout September, Hamilton attempted to devise a core of reform proposals capable of garnering bipartisan support. Dreier confronted analogous challenges, although of less magnitude because of the relative homogeneity of House Republicans on key reform issues. Indeed, House Republicans had handed out a comprehensive reform plan—their "Mandate for Change"—at the Joint Committee's organizational meeting in January 1993. But many House Republicans wanted to promote reform proposals that were clearly unacceptable to the majority party. For that matter, many partisans on both sides of the aisle wanted to walk away from the Joint Committee process and blame its demise on the other party.

The most significant sticking points concerned the rights of the minority party in the House. Without concessions from the majority on certain of these issues, a bipartisan accord on reform would be impossible. The minority Republicans particularly wanted a ban on proxy voting in committee, a guarantee of the motion to recommit with instructions on all bills, and a requirement that the minority be guaranteed one-third of committee staff resources.[10] Support among rank-and-file House Democrats for extending minority party rights was limited, but Democratic leaders were somewhat flexible on these issues. During the deliberations of the House Administrator task force the previous year, for example, Speaker Foley had expressed support for certain of the Republican reform proposals.

However, these efforts to achieve an agreement on House minority party rights were derailed in early October when the issue became linked to filibuster reform in the Senate. On October 12, 1993, an article by Rep. Barney Frank, D-Mass., appeared in the *Washington Post.* Frank attacked the Senate filibuster and juxtaposed the issue of House minority party rights with demands for enhanced majority prerogatives in the Senate. The article impressed key members of the House Democratic Study Group (DSG) task force on reform, who asked Frank to appear the following week at one of their regular breakfast meetings. Immediately following that meeting, Frank, David Obey, and DSG Chairman Mike Synar, D-Okla., circulated a petition requesting that House Democrats on the Joint Committee not agree to any minority party rights concessions in the House until Senate members of the committee agreed to reform the filibuster. The petition also requested a meeting of the full House Democratic Caucus to discuss the proposed linkage. Within a few hours, approximately 60 House Democrats had signed the petition, and the caucus meeting was conducted on October 20.

A large and vocal majority of the Democratic Caucus would not support the inclusion of minority party rights concessions in the Joint Committee mark unless major changes in the filibuster rule were included. Backers of the filibuster reform movement justified their efforts as necessary to promote real reform and strengthen Hamilton's negotiating leverage vis-à-vis Boren and the Republicans. Senator Domenici had a different view: "[W]hat they're really saying is they want an excuse not to have real reform, because they know the Senate is not going to get rid of the filibuster" (Merida 1993, A18).[11]

A filibuster reform proposal of sufficient significance to House Democrats was not forthcoming from Senators Boren and Domenici. And without the inclusion of items relating to House minority party rights, a bipartisan mark would be impossible to achieve among the House members of the Joint Committee. Concerned that problems in the House might endanger and indefinitely delay the Senate portion of the reform effort, Boren and Domenici decided to move ahead on their own and conduct a separate Senate markup.

Joint Committee Action

On November 4 Senators Boren and Domenici unveiled their reform plan, which was based largely on the proposals discussed by the four leaders of the Joint Committee earlier in the fall. It was this package of proposed changes that served as the markup vehicle for the Senate group's drafting session, which occurred six days later.

Senate Markup

The two senators proposed a two-year congressional budget process; committee assignment limitations; a two-hour limit on the motion to proceed to legislation in the Senate (curbing the use of a filibuster to block consideration of measures); the elimination of all joint committees; limitations on the number of Senate subcommittees; reductions in the number of legislative branch staff; ethics reform; and the establishment of an Office of Compliance to bring the Senate into compliance with various laws applied to the private sector and the executive branch. Specific action on ethics and compliance was eventually left to two Senate leadership task forces that had been created to study those issues.

When the Senate members of the Joint Committee took up the Boren-Domenici package on November 10, they moved with dispatch and a minimum of public discord. By a 12-0 vote, the senators endorsed the plan with a few modest changes, such as exempting the Select Intelligence Committee from the committee assignment limitations. Selected reform proposals reported by the senators on the Joint Committee are summarized in Table 5-2. Despite the unanimous vote, several senators made it clear that they opposed various proposals, such as restricting committee assignments and abolishing the joint committees, and would attempt to alter the package as it moved through the legislative process.

House Markup

In the end Representatives Hamilton and Dreier were unable to achieve a bipartisan accord about the contents of their draft bill. The House members' markup began on November 16 and stretched on through five days of fractious meetings before concluding on November 22, just hours before Congress adjourned for the year. The markup draft, prepared by Chairman Hamilton, included among other items limitations on committee assignments, biennial budgeting, the involvement of private citizens in the ethics process, the application of appropriate laws to Congress, oversight planning, changes in bill referral procedures, reductions in the number of subcommittees, and a proposal to curb special interest earmarks. As Hamilton noted in his opening statement at the markup:

> By design, the most controversial reforms mentioned during our six months of hearings are not included in the markup draft. The membership of this committee is equally divided between the two political parties. Even if all of the Republicans or all of the Democrats objected to a provision, they would not be able to delete it from the bill without the support of Members of the other party. For this reason we have decided only to include in the markup draft proposals that are supported by a majority of the House Members on the Joint Committee.

Hamilton argued that the adoption of the recommendations included in the markup draft "would significantly enhance the institutional integrity and effectiveness of Congress." He also said that he expected more controversial proposals to pass during the amendment process in committee and on the floor.

Vice-Chairman Dreier, along with the other Republican committee members, expressed regret that the markup draft did not include additional recommendations. "I have to say that I am frankly very disappointed with the document that we're going to be looking at today as our mark," said Dreier. "Basically, from my perspective, we're back to ground zero." Dreier noted that the markup draft failed to address such issues as comprehensive committee jurisdictional realignment, the abolition of proxy voting, or a requirement for biennial appropriations.

Table 5-2   Selected Proposals of Joint Committee on the
            Organization of Congress

House	Senate
■ limit committee and subcommittee assignments	■ limit committee and subcommittee assignments
■ require that assignment waivers be accepted by relevant party caucus and full House	■ require that assignment waivers be offered by majority or minority leader and accepted by full Senate
■ limit subcommittee assignments to five on major panels (except Appropriations) and four on non-major panels	■ limit subcommittees to three on significant committees (except Appropriations) and two on others
■ require Rules Committee to consider a resolution to eliminate a committee if its size falls below 50 percent of its 103rd Congress size	■ require Rules Committee to report, and Senate to vote on a resolution abolishing a committee that falls below 50 percent of its 102nd Congress size
■ abolish joint committees on Printing and Library and transfer functions to new Joint Committee on Information Management	■ abolish all four joint committees
■ require biennial budget resolutions, biennial appropriations, and multi-year authorizations	■ require biennial budget resolutions, biennial appropriations, and multi-year authorizations
■ guarantee minority party motions to recommit with instructions on all measures	■ limit debate on motion to proceed to two hours
■ require congressional compliance with key employment laws and create an Office of Compliance to explore compliance with additional laws and to issue enforcement regulations	■ urge consideration of recommendations of Senate task force on compliance
■ authorize Ethics Committee to use nonmembers to investigate ethics cases	■ urge consideration of recommendations of Senate task force on ethics
■ create task force to reduce legislative branch employment by up to 12 percent	■ urge relevant standing committees to recommend how to reduce legislative branch employment by up to 12 percent

During contentious and often partisan sessions, the House members of the Joint Committee considered nearly 50 amendments. Fifteen amendments were agreed to either unanimously or by bipartisan votes. For example, a requirement for biennial appropriations, the recodification of House rules, a guarantee to the minority party of the right to offer a motion to recommit with instructions, and publication biannually in the *Congressional Record* of lawmakers' committee attendance and voting records all received bipartisan endorsement.

Roughly 30 other amendments were rejected by 6-6 party line votes, including a committee realignment plan offered by Dreier, as well as GOP-sponsored amendments to ban proxy voting in committees, impose term limits on committee chairmen and ranking members, and provide that one-third of investigative funding for committees be designated for minority staff. Tempers flared when some Democrats stated that their support for Republican proposals to enhance minority rights in the House was contingent on reform of Senate rules, which they argued grant the minority too much power. Angry House Republicans responded that the Senate would never do away with the filibuster and that these Democrats' objectives were to avoid consideration of Republican reform proposals and to continue the status quo in the House. A number of Democratic-sponsored amendments, such as requiring that first-degree amendments in the Committee of the Whole be subject to prenotification requirements, also were rejected on party line votes.

In the end the House contingent voted 8 to 4 to report a package of reforms to the House. To keep the reform process moving, Republicans Bill Emerson of Missouri and Dreier reluctantly voted with the six Democrats to report the package. As indicated in Table 5-2, the reform plans reported by the House and Senate contingents were relatively similar: the major differences were that the Senate plan included more comprehensive committee reforms, and the House package (unlike the Senate plan) included detailed language aimed at reforming the ethics process and applying laws to Congress.

Co-Chairman Hamilton described the package as a major change: "I am confident that in the weeks and months ahead we will make a strong package even stronger." He also promised to work for a "generous rule" from the Rules Committee so that the major reform alternatives could be considered on the House floor. Vice-Chairman Dreier and the other Republican members expressed disappointment in the outcome of the Joint Committee process. Although acknowledging that the package included "some significant elements," Dreier expressed "serious misgivings about these recommendations as a whole. . . . We can do better than this" (JCOC 1993b, 500-501).

The Chambers React to Reform Ideas

On February 3, 1994, Senators Boren and Domenici introduced the Senate reform package as the Legislative Reorganization Act of 1994 (S. 1824). The bill was referred to the Senate Rules and Administration Committee. The same day, Representative Hamilton introduced the House reform package, also titled the Legislative Reorganization Act of 1994 (H.R. 3801). The House bill was simultaneously referred to three committees: Rules, Government Operations, and House Adminis-tration. Representative Dreier chose not to join Hamilton in sponsoring the bill because he did not receive sufficient assurance from the Speaker that Republicans would be allowed to offer floor amendments on the major reform issues.

In February both the House and Senate Rules committees commenced a series of hearings that extended through spring of 1994. On June 14 and 30, the Committee on House Administration also conducted hearings on the compli-ance provisions of H.R. 3801. Substantial opposition emerged to toughen limits on committee and subcommittee assignments and to biennial budgeting.

Particularly controversial was the Joint Committee's de minimis approach to reform of committee jurisdictions (the fourth item in Table 5-2).

Although Co-Chairmen Boren and Hamilton favored comprehensive juris-diction reform, they had come to believe that a major jurisdictional realignment would endanger the entire reform effort. Indeed, Hamilton predicted "a blood bath" on the House floor if jurisdictional issues were directly confronted. As a result, neither the House nor Senate package recommended explicit jurisdic-tional changes.[12] The intention was for tighter committee assignment limits to be implemented, along with a tougher process for securing waivers from these limits. As members gave up assignments on the least popular committees (often having narrow jurisdictions), the number of members on these panels would decrease. If, as a result of the strict assignment limits, a committee fell in size by more than 50 percent of its size at the end of the 103rd Congress, the panel would be considered for abolition, with its jurisdiction potentially transferred to another committee.

Various witnesses who testified before the House and Senate Rules committees asked why a committee's popularity should so influence its continued existence. Some unpopular panels, they argued, are simply too important to be abolished. If the issue of committee jurisdictional realignment is to be addressed at all, these witnesses said, it should be addressed in a straightforward and purposeful manner rather than through an indirect, de minimis approach.

Senate Action

On June 16 the Senate Rules Committee sent its final report on S. 1824 to the floor. With some relief Chairman Wendell Ford said he had washed his hands of reform for the year: "I've done my job. . . . It's Domenici's problem now" (Foerstel 1994a, 3).

The Senate Rules Committee chose to split the Boren-Domenici package into three separate bills: S. 1824 as amended, S. Res. 227, and S. Res. 228. The first dealt primarily with budget reform and the application of laws to Congress. Dropped from the package were the Joint Committee's recommendations for biennial ap-propriations. The Rules Committee also weakened the congressional compliance proposal by adding an amendment that said cost should be considered when ap-plying new laws to Congress. The other two reform bills reported by the Rules Committee dealt with the proposed changes in the committee system and Senate floor procedure. Once again key provisions supported by the Senate half of the Joint Committee were modified or dropped. According to Senator Boren, the resulting legislation was "about two-thirds of what I hoped it would be." Nancy Landon Kassebaum of Kansas, another Joint Committee member, also expressed disappointment: "It isn't what I had hoped. . . . I don't think it will be any major change" (Foerstel 1994a, 30).

In mid-September the Senate Governmental Affairs Committee addressed a key aspect of the reform agenda—the issue of applying laws to Congress—when it reported out a version of the Congressional Accountability Act, sponsored by Sen. Joseph Lieberman, D-Conn. and Sen. Charles Grassley, R-Iowa. According to Lieberman, "We're open to attaching . . . [our version] to anything that's moving" (Foerstel 1994a, 30).

From June through late September, there was not much movement on reform in the Senate. As a result, on September 29 Senators Boren and Domenici took the unusual step of offering all the Joint Committee's recommendations as a floor amendment to a pending amendment on the District of Columbia appropriations conference report. As Senator Boren explained:

> Because of procedural problems on the Senate floor, we have been unable to bring . . . those important recommendations . . . to this body for consideration. Out of frustration, the Senator from New Mexico . . . and I decided we should not allow this Congress to adjourn without giving the Members of the Senate an opportunity to vote on these reform recommendations.[13]

The Boren-Domenici maneuver raised several objections. Opponents argued that an appropriations measure was the wrong way for the Senate to consider congressional reorganization. "I cannot support [the Boren-Domenici] effort to circumvent the committee process," said Sen. Mark O. Hatfield, R-Ore., a member of the Rules Committee as well as ranking minority member on the Appropriations Committee. Senate Rules Chairman Wendell Ford, D-Ky., raised an institutional argument:

> As this amendment is drafted, it permits the House to legislatively change the committee structure of the Senate—I do not think we want that. . . . That is the reason we separated these out into resolution form so the Senate could vote on what applied to the Senate and the House could then vote on what applied to the House.[14]

In the end, Appropriations Chairman Byrd raised a point of order (or parliamentary objection) which failed by a vote of 58 to 41, two votes short of the waiver requirement of 60.[15] The following week independent efforts to apply private-sector laws to the Senate also died when George Mitchell, then the majority leader, was unable to bring the Lieberman-Grassley measure to the floor for a vote. None of the Joint Committee's recommendations passed the Senate in the 103rd Congress, and they fared only somewhat better in the House (see Love 1994c).

House Action

As the House Rules Committee concluded its hearings on reform, a key strategic question was whether to divide the legislation into two or more pieces. An important "sweetener" in the House package was a proposal to apply laws to Congress, based largely on the Congressional Accountability Act introduced by Rep. Christopher Shays, R-Conn., and then representative Dick Swett, a Democrat from New Hampshire who was defeated in November 1994. The Shays-Swett measure was supported in the House by a broad-based, bipartisan coalition (and it also was the model for the Senate bill introduced by Lieberman and Grassley).

In mid-June Shays and Swett sent Speaker Foley a letter in which they threatened to introduce a discharge petition on their legislation if the issue of congressional compliance was not considered by the House before the August recess. In a meeting the following week, Foley agreed to their request. Rumors soon began circulating that the congressional compliance issue would be split off from the rest of the House reform package, with the remaining reform proposals to be considered after the recess—if at all. As one House Democratic leadership aide said, "You're not going to get this thing done in short order unless it's done in various pieces."[16]

In a letter to the Speaker, Representative Hamilton argued against splitting the bill, pointing out that the compliance provision was a critical sweetener for less popular reform proposals in the congressional reorganization package. "If the reform package is divided, it will be harder to concentrate the attention of members and the public on institutional reform," Hamilton warned. Former vice-chairman Dreier also sought to hold the package together, arguing that "dividing . . . [the package] is little more than a divide-and-conquer strategy . . . [and] a great disservice to a year of effort" (Foerstel 1994d, 26). But pressure to expedite the congressional compliance proposal was too great. In exchange for an explicit promise from Speaker Foley that remaining reform provisions would be considered by the full House in September, Hamilton agreed to separate the congressional compliance proposal from the rest of the reform package. Hamilton remarked after the meeting, "My preference is not to break [the bill] up [but under the agreement] Members will get a chance to look at each of the reform proposals" (Foerstel 1994d, 26). Dreier, however, opposed the division, arguing that it would endanger the rest of the reform package.

A revised version of the Shays-Swett congressional compliance proposal passed the House on August 10, 1994 by a vote of 427 to 4. The legislation applied to Congress 10 workplace laws (including the Occupational Safety and Health Act) and created a bicameral Office of Compliance within the legislative branch to enforce the laws. However, the legislation required Senate passage, which, as mentioned, never occurred. Consequently, House Democratic leaders drafted a resolution applying the 10 workplace laws to the House via an amendment to House rules. After a last-minute compromise with Republican leaders, the resolution passed the House by a wide margin on October 7.

The House Rules Committee did not complete markup of the rest of the reform plan. After an abortive beginning to the markup in August dominated by partisan infighting, the panel continued markup on September 21. That session was repeatedly interrupted as Rules Committee Democrats caucused privately in Chairman Moakley's office. Speaker Foley joined them, arguing against jurisdiction changes or an outright ban on proxies—two measures advocated by California Democrat Anthony C. Beilenson, a member of the Rules Committee. Waiting in the committee room were staff from the panels potentially affected by Beilenson's realignment proposals, as well as two high-ranking officials of the American Legion (obviously concerned about the fate of the Veterans' Committee). Late in the afternoon Moakley stepped briefly into the meeting room and announced that the panel would not be conducting any further business that day.

Although the Legislative Reorganization Act of 1994 remained on the House floor schedule for the remainder of the 103rd Congress, the Rules Committee never resumed its markup and floor action on the measure did not occur. Both Hamilton and Dreier expressed disappointment at the outcome, each vowing to push for congressional reform during the 104th Congress.

Lessons

Meaningful reform of Congress affects the distribution of power, and proposals to redistribute power on Capitol Hill are inherently controversial. But beyond the inherent difficulty of congressional reorganization, the work of the Joint Committee on the Organization of Congress suggests certain lessons for would-be reformers.

First, congressional reform can proceed in a variety of ways and in a variety of forums. Reform can emerge from House or Senate select committees, party task forces, informal groups, party caucuses, or, as in this case, a bipartisan joint committee. Clearly, the appropriate forum for reform depends on the larger political context and the reform agenda. Adopting the Joint Committee approach facilitates a high-profile, comprehensive effort to revamp the legislative branch. Unfortunately, during the 103rd Congress, there were especially sharp disagreements between the chambers on procedural questions even though both were controlled by the same party, the Democrats. Furthermore, the period was suffused with intense partisanship. In short, the underlying structure of the Joint Committee made it suspect in the eyes of many lawmakers, particularly on the House side. The panel's structure also limited the ability of Joint Committee members to reach agreement on the specifics of reform at the crucial early stages of the reform process.

> • *A bipartisan, bicameral committee (such as the Joint Committee on the Organization of Congress) is most appropriate as a vehicle for devising reform proposals when an actual or potential consensus about the substance of reform is apparent between the parties and across the chambers. Otherwise, alternative forums (select committees, party task forces, informal groups) probably should be employed.*

Second, when the Joint Committee began work in January of 1993, nearly every major reform topic was on its platter, from committee assignment limitations to the administrative practices of Congress. In retrospect, it may have been preferable to narrow the agenda somewhat, shorten the hearings process, and focus members' attention earlier on devising some consensus on the specifics of reform. For example, the Joint Committee could have met more frequently in informal settings to discuss what the fundamental, bottom-line reform priorities should be for Congress, as well as whether a winning coalition could be assembled for any reform package. In short, more attention might have been spent assessing where the Joint Committee wanted to go.

> • *Future reform panels might consider something narrower than a comprehensive reform agenda, facilitating efforts to focus the attention of members of Congress and the public on specific proposals.*

Relatedly, a comprehensive effort to reorganize Congress necessarily takes time. An issue that needs careful consideration, especially for a reform panel with a limited life span, is the appropriate balance between deliberation and decision. Too much time spent in studying and gathering information on a wide array of topics could leave too little time for crucial decision making: identifying the priority reforms, making specific reorganization choices among them, reporting a reorganization package to Congress, and mobilizing internal and external support for the recommendations.

The informal retreat in Annapolis conducted by the Joint Committee may have been the high point of the reform process in 1993, with members freely exchanging views about the specifics of reform. Perhaps such a retreat should have been scheduled earlier in the reform process.

> • *Future reform entities should proceed more quickly than did the Joint Committee from the information-gathering to the decision-making stage of the reform process.*

Third, any congressional reform effort must balance the ideal with the politically feasible. Bold reform recommendations have certain advantages. They generate media attention and designate the high-water mark for reform, providing a benchmark from which to judge the success or failure of a reorganization effort. It may be easier to generate public support for bold recommendations than for proposals grounded in political feasibility. Furthermore, a bold plan provides bargaining leverage when the inevitable negotiations begin with opponents of change.

However, in the reform game there also are certain disadvantages to boldness. Most important, proposing too substantial a departure from the status quo may make a reform plan irrelevant, particularly in the House where the majority leadership has strong control over access to the floor. As mentioned, both Senator Boren and Representative Hamilton favored major jurisdictional realignments in principle, but opposed including such proposals in the Joint Committee's package because doing so might bring down the entire reform effort.

In particularly controversial reform areas, such as committee realignment, a menu of reform options could be proposed rather than a single recommendation. Under this strategy—suggested by Rep. John Spratt, D-S.C.—a modest and a more radical alternative would be presented to the full chamber for consideration. The bolder alternative could help generate media attention and public support, while the presence of a more politically realistic alternative might reduce the chance that the entire package would be viewed as unachievable and irrelevant.

> • *The art of reform is finding the proper mix of boldness and political feasibility. Future reform entities should offer a menu of reform options.*

Fourth, party leaders play a pivotal role in congressional reform plans. From the creation of reform panels to their composition and leadership, from the content of reform recommendations to influencing when (or if) reform bills are scheduled for floor action, party leaders are well positioned to affect the passage, modification, delay, or defeat of congressional reform.

Party leaders, however, are not necessarily sympathetic to reform initiatives or objectives. The 1945 and 1965 joint reform panels, for instance, encountered resistance to change from their respective party leaders. It is one thing for leaders to say they are for change in the abstract and another thing for them to work hard to pass specific recommendations. A major impediment to passing comprehensive reform during the 103rd Congress was the difficulty of securing floor time for consideration of the House and Senate reform packages. Another hurdle was crafting a reorganization package that would be favorably reported by the standing committees of jurisdiction, certain of which were dominated by leadership loyalists.

> • *Future reform entities should push hard for original jurisdiction and the right to go directly to the floor with their recommendations. Efforts also should be made to secure a date certain for floor consideration, perhaps included explicitly in the entity's authorizing resolution.*

Fifth, every reform effort requires some combination of outside pressure and inside frustration to produce major changes. The public climate during the 1990s appeared conducive to making major alterations in the internal operations of Congress. Many lawmakers, especially the newcomers to the 103rd Congress, campaigned on the need for reform. Yet toward the end of the 103rd Congress, this headline ran in a Capitol Hill newspaper: "Hill Reform in Graveyard" (Love 1994c).

A key reason for the failure to pass comprehensive reform during this period was the dissonance between what the public viewed as reform (less perks, pay, and pork for lawmakers, and the imposition of term limits) and what a wide range of members, scholars, and other informed observers perceived as worthwhile change. What lawmakers, responsible journalists such as David Broder, and participants in the Brookings-AEI Renewing Congress Project emphasized were not perks and privileges but committee reform and the need to make better use of members' time.

This "disconnect" between the outside and inside reform agendas made it easier for reform opponents to argue that doing nothing was preferable to the conflict accompanying meaningful change. Because the public reform agenda was diffuse and not fully supported by many change-oriented lawmakers, it was relatively easy for opponents to portray the broader political gains from reorganization as minimal. And the case against moving a reform package was reinforced by significant divisions between parties, factions within parties, the House and the Senate, junior and senior members, and party leaders and reform advocates. On institutional reform, like health care reform, lawmakers came to believe there was little price to be paid electorally or politically for failing to pass legislation, while the price of supporting something radically new was high.

> • *Outside demands for reform are likely to create the primary momentum for structural change in the years ahead. Therefore, reformers should highlight issues that are salient to the public, particularly those relating to ethics and institutional integrity and efficiency (such as campaign finance and lobbying reform and further streamlining of the legislative process).*

In brief, the attentive public should better grasp the realities of legislative decision making (despite Bismarck's adage that one shouldn't watch laws or sausages being made because each is typically a messy process) and the roles of Congress. Members need to educate their constituents about the complexities of the committee system, procedural problems that arise on the House and Senate floor, scheduling issues, and other key reform needs and features of Congress.

> • *Success in passing responsible reform may depend, in the end, on enhanced public understanding of our national legislature.*

Epilogue

On November 8, 1994, Republicans won majorities in both the House and Senate for the first time in 40 years. In the House the cohesive new majority pledged major congressional reform as part of its landmark "Contract with America." In the more informal and bipartisan Senate the momentum for reform was less pronounced. But the sheer intensity of reform sentiment in the other chamber placed additional pressure on Senate Republicans to likewise consider meaningful rules changes.

In the House

On the morning after the election, incoming Speaker Newt Gingrich asked former Joint Committee vice-chairman David Dreier to develop a comprehensive plan that refined and expanded the eight reform items explicitly listed in the "Contract with America." Among these reform items were the application of laws to Congress, a ban on proxy voting in House committees, the streamlining of House committees and a one-third reduction in committee staff, open meeting requirements, and a three-fifths requirement for the passage of income tax rate increases. Gingrich also appointed Rep. Jim Nussle of Iowa to head a Republican transition team charged with reforming the administrative functions of the House and coordinating the overall reform effort.

Working with the other House Republicans who had served on the Joint Committee, Dreier formulated four option plans for realigning committee jurisdictions, as well as a range of additional committee reform proposals. One of the jurisdiction plans—reportedly found in a wastebasket and promptly circulated around Capitol Hill—would have abolished five committees, substantially reduced the jurisdictions of the powerful Energy and Commerce Committee and Ways and Means Committee, and fundamentally reshuffled the jurisdictions of most remaining panels. The leaked jurisdiction plan sparked a firestorm of opposition among incoming chairs of the affected panels. An aide to Virginia representative Thomas J. Bliley, Jr., Republican heir to John Dingell's chairmanship on Energy and Commerce, remarked that "Mr. Bliley has not spent 14 years toiling in the vineyards trying to uphold the Republican principle against the best the Democrats had to offer so that we could be robbed of the opportunity of enacting the Republican agenda" (Roman 1994, A3). Other Republican committee leaders felt similarly protective about their own jurisdictions.

After weeks of negotiations, the new Republican leadership embraced relatively modest (but still significant) jurisdictional changes rather than a comprehensive realignment. Included in the Republican package were the abolition of three narrow panels of particular importance to Democratic constituencies—the committees on the District of Columbia, Merchant Marine and Fisheries, and Post Office and Civil Service. Interestingly, two narrow committees long considered as candidates for abolition by reformers—Small Business and Veterans' Affairs—were maintained, in part because they represent powerful constituencies important to House Republicans. Approximately 20 percent of the Energy and Commerce Committee's huge jurisdiction was transferred to other panels and most House committees were renamed to better reflect Republican agenda priorities. Also included among the committee reform recommendations were proposals to reduce the number of subcommittees, restrict committee assignments, and limit the terms of committee chairs to six years. Although Dreier was unable to advance as bold a reform plan as he originally sought, the changes he did secure constitute the most sweeping reforms of the House committee system in decades. Certain minority party rights provisions, which Republicans had pushed during their long years in the minority (for example, equitable member ratios on committees), were not included in the new Republican reform package.

The transition group led by Representative Nussle proposed a fundamental reorganization of the administrative functions of the House. The Nussle group's report, entitled *The GOP's Open House,* cited recommendations made by the Joint Committee for enhanced coordination of nonlegislative services in the House. The Committee on House Administration, renamed the Committee on House Oversight, was downsized and placed under the purview of the leadership. Day-to-day management of the chamber shifted to a chief administrative officer, who supplanted the bipartisan director of nonlegislative services and reported directly to the Speaker.

The congressional reform proposals mentioned in the "Contract with America," the committee reforms developed by Representative Dreier, and the administrative reforms proposed by the Nussle transition group were all adopted by the full Republican Conference in December 1994 and by the House (with bipartisan majorities) on the first day of the 104th Congress.[17]

In the Senate

Senate Republicans proceeded more deliberately with reform than did their House counterparts. During the transition period following the November elections, incoming majority leader Robert Dole appointed a task force of Republican senators to explore reform options, with former Joint Committee leader Pete Domenici and Connie Mack of Florida serving as co-chairmen. The Senate Republican task force released its reform agenda on January 23, 1995. As noted by Domenici, "The working group based its recommendations on the proposals made by the Joint Committee on the Organization of Congress in 1994."[18]

Included among the working group's recommendations were proposals to reduce the number of subcommittees, clamp down on excessive committee assignments, curtail proxy voting in committee, cut staff resources, and implement a two-year budget and appropriations process. Like the Joint Committee, the group supported a two-hour limit for debate on motions to bring up legislation, removing one of the opportunities for senators to filibuster a measure. The working group proposed that its recommendations be presented to the Senate in three separate measures: (1) committee structure, staffing, administration and support agencies; (2) budget process; and (3) floor procedure. In May 1995, prospects for this package were mixed; however, Senate Republicans were considering an alternative package of party rules changes that would, among other things, limit the terms of committee chairmen.

The Contribution of the Joint Committee

The groundwork for institutional change in 1994 and 1995 had been done by the Joint Committee in 1993. Many of the reforms passed or under consideration during the 104th Congress were previously proposed by the Joint Committee. Other reforms embraced by the Republican majority had been developed, refined, and publicized, if not adopted, during the reform committee's deliberations. Representative Dreier and other Joint Committee Republicans were able quickly to devise detailed options for jurisdictional reform because of the months of work they had done earlier. Asked about the House rules changes implemented in January 1995, Dreier responded that 90 percent of the amendments he offered during the Joint Committee's deliberations ended up in the Republican package: "I could not be happier. . . . If you go back and look at the amendments I offered to the JCOC, this is very close" (Kahn 1995, A44).

Perhaps most important, the Joint Committee focused the previously diffuse agenda for congressional reform and provided a degree of bipartisan legitimacy. Dissonance between what the public views as reform and what members and other elites view as constructive change still constitutes a key feature of the reform process. But the new Republican majority in the House was able to pass a comprehensive reform plan quickly—and one with substantial bipartisan credibility and support—in part because of the previous efforts of the Joint Committee.

In sum, congressional reform occurs in a variety of ways and forums and under diverse circumstances. Sometimes the reform process is like a 100-yard dash; proposals are swiftly agreed to by the House or Senate. Other times the process is like a marathon; it may take months, years, or even decades before fundamental change occurs in the organization and operation of Congress. The pace and purpose of congressional reorganization are also influenced by numerous factors, such as the change-oriented mood of members and the public-at-large or the influx of new lawmakers who have no stake in the status quo. However the race is run, reform is not for the short-winded because the effort to change Congress is never ending. The House and Senate will continue to adjust to new conditions, challenges, and pressures.

Notes

Authors' Note: The authors gratefully acknowledge the help they received from the four leaders of the Joint Committee: Lee H. Hamilton, David Dreier, David Boren, and Pete V. Domenici. Our staff colleagues on the Joint Committee also enriched our understanding of the congressional reform process, especially Kim Wincup, Phil Grone, Nick Wise, John Deeken, Kelly Cordes, Paul Rundquist, Carol Hardy Vincent, Maureen Groppe, James Saturno, Diane Lampert, and Mary Lou Smullen. Ken Nelson of Representative Hamilton's staff provided invaluable insights into the workings of the legislative process. In addition, scores of other expert professional staff and academics, too numerous to mention here, expanded our knowledge of Congress and its members.

1. *Congressional Record,* June 18, 1992, H 4867-4868.

2. Floor statement of Rep. Lee H. Hamilton, *Congressional Record,* June 18, 1992, H 4893.

3. Hearings and Markup Before the Committee on Rules, U. S. House of Representatives, 102nd Congress, 2nd Session, p. 155; *Congressional Record,* June 18, 1992, H 4897.

4. Michel appointed freshman Republican Jennifer Dunn of Washington to fill the open slot on the Joint Committee created by Gradison's resignation.

5. Clinton's election also reduced the bargaining leverage of congressional Republicans on reform issues.

6. House freshmen did contribute to House passage of a measure applying federal workplace laws to Congress, as well as to lobbying reform.

7. Associated Press wire; July 13, 1993.

8. For example, Vice-Chairman Dreier presided over Joint Committee hearings in the absence of the two co-chairmen, an unusual practice in the House.

9. Similarly, recommendations could be added to the mark only with bipartisan support.

10. In most House and Senate committees, if a member was absent from a meeting he or she could vote by proxy. Many members of both parties and both chambers favored banning the practice, but many committee chairmen argued that proxy voting was crucial for managing their committees and processing legislation. The motion to recommit with in-

structions is essentially an opportunity to amend legislation on the House floor. Republicans sought a guarantee of their right to offer such amendatory instructions so that they could participate more effectively in floor deliberations. On most House committees, the distribution of staff resources is tilted heavily in favor of the majority party. When in the minority, Republicans wanted the House to adopt the Senate practice of guaranteeing the minority party at least one-third of committee staff resources.

11. In fact, the authorizing resolution that created the Joint Committee (H. Con. Res. 192, 102nd Congress) explicitly stated that any "recommendation with respect to the rules and procedures of one House which only affects matters related solely to that House may be voted on by the members of the committee from that House." Ironically, the provision was included in the authorizing resolution to address House Democratic concerns that senators might attempt to alter House rules. But by the fall of 1993, many House Democrats were concerned about how Senate procedures could kill House-passed legislation.

12. On the Joint Committee only House Republicans solidly supported a jurisdictional realignment. Representative Dreier offered a jurisdictional reform proposal at the House markup of the Joint Committee, and it lost on a party line vote.

13. *Congressional Record,* September 29, 1994, S13665.

14. Ibid., S13694.

15. Under Section 306 of the Budget Act, explained Senator Byrd, "it is not in order to consider matters in the jurisdiction of the Budget Committee unless it is on a measure reported from the Budget Committee." *Congressional Record,* September 29, 1994, S13697. Boren and Domenici urged their colleagues not to defeat congressional reorganization on a procedural vote; they had also asked Majority Leader George Mitchell to refer S. 1824 to the Budget Committee for a limited period so as to obviate the point of order. The request was denied.

16. *National Journal's Congress Daily,* July 13, 1994, 4.

17. An important exception was the proposal to require a three-fifths supermajority to increase taxes. Although the proposal was narrowed by Republicans to only cover income tax rate increases, there remained substantial opposition to it among House Democrats on both policy and constitutional grounds.

18. News release, Sen. Pete V. Domenici, January 23, 1995.

6

THE STRUGGLE OVER REPRESENTATION AND LAWMAKING IN CONGRESS: Leadership Reforms in the 1990s

Barbara Sinclair

Seldom popular, Congress in the early 1990s sank to a new low in the public's regard. Mark Twain's characterization of Congress as the only native American criminal class was taken literally by many angry voters in the 1994 elections. The problem, as the public sees it, is that Congress doesn't listen and doesn't perform. It doesn't produce policy that speaks to people's needs, that addresses the big problems facing the country, and it certainly doesn't act with dispatch.

In response to public disaffection, Congress launched a multifaceted reform effort in the 1990s. This chapter examines those reforms—proposed and enacted—with a significant bearing on congressional party leadership. It also assesses the effect of the 1994 elections on the leadership-related reform agenda and on the functioning of majority party leadership. First, however, some discussion of the appropriate criteria for judging Congress is necessary. Public criticisms and the congressional reform effort itself have been characterized by a lack of clarity about criteria. Yet unless we are clear about what it is we want Congress to do, any reforms are bound to disappoint.

Certainly we expect Congress to represent; we expect members to bring into the legislative process the views, needs, and desires of their constituents, and we expect the Congress as an institution to provide a forum where the interests and demands of all segments of society are expressed. But while we want Congress to be an open forum for wide-ranging debate, we also want Congress to make decisions—to pass laws.

Obviously, not just any laws will do. In characterizing what sort of laws Congress is expected to pass, people frequently mention (and often combine) two criteria. First, Congress should pass laws that reflect the will of the people; that is, Congress should be responsive to popular majorities. Second, Congress should pass laws that deal promptly and effectively with pressing national problems. These two criteria, which can be labeled responsiveness and responsibility, are distinct. Only in a perfect world would what the majority wants always accord with what policy experts deem most likely to be effective, especially in the long run. In recent years much elite discourse has assumed that, when a conflict exists, responsibility should take priority. Yet the uncertainty inherent in the best experts' policy predictions, as well as the cost in legitimacy if Congress regularly thwarts popular majorities, make that questionable as a general rule. Furthermore, uncertainty about the link between a specific policy choice and the societal outcome means that, in most policy areas, legitimate differences of opinion as to what constitutes good public policy can and do exist. Both responsiveness and responsibility are values we would like Congress to further in its lawmaking, yet at times they may come into conflict.

Even were the criteria for appropriate lawmaking unproblematical, a tension between lawmaking and representation would exist. In institutional design terms, the requisites of representation and those of lawmaking are different. A decentralized, open permeable body in which individual members have considerable resources and autonomy of action has great potential for articulating the broad variety of opinions and interests in our society. A more centralized, hierarchical body is better suited to expeditious decision making. In process terms, representation takes time, especially when there are many viewpoints; by definition, lawmaking requires closure, an end to debate and, implicitly or explicitly, a choice among competing alternatives.

Although the values of representation, responsiveness, and responsibility can conflict, they are not strict alternatives. Appropriate decisions about institutional design (and processes of education, deliberation, and compromise that institutional design can further) can make possible an acceptable balance among them. But whether considering questions of institutional design or evaluating member behavior or outcomes, we must remember that all three values cannot be maximized simultaneously.

As the only central leaders in the institution, congressional party leaders potentially play a critical role in enabling the Congress to legislate. Representation as defined here can be achieved by members acting as individuals. Lawmaking requires collective action, and party leaders have traditionally been expected to perform key coordinational and coalition-building tasks that make it possible. Usually the goal of reforms affecting party leaders is to facilitate lawmaking. Yet reforms that significantly strengthen the central leadership may lessen members' opportunities to articulate and promote the full range of views in society.

Party Leadership and Lawmaking: Conflicting Diagnoses and the Historical Context That Shaped Them

The diagnoses of what ails Congress, certainly as they relate to leadership, vary significantly across chamber, party, and time. To understand why requires a brief examination of the impact on the two chambers of the institutional changes of the 1970s and the political experiences of the 1980s and early 1990s.

The House

In the House of Representatives, which Democrats controlled continuously from 1955 through 1994, the reforms of the 1970s massively redistributed influence; control over key institutional powers and resources previously in the hands of committee chairmen shifted to subcommittee chairs and rank-and-file members on the one hand and to the majority party leadership and the party caucus on the other. The power to make subcommittee assignments and appoint subcommittee chairs was taken away from the chair of the full committee and vested in the committee's majority party caucus. Chairs lost some of their control over committee staffs with the requirement that each subcommittee chair be assigned a professional staffer and a subcommittee budget. The stipulation of open markups and conference committee meetings reduced committee leaders' control over information. The supply of the single most critical resource—staff—expanded enormously and was broadly distributed across members.

The majority party leadership's institutional powers were also augmented. The leadership role in committee assignments was increased with the shifting of that function from Ways and Means Democrats to the new Steering and Policy Committee, chaired by the Speaker. The Speaker was given sole authority to nominate all Democratic members of the Rules Committee subject only to caucus ratification. The new multiple referral rule gave him power to set reporting deadlines for committees. The party leadership also benefited from staff increases.

Committee chairmen were deprived of their autonomy when all chairmanships were made subject to ratification by the party caucus. Appropriations Committee subcommittee chairs were also made subject to such review. These reforms forced committee leaders to be more responsive to the party membership and its elected leaders.

Both policy and participation concerns had motivated the reforms. Northern liberals' policy dissatisfaction provided the initial impetus for the reform movement and drove it along. These members also were dissatisfied with the meager opportunities for rank-and-file participation in the legislative process. As the junior liberal Democrats saw it, seniority-based committee government gave disproportionate decision-making power to an unrepresentative cadre of conservative southerners. This deprived the more numerous but junior liberals of their fair share of influence. The result, in their view, was public policy unresponsive to the preferences of a party majority. If participation in the making of legislative decisions was broadened, liberals believed better—meaning more liberal—public policy would result (Sheppard 1985).

The reforms transformed a committee-centered institution into a body that broadly distributed decision-making responsibilities (Sinclair 1983; Sinclair 1995; Smith 1989). Committee chairmen could no longer dominate their committees, and committees could no longer count on their bills receiving only pro forma scrutiny on the floor. Increased participation by rank-and-file members at both the committee and the floor stages of deliberations, the growing attractiveness of the free-lance entrepreneurial style, and large numbers of inexperienced subcommittee chairmen multiplied the significant actors and radically increased uncertainty. Democratic committee contingents, Democratic committee leaders, and the Democratic membership found that they now needed help passing their legislation, and they began to look to their party leaders for that help.

Party leaders are, after all, the elected agents of their members and the only central leaders in the institution. A number of the rules changes in the 1970s were clearly and directly aimed at making the party leadership more capable of furthering the party majority's legislative goals. The problem the party leadership faced was providing the legislative help their members wanted without constricting the participation opportunities those same members prized.

The leadership team of Speaker Tip O'Neill and Majority Leader Jim Wright, which served from 1977 to 1987, developed a set of strategies for coping with the new House. Including as many members as possible in the coalition-building process became a key modus operandi. This "strategy of inclusion" entailed expanding and using formal leadership structures, such as the whip system, and bringing other Democrats into the coalition-building process on an ad hoc basis, through bill-specific task forces, for example. In the new House environment, the core leadership was too small to undertake the task of successful coalition building alone; including other members provided needed assistance. The strategy of inclusion was also a way for leaders to satisfy members' expectations of significant participation in the legislative process, but to do so in a manner beneficial to the party and the leadership.

The leadership refined the quintessential legislative strategy of using its control over procedure to structure the choices members confront. By giving the Speaker control of the Rules Committee, the reforms greatly enhanced the leadership's tools for structuring floor choices. In the mid-1970s, members' desires for maximum participation opportunities constrained the leadership's use of this resource. By the late 1970s, however, many Democrats were having second thoughts about the wide open amending process on the floor. The unrestricted amending process was resulting in lengthy and late sessions; Republicans were becoming adept at drafting amendments that confronted Democrats with a no-win choice; and legislative compromises, carefully crafted in committee, were being picked apart on the floor. In August 1979 over 40 Democrats signed a letter to the Speaker complaining about the length of floor sessions and calling for more frequent use of restrictive rules. The Rules Committee, in concert with the party leadership, increasingly reported rules that restricted amending activity to some extent. During the 1980s such rules were to become a key element of leadership strategy.

The wide open, participatory process that the reforms established became even more legislatively problematical in the political environment of the 1980s. With the 1980 election of Ronald Reagan, House Democrats faced a conservative, confrontational president who threatened all their goals. Advantaged by a widespread perception of a policy mandate and a Republican Senate, Reagan was a formidable opponent. Even after the mandate perception faded, passing legislation Democrats favored continued to be difficult. Republicans controlled the Senate from 1981 through 1986, and the large and growing budget deficits severely constrained legislative activity as they continue to do today. This political climate further increased Democrats' need for leadership help to pass even minimally satisfactory legislation.

The 1970s and 1980s, in addition, witnessed a change in the structure of legislation that contributed to majority party members' greater need for the sort of assistance that only the party leadership can provide. Jurisdictional conflicts among committees and the House's inability to realign jurisdictions created a need for an outside arbiter when committee leaders could not agree. The multiple referral rule, instituted in 1975, formalized the Speaker's role and gave him new powers to set reporting deadlines for legislation referred to more than one committee.

In the 1980s and early 1990s, deep policy divisions between the president and House Democrats resulted in much more frequent employment of omnibus measures. The major battles revolved around budget resolutions, reconciliation bills, and other omnibus measures centering on questions of basic priorities. Because of the number and magnitude of issues and sometimes also the number of committees involved in omnibus measures, putting together and passing such legislation often requires negotiation and coordination activities beyond the capacity of committee leaders. Furthermore, on such high-stakes, broadly encompassing measures, committee leaders lack the legitimacy to speak for the membership as a whole. Thus, as omnibus measures became more prominent on the congressional agenda, the need for leadership involvement increased.

The reformers of the 1970s had given their party leadership new powers and resources that, aggressively used, could significantly increase the probability of legislative success. In the immediate postreform period, Democrats had been unwilling to allow their leaders to employ those new resources expansively. This changed in the 1980s. Members increasingly relied on party leaders to help them pass legislation and advance their policy and reelection goals.

This change in members' expectations of party leaders was almost certainly dependent upon an increase in the Democratic membership's ideological homogeneity, which reduced the potential costs of stronger leadership. The change in southern politics set off by the civil rights movement and the Voting Rights Act had resulted, by the early 1980s, in a less conservative House contingent of southern Democrats. After the 1982 elections the voting cohesion of House Democrats began to increase and in the late 1980s and early 1990s reached levels unprecedented in the post–World War II era (Rohde 1988; Congressional Quarterly various years). As policy differences among Democrats declined, so did fears that the exercise of strong leadership would pose a threat to individual members' policy or reelection goals.

Responding to its members' desires for both legislative results and opportunities to participate broadly in the legislative process, the Democratic party leadership became more active and more central in the legislative process but also more inclusive. One study shows that party leadership involvement on the 40 to 50 most significant bills of a Congress increased from 46 percent in the 91st Congress (1969-1970) to 83 percent in the 100th (1987-1988) and 68 percent in the 101st (1989-1990); major involvement by the Democratic leadership on this same legislation increased from 28 percent in the 91st to 60 percent in the 100th and 54 percent in the 101st (Sinclair 1995, 48). Whip task forces charged with whipping support for a specific bill, functioned in about 70 instances in each of the 100th and 101st Congresses. The leadership has vigorously pursued the strategy of structuring floor choices through rules; rules that in some way restrict amendments have steadily increased from 15 percent of all rules in 1977-1978 to 66 percent in 1991-1992 (Wolfensberger 1992). On the most major legislation the likelihood of a restrictive rule is even higher.

At the same time, the leadership has continued to pursue the strategy of inclusion. In the 102nd Congress almost 40 percent of all House Democrats were members of the whip system. The task forces are made up of Democrats who volunteer. In the 100th Congress about 60 percent of all Democrats served on one or more task forces. Other forums under the auspices of the leadership also provide Democrats with opportunities to participate.

Given this historical context, it is hardly surprising that House Democrats and House Republicans offered radically different diagnoses of what's wrong and what appropriate remedies are. As a long-standing and increasingly cohesive majority, Democrats were more concerned with enhancing lawmaking than representation. The 1970s reforms had made the House a more open forum for the articulation of societal views, and, during the 1980s, House Democrats had worked out ways within the party of reconciling members' desires to participate broadly in the legislative process with the requisites of lawmaking. Thus, the reforms proposed by Democrats had the aim of directly or indirectly enhancing the party leadership's capacity to facilitate lawmaking. However, since Democrats had already strengthened their leadership significantly, most of the proposals were modest.

When an activist legislative majority attempts to make law under conditions of divided control in a media age, frustrations result. These frustrations drove Democrats' major proposal for leadership-related reforms. During the long period of divided party control, congressional Democrats were usually strongly dissatisfied with the president's agenda. Yet even with his party a minority in Congress, the president has a great advantage in the struggle to define the national and the congressional agenda, an advantage that seemed to increase in the media-dominated 1980s. Thus, a mechanism for agenda setting headed Democrats' priority list of leadership-related reforms in 1992.

Not surprisingly, House Republicans' diagnosis of Congress's ailments was fundamentally different. The House is a majority rule chamber: when the majority party is cohesive, it is the majority that rules. The increase in Democratic cohesion and the related increase in the strength and centrality of the Democratic party leadership cut Republicans out of the action, especially at the postcommittee stage in the House. The problem, Republicans argued, was that a corrupt, power-mad majority party heavy-handedly ran the House in such a way as to unfairly exclude the minority party, from decision making and from having a fair chance to win (Connelly and Pitney 1994). The majority party leadership accomplished this primarily by manipulating the rules, especially special rules from the Rules Committee.

Republicans argued that the increased use of restrictive rules hindered both representation and responsiveness, that it limited the diversity of views expressed, and that it prevented the House from responding to the public will. Therefore, Republican priorities for reform were aimed at lessening the majority party's control of the floor agenda.

The Senate

The Senate and the House have always been distinctly different legislative bodies; institutional developments and political factors, by the late 1980s, had magnified the differences between the two chambers. As a result, the Senate's leadership-related problems are also very different from those of the House (Sinclair 1989).

Senate rules have always conferred great power on the individual senator. In most cases any senator can offer an unlimited number of amendments to legislation on the Senate floor and those amendments need not even be germane. A senator can hold the Senate floor indefinitely unless cloture is invoked, which requires an extraordinary majority—now 60 votes.

In the Senate of the 1950s and before, norms limited the extent to which senators exploited the powers rules gave them. Since floor time was relatively plentiful, the disruptive potential of these powers was less (Oppenheimer 1985). The typical senator of the 1950s was a specialist who concentrated upon the issues that came before his committees. His legislative activities were largely confined to the committee room; he was seldom active on the Senate floor, offering few amendments to legislation outside his area of expertise. Senators seldom resorted to extended debate and then only on the most momentous issues.

During the late 1960s and the 1970s, the Senate underwent a transformation. The body increased the supply of staff and of desirable committee assignments and began to distribute those resources much more equally among its members. Norms dictating specialization, and a highly restrained use of the great powers the Senate rules confer upon the individual, lost their hold. Senators increasingly involved themselves in a broad range of issues, including ones outside the jurisdiction of their committees. They became highly active both in the committee room and on the Senate floor (Sinclair 1989). Extended debate became more frequent, and senators increasingly became willing to use that power on issues of lesser importance.

In the Senate, unlike the House, rule and norm changes that increased rank-and-file members' opportunities to participate were not accompanied by leadership-strengthening changes. The Senate majority party leader, always institutionally weaker than the Speaker of the House, was given no significant new powers for coping with the more active, assertive, and consequentially less predictable membership. As a result, the majority leader's control over the floor schedule is tenuous. A single senator can disrupt the work of the Senate by exercising the right of unlimited debate or objecting to the unanimous consent requests through which the Senate does most of its work. Clearly, a partisan minority of any size can bring legislative activity to a standstill.

Data show that filibusters have become commonplace. In the 1950s and before, filibusters were rare; the period 1951 to 1960 saw an average of 1 per Congress. In the 1960s the average per Congress was 4.6; in the 1970s (1971-1980) it rose to 11.2. From 1981 through 1986 the average per Congress was 16.7, and for 1987 through 1992 it was 26.7 (DSG 1994). As Majority Leader George Mitchell said in 1993, "Now we see that a filibuster is used almost every day on almost everything that comes before the Senate. Right now in this Senate there are six different filibusters going on at one time" (November 3, 1993, quoted in DSG 1994). During the 103rd Congress, the filibuster became an increasingly partisan tool, used over and over again by minority Republicans to thwart a new Democratic president and the majority in the chamber.

Even more consequential for Senate decision making than actual filibusters are threats to filibuster. Full-blown filibusters are vastly outnumbered by implicit or explicit threats to filibuster. When floor time is tight—before a recess or near the end of the session—a single senator's threat to engage in extended debate is often sufficient to prevent the leadership from bringing up any bill that is not "must" legislation. As a tacit recognition of this fact, the meaning of "holds" has changed. According to a Republican leadership manual of procedure: "When a senator has particular concerns about a measure, he may ask that a 'hold' be placed against it. It will be honored for so long as the majority leader can do so, but at some point the leadership may move the legislation notwithstanding the hold which has been placed against it" (Gold 1981, 25).

However, over time, holds have become more nearly absolute. As a long-time staffer explained in the mid-1980s:

> It used to mean that putting a hold on something meant simply that you would be given twenty-four hours notice that this thing would come up, so you could prepare for that. And, of course, when you put a hold on something, it puts the people, the sponsors, on notice that you had some problems and it would be in their interest to come and negotiate with you. But four or five or six years ago it started to mean that if you put a hold on something, it would never come up. It became, in fact, a veto. (Sinclair 1989, 130)

By custom, holds can be placed anonymously; the leadership does not release the name of the senator who is responsible for blocking action. This secrecy thwarts accountability and makes imposing a hold cost-free to the individual senator, thus encouraging frequent and broad use. As Mann and Ornstein (1993, 50) explain, "Increasingly, senators are subject to sophisticated demands by lobbyists to use holds on behalf of their causes: and senators have been more than willing to fully exploit the notification process on behalf of interest groups, constituents, and personal agendas. At times the practice degenerates into rolling anonymous holds as lobbyists persuade one senator after another to hold up legislation they oppose."

The contemporary Senate is a superb forum for the articulation of the American public's broad array of interests and opinions. The enormous power and autonomy the body gives each of its members furthers representation. That distribution of influence, however, makes lawmaking highly problematical. Large minorities can block action that majorities support. The partisan use of the filibuster in 1993 to kill elements of a new president's program highlighted the antimajoritarian character of the body. Even when they cannot stop legislation entirely, a determined minority can often extract substantive concessions. And a single adamant or disgruntled senator can disrupt the work of the body and often affect outcomes.

Reform proposals in the early 1990s focused on enhancing the leadership's control over the floor agenda, especially but not exclusively by curtailing opportunities for extended debate. Proposals seriously advanced by senators were, however, quite modest. Various outsiders advocated major change, but senators did not (Dewar 1994a). With all its frustrations, the current structure that gives each senator so much latitude is very attractive to senators as individuals. Even majority Democrats seemed less than highly enthusiastic about fundamental change; of course, their experience of minority status from 1981 through 1986 may have tempered their desire for radical, majority-empowering reform.

Different Diagnoses Lead to Different Prescriptions: Reform in the 103rd Congress

The House

"Reforms adopted by the Democratic Caucus this week will give House leaders greater leverage in conducting the nation's legislative business. The reforms will provide leaders with a greater capacity to construct a single comprehensive legislative agenda and new powers to deal with committees to ensure cooperation in efforts to adopt that agenda." Thus read the first paragraph of the Democratic Study Group's report on the rules changes adopted by the House Democratic Caucus in December 1992 (DSG 1992, 1). Specifically, House Democrats created a Working Group on Policy Development "to assist the Leadership, the Steering and Policy Committee, the individual committees and the Caucus in the establishment and implementation of a consensus policy agenda" (Caucus rule 43E). The Speaker appointed the members, with at least half coming from the Steering and Policy Committee.

Caucus rules admonished the Working Group to work "in close consultation with the chairmen of each of the committees," and Speaker Foley's 31 appointees included 8 committee chairs. Yet the chairmen had initially opposed such a group altogether and then had argued for inclusion of all 21 standing committee chairs.

The second major rules change by the Democratic Caucus in 1992 came at the expense of committee leaders as well. Under the new rules, the Steering and Policy Committee or 50 members could request a vote of the caucus to remove the chair of a committee or subcommittee at any time during a Congress. As the DSG report stated, "Chairs will not only be subject to a vote at the beginning of each Congress, they will be presented with a clear set of expectations for legislation action in the area of their committee's jurisdiction, and they can be removed during the course of a Congress for failure to adequately respond to Caucus demands for action" (DSG 1992, 3).

The frustrations of lawmaking under divided party control and, by the time of the actual caucus organization sessions, the prospects of having to deliver legislatively under united control, motivated House Democrats to institute reforms enhancing their party leaders' capacity to facilitate lawmaking. Clearly, these changes represented not a radical departure but a continuation of a now well-established trend: toward a party leadership with greater responsibilities and leverage but one expected to lead through a highly inclusive style and toward all leaders, committee as well as party, being perceived as agents of the Democratic membership and being expected to act accordingly.

The Joint Committee on the Organization of Congress made modest proposals that directly affected party leadership in the House. It proposed that the Speaker designate a "primary" committee of jurisdiction in joint referral cases. It also recommended time or subject matter restrictions on the other committees of referral after the committee of primary jurisdiction reports the matter (JCOC 1993f, 6). Unable to realign jurisdictions or tighten the multiple referral rule, the JCOC urged the Speaker to make more aggressive use of his referral powers to facilitate lawmaking.

Another JCOC proposal guaranteed the minority party a motion to recommit with instructions on all legislation. In contrast to the relative lack of controversy on the multiple referral provision, the debate over floor procedure was highly contentious and strongly partisan. That debate focused primarily on the special rules used to bring most major legislation to the floor.

As restrictive rules became more and more standard, Republicans became increasingly and vocally unhappy about House floor procedures. Rules that deny the minority a motion to recommit with instructions had been the special target of Republican displeasure up to 1995. Republicans argued that the standing rules of the House guaranteed the minority a motion to recommit with instructions—a last opportunity to amend the legislation at issue before 1995. Democrats argued that the rules guarantee the minority only a motion to recommit in *some* form. (A motion to recommit without instructions, another way of attempting to kill the legislation, generally has little chance of success.) Rules denying a motion to recommit with instructions are relatively rare, but Democrats did use them when they believed Republicans had a proposal likely to split their ranks.

For example, the rule for the reconciliation bill implementing President Clinton's economic program in 1993 allowed only a vote on a comprehensive Republican substitute. It did not allow amendments to delete various unpopular elements of the package—the BTU tax and the tax on social security payments to high-income recipients. Nor did it allow a motion to recommit with instructions by which Republicans could and undoubtedly would have offered those same amendments. Many Democrats would have found it very difficult to explain votes against such amendments back home. Allowing the amendments, either directly or via a motion to recommit with instructions, would have confronted Democrats with an unpalatable choice: cast a series of politically dangerous votes or contribute to the picking apart of the package on the floor.

Special rules evolved into highly flexible and powerful tools that can be used to manage floor time and prevent obstructionism, to focus debate on the major alternatives, and to structure floor choices so as to advantage some outcomes over others. From the Democratic Party's perspective, special rules were an indispensable leadership instrument for facilitating lawmaking. Strategic use of special rules sometimes allowed the majority party leadership to further responsible lawmaking on inflammatory issues; an appropriately structured rule might allow Democrats to vote on the basis of their policy goals rather than on the basis of their reelection fears (Sinclair 1993; Arnold 1990).

From the Republican Party's perspective, restrictive rules limited representation and responsiveness. In the words of Gerald Solomon of New York, a Republican member of the JCOC and of the Rules Committee, "'restrictive rules' ... limit the ability of members to fully represent their constituents by offering amendments" (JCOC 1993f, 159). And because the minority's view of what constitutes good public policy differs from the majority's, Republicans before 1995 saw strategic special rules as thwarting responsiveness rather than furthering responsibility.

From the majority Democrats' perspective, the restrictive rule on the reconciliation bill made it possible for the majority to make the hard but necessary choices, to legislate responsibly. From the minority Republicans' perspective, the rule fostered a lack of responsiveness by not requiring members to vote on the unpopular provisions individually. (In 1981, on the Reagan reconciliation bill, the roles and the arguments of the two parties were reversed.)

JCOC House Republicans proposed requiring a supermajority to waive the standing rules of the House via a special rule; they also wanted to make it easier to amend rules on the floor (JCOC 1993f, 155). (In addition, their proposal restricted the use of the suspension procedure, thus further eroding the majority leadership's control over the floor schedule.) JCOC Democrats agreed only to guarantee the minority the right to offer a motion to recommit with instructions if offered by the minority leader or his designee; they did so to get some Republican support for the reform package as a whole. Most rules gave Republicans the opportunity to offer a substitute, and such a vote on the Republican alternative is a clearer, easier-to-understand vote. Crafting language guaranteeing the minority this opportunity proved extremely difficult, and the motion to recommit with instructions had taken on a symbolic importance with Republicans. Because it is a procedural vote, it is usually easier for the majority to defeat—an advantage from Democrats' point of view in 1993. Beyond the symbolism, Republicans found it attractive because it gave them the element of surprise. A substitute usually must be made public before the rule is granted; the amendatory content of a motion to recommit with instructions need not be determined or revealed until the last moment. The JCOC did write into the rule a stipulation allowing the Speaker to postpone the vote on such a motion for up to two hours.

Republicans' dissatisfaction with the majority party's tight control over the floor agenda extended well beyond the issue of special rules. In late 1993 a Republican House member, with the help of conservative hosts of radio talk shows and the *Wall Street Journal,* forced a change in House rules that could weaken the majority party leadership's control of the floor agenda.

The House has long had a rule that allows a majority to discharge a committee and thus force a measure to the floor. The names of the members who signed a discharge petition were kept confidential until the requisite 218 signatures had been obtained. Rep. James Inhofe, an obscure junior member from Oklahoma, proposed making signatures on a discharge petition immediately public. He and other proponents based their argument on the people's right to know and claimed that the change would make the House more responsive to the will of the people; secrecy allowed members to mislead their constituents, to "vote liberal and press release conservative" as Inhofe put it (House Committee on Rules 1993, 7).

Opponents worried that the change would make it harder for the House to act responsibly, to make sound decisions. In a perfect world, they conceded, the proposed change in the discharge rule probably would not present a threat to responsible decision making. But a world of 8-second sound-bites and 30-second attack ads is far different. Members often must choose between a position they believe to be good public policy, what their constituents would themselves support had they time to examine the issue, and a position that because of its simplicity and emotional appeal is very hard to oppose. In fact, on complex policy issues (most of Congress's workload), a responsible position is likely to be complicated and thus more difficult to explain to constituents than a simple-minded gut response. Committees and the party leadership can sometimes protect members from having to make such choices by preventing hot button issues from coming to the floor. In the contemporary House, leaders cannot thwart the will of a majority that really wants an opportunity to act on an issue. Party and committee leaders are responsible to their caucuses, which can remove them, and in any case the discharge rule is always available. Leaders *can* provide a little insulation against hotburning but often short-lived popular issues; they can provide a little time for passions to cool and for members to assess the wisdom of the proposal. The change in the discharge rule weakened the ability of leaders to perform this function.

Inhofe used the discharge petition to get the proposed rules change to the floor; he and his allies compiled a list of the members who had signed the petition and leaked it to the *Wall Street Journal,* which published the names of those who had refused to sign. Under pressure generated by "wildly erroneous *Wall Street Journal* editorials and sensationalized talk show hysteria," opposition collapsed. The measure came to the floor and passed easily (Pincus 1993, 151).

The change in the discharge rule makes it easier to pressure members to act in the heat of the moment. Legislation and constitutional amendments dealing with highly emotional issues are more likely to get to the floor. The rule change also benefits well-endowed special interests, opponents argued. In a world where lobbyists, often representing narrow interests, are much more attentive to the legislative process than is the public at large, the change in the discharge rule may give lobbyists a potent new tool for moving special interest legislation.

The Senate

For the Senate the central question at the beginning of the 103rd Congress was whether to alter Rule 22, the rule giving members the formal means (cloture) to end extended debate. Senators favor more efficient use of floor time and greater predictability in the floor schedule. This is unobtainable without some curbs on extended debate. So long as a single disgruntled senator can disrupt the party leaders' legislative schedule, party leaders are forced to defer to individual senators even at the expense of inconveniencing a majority. Leaders lack the control over floor proceedings necessary to make possible efficient use of time or scheduling predictability. And, of course, extended debate can thwart a Senate majority from working its will and thus hinder the Congress in lawmaking.

Many outsiders—including House Democrats and a number of prominent former senators—urged substantial reforms in Rule 22. The proposals of most senators, however, were modest. Senator Tom Harkin's plan to decrease the number of votes needed to invoke cloture with each successive vote until eventually 51 votes could cut off debate was the most radical recommendation offered and similar to ones suggested by a number of outsiders. Not surprisingly, Republican senators were prominent opponents of limiting extended debate, but majority Democrats did not make a concerted effort for major change. To be sure, changing Senate rules over opposition is enormously difficult; to impose cloture on a change in rules requires a two-thirds vote. However, at least until the Republican strategy of attempting to block almost everything became evident, Democrats displayed limited enthusiasm for significant change, and, of course, by then the impossibility of effecting such change was obvious.

Majority Leader George Mitchell proposed a package of changes that he said would not "change the basic nature of the filibuster nor of the institution of the Senate itself [but would] significantly reduce delay and obstruction" (JCOC 1993e, 51). Specifically, Mitchell recommended (1) that debate on the motion to proceed, made by the majority leader or his designee, be limited to two hours; (2) that a ruling of the chair (that is, the presiding officer) be overturned only by three-fifths votes; (3) that amendments reported by a committee be considered germane in a post-cloture situation; (4) that time consumed on quorum calls in a post-cloture situation be counted against the senator who suggested the absence of a quorum; (5) that the Senate request or agree to a conference through the adoption of a single motion, rather than three, each of which is debatable and subject to a filibuster; (6) that conference reports be considered as having been read when called up for consideration; and (7) that 60 senators could require that amendments to a measure be relevant and that, under this procedure, "sense of the Senate," resolutions be considered nonrelevant per se.

In its reform package the JCOC included some but not all of these rule changes. (It endorsed the first, second, fourth, and sixth, the latter with a layover requirement.) The committee was not willing to reduce from three to one the number of opportunities to filibuster a conference report nor to institute a new motion by which 60 senators could require amendments to a measure to be relevant. For a sense of the Senate resolution to be considered, the JCOC recommended by 10 Senate cosponsors, unless the resolution was offered by the majority or minority leader—a weaker control than Mitchell had proposed on these nonlegally binding but time-consuming resolutions.

In terms of enhancing the majority leader's control over the floor, the most significant of the proposals adopted by the JCOC was the limitation on debate on the motion to proceed. Currently, if senators filibuster a motion to proceed and cloture is invoked, they bear no parliamentary cost for having filibustered: the floor situation is identical to what it would have been had they not done so. However, if a filibuster must take place on the legislation itself, the requirement that amendments must have been filed and must be germane when cloture is invoked means the filibusters do pay some price in parliamentary flexibility for having filibustered and lost. Furthermore, since filibustering or threatening to filibuster a motion to proceed often seems aimed at securing favorable terms in the unanimous consent agreement that will govern floor consideration of legislation, eliminating this possibility would reduce individual senators' leverage and thus increase the majority leader's control over the floor agenda (Beth 1993, esp., 32-34).

Limiting the use of holds explicitly was much discussed during JCOC hearings. Increasing the number of senators required to place a hold, imposing limits on the length of time that a hold remains in effect, and requiring that the names of senators placing holds be made public were suggested. In the end the JCOC made no recommendations on holds. Although most senators seem to agree that something should be done about holds, doing so through the mechanisms of a formal Senate rule has the disadvantage of giving formal recognition to what is now only an informal practice. Furthermore, such restrictions are unlikely to be enforceable or effective so long as the big gun that undergirds holds—extended debate—remains available.

The Senate Rules and Administration Committee further weakened the modest JCOC proposals. The provision changing the time consumed on quorum calls in a postcloture situation against the senator who suggested the absence of a quorum was stricken on a motion from Sen. Robert C. Byrd, D-W.Va. In another demonstration of the adage that where you sit determines where you stand, Byrd successfully moved to strike a provision specifying that "the Senate Majority and Minority Leaders should make assignments to committees under rules adopted by their respective caucuses" (JCOC 1993f, 4). The party caucuses, not the Senate as a whole, assign senators to committees in the contemporary Senate, and the purpose of this change, as its wording made clear, was to bring the rules into conformity with practice. Nevertheless Appropriations Committee Chairman Byrd objected. The committee approved other changes in floor procedures (most importantly the limitation on debate on the motion to proceed), but all committee Republicans voted in opposition.

Why So Little Reform?

Given the extent of public dissatisfaction with Congress, why were the leadership-related reforms proposed during the 103rd Congress—especially those of the JCOC—so modest? In the House, a chamber whose essential character is majority rule, the majority and minority offered radically different diagnoses of what was wrong, diagnoses that grew out of their very different situations in the chamber. The lack of common ground precluded the JCOC from recommending any but the most modest changes. The Senate, in contrast, is a quintessentially individualist chamber—a characteristic enormously amplified during the past several decades. Changing rules requires a consensus, and for most senators, regardless of party, the individual benefits of the contemporary Senate outweigh the collective frustrations. Even heightened partisan tensions and obstructionism of the 1980s and early 1990s did not produce a substantial number in favor of fundamental reform. In neither chamber did the JCOC proposals, despite their modest scope, even receive floor consideration.

Come the Revolution?
The New Republican Majorities and Reform

The 1994 elections gave Republicans control of both chambers for the first time in 40 years. What is the likely impact on leadership-related reforms? More generally, whether driven by rules changes or not, what alterations in the functioning of majority leadership are we likely to see?

The change in party control should have a greater impact on the House than on the Senate because Republicans have been out of power so much longer in that chamber and because the parties differed so radically in their proposals for reform. Circumstances and inclinations dictate that Newt Gingrich, R-Ga., be an activist Speaker. The members that make up the new Republican majority are ideologically quite homogeneous, and they believe the elections gave them a mandate to change public policy. Before the elections, House Republicans under Gingrich's lead pledged to uphold a legislative agenda they dubbed their "Contract with America." Even as a leader of the minority, Gingrich engaged in the sort of agenda setting that Democrats were increasingly demanding of their leadership during periods of divided party control. House Republicans have given their leaders many of the same tools that Democratic leaders utilized when they were in the majority. For example, the Republicans have an elaborate whip system, and the Speaker has the authority to nominate the Republican members of the Rules Committee and to influence committee assignments and the selection of chairs.

Relying on his enormous prestige with House Republicans, Gingrich, in the early days after the elections, exercised power well beyond that specified in Republican Conference rules. He designated Republicans to serve as committee chairs, bypassing seniority in several instances. According to the rules, the party Committee on Committees nominates chairs, and the Conference approves them; Gingrich preempted that process, assuming that his stature would prevent anyone from challenging his choices. He also engineered a rules change to increase the party leadership's voice on the Committee on Committees, and he used that new influence to reward junior Republicans, his strongest supporters, with choice assignments (Rules, Ways and Means, Appropriations, and Commerce). The three-term (six-year) limit on committee chairs, already a Conference rule, was written into House rules and will make committee chairs less formidable competitors for power in the chamber.

To legislate successfully, especially when the president is a member of a different party, the contemporary House needs an activist Speaker. Political circumstances, by and large, are conducive to the exercise of strong party leadership. Gingrich and his leadership team have the institutional tools and, most critically, the member support to lead aggressively. Strong leadership depends on both, but it is the latter that is essential.

Although the new Republican leaders may be pushing the envelope in some respects, they do not appear to be innovators in developing new tools or new strategies, except perhaps in their use of the media. To this point, they are relying on those developed by Democratic leaders in the past. Furthermore, House Republicans' rhetoric while in the minority may constrain their use of restrictive rules, one of the most potent and flexible leadership tools of the majority party.

The Republicans' critique of Democratic majority leadership centered on the leaders' use of procedure in what Republicans claimed was a dictatorial fashion; specifically, restrictive rules were excoriated as devices for stifling debate and preventing the majority from working its will. Since winning control, Republicans have dropped their proposals to require a supermajority for restrictive rules and to narrow the use of the suspension procedure. However, in their "Contract with America," Republicans promised to bring up their legislative proposals under open rules, and, after so many years in the minority, Republican House members have high expectations of participating fully in the legislative process. Yet the Republican majority is narrow and Democrats are likely to make good use of the opportunities that open rules provide. After the euphoria of having taken control fades, the Republican Party and its leadership will face a choice: reverse themselves and invite charges of gross hypocrisy or eschew one of the majority party's most potent tools, one that may well be necessary to keep the contemporary House functioning. In fact, Republicans confronted that choice on the first day of the 104th Congress. To meet their self-imposed schedule on the first day, Republicans reneged on campaign promises and brought their first two items to the floor under closed rules.

Over the long haul, if Republicans maintain their majority, the four-term limit on the Speaker, passed at the beginning of the 104th Congress under pressure from junior Republicans, may come back to haunt them and the House. While few Speakers have served longer, the limit will make the Speaker a lame duck and foster succession struggles well before the term limit actually goes into effect.

In the Senate, neither rules nor the exercise of leadership is likely to change much. The consensus required to rein in senators' right to engage in extended debate does not exist. And so long as Rule 22 remains unchanged, majority party leadership will perforce require deference to and accommodation of senators as individuals. To be sure, Senate Republicans may display considerable cohesion for a time, and Democrats may be more selective in the use of the filibuster than Republicans were. But when the political impetus to such restraint fades, as it inevitably will, the severe constraints that Senate rules impose on majority party leadership in that chamber will again become glaringly obvious.

7

CONGRESS BASHING:
External Pressures for Reform and
the Future of the Institution

Norman J. Ornstein and Amy L. Schenkenberg

If the 1994 midterm elections told us anything about the state of our country, it was that the public's—and the members'—attitudes toward Congress are abysmally negative. When asked by the *Washington Post* about the race between then House Speaker Tom Foley, D-Wash., and his challenger, George Nethercutt, one voter quipped, "I think it's time for a new liar" (Kenworthy 1994, A1). The nation met the elections with a disapproval rating of Congress of 73 percent and an approval of only 20 percent, resulting in a Republican majority in both the House and Senate for the first time since the 83rd Congress (1953-1954) (CBS News/*New York Times* 1994). Among the victims were 16 Democratic freshmen rejected for a second term because their constituents had not seen the results they desired. The members went in one term from a part of the solution to a part of the problem.

Not surprisingly, the election, even with its dramatic outcome, did not immediately erase all public cynicism. After a stunningly successful first day, the 104th Congress went sharply up in public approval—to 31 percent, with 50 percent continuing to disapprove (*Time*/CNN 1995). The extent to which the new Congress can lessen public disdain remains to be seen. Republicans pledged a very productive first 100 days of the 104th Congress, but whether the public will deem their legislative accomplishments worth applauding remains in question—as does the course of the 104th Congress in the remaining 630 days.

The public now finds very little for which to commend our government. Even though a Congressional Research Service study released in April 1994 indicates that the laws, regulations, and rules respecting the financial interests and conduct of U.S. legislators are "substantially more restrictive than the countries surveyed" (Maskell 1994, 1), 60 percent of the public think members lack a high personal moral code (ABC News/*Washington Post* 1994b). Elementary school kids just learning about our government are predisposed to think negatively of it. When Rep. Ted Strickland, D-Ohio, defeated in 1994, asked an eighth grade social studies class how many of them hoped to serve in Congress, not one hand went up (Merida 1994, 1A). The college educated, who have a better understanding of Congress and how it operates, formerly were the most supportive of Congress. Now they are among the most critical. Even among the elderly, criticism of

Congress flourishes. One Times Mirror Center survey found that 69 percent agreed that elected officials in Washington lose touch with people quickly (Times Mirror Center 1994b, Question 22B).

Members' frustrations are apparent in the escalating number of departures. The 1992 elections saw the greatest number of retirements in the post-World War II era. And the 27 representatives and 9 senators who departed voluntarily at the end of the 103rd Congress, many of them well before any standard retirement age or lengthy service, confirm the trend.

The public today is not only discontented with Congress but increasingly determined to do something about it. We saw this initially in the primary and general election results of 1992. Voters ousted 43 House incumbents, 19 in the primaries and 24 in the general election. Then in 1994, public discontent with the status quo turned into hostility toward the Democrats, and voters unseated 34 Democratic House incumbents in the general election and 3 in the primaries, as well as 2 Democratic senators. (Not a single Republican incumbent running in the general elections for House, Senate, or governor races was defeated.)

Voters manifest their discontent with Congress in other ways than simply striking out at individual lawmakers at the polls. Seventy-two percent of Americans support term limits (ABC News/Washington Post 1994b). And in most states where they have been brought to a vote, term-limit measures have been supported by large margins. In the 1994 elections, seven new states voted for congressional term limits, bringing the total number of states with term limit legislation up to 22.[1] In their "Contract with America" written during the campaign, House Republicans promised a vote on term limits in the first 100 days of the 104th Congress. While it was originally thought that the measure would pass easily, a wide range of members began voicing opposition, and the measure was rejected in the House on March 29, 1995. Senate Majority Leader Bob Dole, R-Kan., has still vowed to hold a vote on it.

In an April 1994 survey, 64 percent of respondents favored conducting national referendums on major issues and requiring the government to give a referendum approved by a majority the same weight as legislation passed by Congress (American Talk Issues 1994, 51). Yet to many analysts' relief, this sentiment did not surface strongly in the elections. Four states carried initiatives on whether voters should be allowed to approve all future tax increases through statewide referendums; only one state, Nevada, passed its initiative.

In the 1992 presidential election, Ross Perot skillfully capitalized on the pervading negative attitude. Though he offered almost no concrete substantive policy platform, Perot was able to combine successfully voters' negative attitude toward government with their growing financial concerns sparked by the 1990-1991 recession. He honed in on public cynicism, raised it even higher, and then announced that *he* cared even if those in smug, pampered, insulated, and corrupt Washington did not. In the end, Perot captured 19 percent of the popular vote, the highest for an independent candidate for president since Teddy Roosevelt in 1912—even more remarkable because Perot entered the race declaring, "I have no desire to be president." Even though he lost the election and received wide criticism for his opposition to the North America Free Trade Agreement, Perot has endured and remains a threat in 1996. While pursuing a platform based on hostility to Congress, he continues to command roughly 20 percent support from voters in polls looking toward 1996. In 1994, a year of campaigns that attacked the "Washington insider" as never before, Ross Perot voters sided heavily with the Republicans, making themselves largely responsible for the Republican tidal wave.

Though many of the members elected in 1994 campaigned on the reform agenda pushed by Perot, and supported in many cases by a majority of the public, numerous senior members of Congress do not believe that it fits what the country needs. But voters' zeal for change and public hostility, both fanned by the likes of Ross Perot, have pressured legislators to do something to assuage public distrust. One way in which they responded was legislative activism. In the 102nd Congress, the House introduced the most bills (7,771) since the 97th Congress, and the Senate introduced the most since the 93rd (Ornstein, Mann, and Malbin 1994, 153-155). In the first two months of the second session of the 103rd Congress, there had already been 80 nonprocedural roll call votes in the House and 77 in the Senate, something few outside the institution realized (Congressional Quarterly 1994, 30-32). (This number did taper off further into the session as health care reform legislation became the primary focus.)

Another way members respond to public cynicism is by redoubling their efforts to find out what voters think, and responding to any and all concerns. Lawmakers have increased substantially the number of staff members they employ in district offices. In 1994, at the start of the second session of the 103rd Congress, House members had 3,335 staffers—47 percent of their total staffs—in district offices, compared with only 33 percent in 1978. During this period, Senate staff in district offices increased from 25 to 36 percent (Ornstein, Mann, and Malbin 1994, 130-131; Brownson 1994). And any visit to Washington National Airport on a Thursday or Friday evening of a week when Congress has been in session will show a large collection of members from all regions of the country racing to catch planes for their weekly—or more frequent—visits back home to take the public pulse. It has not always been this way. Before 1970, members of Congress were much less peripatetic, and much less avidly and continuously wired into minute-to-minute public concerns.

In the pre-C-SPAN era, when air travel from Washington to all parts of the country was much less the norm, the public was less directly engaged in watching Congress, members mostly came to Washington early in the year and stayed until summer recess, and lawmakers paid at least as much attention to the attitudes of fellow members as those of the public (Elving 1994, 176).

Ironically, the reduced hypersensitivity to public sentiments meant more praiseworthy and less harsh public judgments about Congress. In a 1970 poll that asked respondents to rate several institutions on a scale from -5 to +5, only 10 percent gave Congress a negative score of any kind (Ladd 1990). And, even though there was far less extensive direct communication between constituents and legislators, a poll from 1964 reported that 40 percent of the public said members of Congress pay a "good deal of attention" to the people who elect them (Ladd 1990). By contrast, in April 1994, with C-SPAN entering over 60 million homes and members regularly returning to their districts for town meetings, 82 percent of respondents to a poll agreed that those we elect to Congress lose touch with the people pretty quickly (ABC News/*Washington Post* 1994a).

Between 1975 and March 1993, Gallup polls reported that favorable opinions about Congress dropped 21 percentage points (Bowman and Ladd 1994, 11). Since then, the news has gotten, if anything, even grimmer. What has caused the dropoff? Can anything be done about it? These are questions we will try to address in the remainder of this chapter.

Origins of Discontent

Why is the public so sour on Congress? Part of the answer is that Americans are nearly *always* sour on Congress. Hostility to politicians and the institution that houses them is ingrained in American culture; periods when Americans feel good about Congress are the rarity, not the rule. But there is, over time, a range of sour opinion, and we are clearly at the lower end of the range. Real performance does have something to do with the negative views. Americans see a Congress that spent more than a decade, from 1981, decrying the deficit, pledging to solve the problem, and spending year after year looking foolish and acting futilely. Americans see a Congress that spent 1993 and 1994 heatedly discussing health care, raising expectations for sweeping reform, then dashing them when it passed nothing at all.

To be sure, the deficit and health care are extraordinarily difficult, nearly intractable, problems. In fact, Congress made huge strides throughout the 1980s and early 1990s on the budget, changing its composition—and the nation's priorities—sharply. It passed tax increases and budget cutbacks and built discipline into the discretionary component of the budget. Without these tough and frequently unpopular decisions, the deficit would be $600 to $800 billion today. Moreover, enacting sweeping health care reform, in the absence of a broad economic crisis or a huge partisan majority in both houses of Congress, was simply unrealistic given the political process designed by the Framers of the Constitution. That process was precisely crafted to keep such sweeping change from occurring. Nevertheless, leaders in Congress set standards concerning the deficit, health care, and other national priorities, repeated them frequently, and just as frequently failed to meet their self-created standards.

Any uncertainties Americans have about Congress are exacerbated by the lack of information given to them when they visit the Capitol. The current visitors' center and tour in the U.S. Capitol offer almost no information on the procedures, dynamics, and meaning of Congress. The tour teaches much about the Capitol building, but little about what Congress is supposed to do, what it does, and how it does it. Visitors to the House and Senate galleries receive brochures that explain why many members are not present on the floor of the chamber at any given moment but say little about what they are seeing. They are told not to read and not to talk. Shuffled in and out quickly, given no sense of who is talking or about what, they cannot be learning much.

Even so, real performance is only a small part of the explanation for the public's unhappiness with Congress. General unhappiness about the state of the nation, including unhappiness with the current and past performance of the economy, matters as does unhappiness with the state of the presidency and other governing institutions. Yet all of these factors fail to provide anything near a complete explanation for why opinion of Congress is at a sharply lower point than usual.

There are two other factors to consider here. One is the role of the members of Congress themselves, aided and abetted by other actors in the political process. The second is the role of the press. And both these factors have to be considered in the broader context of the political, economic, and social backdrop of the times, which reinforce daily the average American's worst thoughts and fears about Congress and its members.

Events, from Watergate and Vietnam to ABSCAM and the brouhaha over the House banking system, have helped to shape public attitudes toward Congress. In addition to these real events, Congress itself has contributed mightily to its own perceptual problems. In their campaigns and communications with constituents, many members of Congress separate themselves from the rest of the institution— defining Congress as, in effect, 434 miscreants and one reformer. This kind of approach began in response to a peculiar phenomenon: Americans tend to hate Congress but love their own representatives or senators.

In recent years, the volume and intensity of Congress-bashing by the members have increased sharply. Fewer and fewer individual lawmakers are willing to stand up and say anything good about the institution to which they belong. More and more, lawmakers engage in shrill, harsh, and unrelenting attacks on their colleagues and their chambers. Few candidates for Congress run on the pride they feel about attempting to become a part of history in the greatest legislative body on earth. Most candidates run as Elliot Ness trying to win a license to clean the Al Capones out of the Capitol. House Speaker Newt Gingrich of Georgia and Majority Leader Dick Armey of Texas were among those who engineered this anti-institutional behavior. Their challenge will be whether they, as new leaders of the majority party, can revise their message to unite Republicans behind the institution that they now lead. The criticism of Congress by members of Congress encourages Congress-bashing by the press, fuels negative campaigning, and does much to expand and reinforce public rage and cynicism.

Still, one cannot look at the public's opinion of Congress without directly considering the mass media—the central source of public knowledge on candidates, issues, and the institution and the prism through which most citizens see Congress. The issues reporters and editors choose to cover or not to cover, and any slant or framework journalists as a whole put on their reporting of politics and leaders, will inevitably get reflected in public views.

The "watchdog" function has always been a mainstay of American journalism, but it was not until Watergate that the focus of the press moved decidedly to Washington. Among other things, Watergate increased the sheer physical presence of the media in Washington. To pick only one example, *Newsweek's* August 1965 masthead listed 17 reporters in its Washington bureau; by August 1975 there were 25—a near 50 percent jump. More reporters, generated by Watergate, in turn generated stories on new scandals. The 1976 scandal of Democratic representative Wayne Hays of Ohio, who was forced to resign after a House Administration Committee employee accused him of keeping her on the payroll to obtain sexual favors, projected this style of coverage onto Congress. A string of congressional scandals soon followed including the financial scandal of Rep. Robert Sikes, D-Fla., the Gulf Oil political contribution investigation involving several senators, and the sex-for-hire scandal involving Rep. Allan Howe, D-Utah.

Even when economic strains forced news agencies to cut back their Washington staffs in the 1980s, and the total number of stories on Congress decreased, coverage of congressional scandals continued to rise. Journalistic norms had changed; one print journalist remarked:

> In terms of [journalists'] mission, things changed with Watergate. Our role models when we were growing up, cutting our teeth as young journalists, were not the guys drinking bourbon in the back room at the White House, and not telling the story; it was the long-haired guys who were out there digging the facts and knocking on the doors, who were bringing down the President. They became our models and our heroes.[2]

Competition and cost pressures brought overall coverage of Washington and Congress down sharply in the 1980s and 1990s—but because of this change in journalistic norms, the balance of coverage shifted. Robert Lichter at the Center for Media and Public Affairs in Washington, D.C., conducted a study for the AEI-Brookings project on renewing Congress. He found that from 1987 to 1994, policy stories, which had previously dominated television news coverage, dropped sharply to barely more than half of all broadcast stories, while stories of scandal and other ethics issues have more than doubled. As of 1992 they had reached one in every six stories (see Figure 7-1). In 1993, 60 percent of network news stories covering Democrats were negative as were 75 percent covering Republicans, according to another Center for Media and Public Affairs Study. Coupled with this shift in topic, television media's attention to conflict both among members and between one member and another political figure nearly doubled from 1986 to 1992 (Lichter and Amundson 1994, 135, 136).

Scandals and reports of scandal helped to precipitate reforms, which in turn led to more scandals and reports of scandal, as disclosure, new standards, and new enforcement mechanisms were created. The Department of Justice created in 1976 a Public Integrity Section geared to cracking down on corruption among public officials. Its charge was to indict politicians, and it answered the call. Between 1975 and 1991 the number of federal officials indicted on charges of

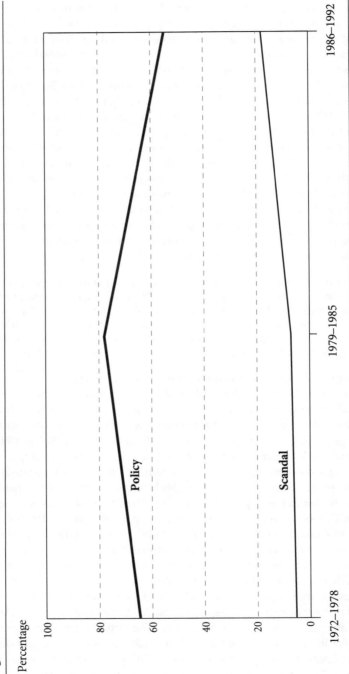

Figure 7-1   Stories on Congress Focusing on Policy and Ethics Matters, 1972–1992

Source: Lichter and Amundson (1994, 13b).

corruption increased by 1515 percent (Statistical Abstract of the United States 1994, 212). Corruption itself certainly could not have risen anywhere near that percentage. But just as journalists found that scandalous reports were much more likely to receive prominent placement in the paper or on the newscast, prosecutors learned that landing a case against a federal official produced abundant press attention, registered highly among colleagues, and proved a reliable path to career enhancement and advancement.

One root cause of this feeding frenzy, as it has been so aptly termed by Larry Sabato (1991), is the tension between demand for action and brief explication in the media, on the one hand, and the intricate and difficult to explain processes of Congress, on the other. Whether in print or video, action draws public attention. People "are more interested in things that they can relate to, like House Bank scandals and pay raises, and so on, rather than process stories," asserted Nancy Nathan, Washington producer of the *Today* show.[3] This chasm steadily widens as television increasingly becomes the medium of choice, reducing attention spans even more. Stories of action, scandal, and conflict are the ones that will be noticed, remembered, discussed.

Editors know this and—since they want their paper read or their program watched—are strongly inclined to assign stories on scandal or conflict instead of stories on what happened and why. Congressional specialist reporters, who must rely on their editors or producers for advancement, soon realize that they will have a much better chance of receiving prominent placement for their story or even of getting it run at all if they stress scandal or conflict.

This is a true source of concern for congressional journalists who know and respect the institution. The Times Mirror Center for the People and the Press conducted an in-depth study of the knowledge about and attitudes toward Congress held by congressional specialists and by prominent editors and producers, the so-called "powers that be" (Times Mirror Center 1992). The editors and producers had significantly less knowledge of the institution and its individual members than did congressional specialists—14 percent could not even name their congressman, compared with just 2 percent of congressional specialists. When asked to consider how the press covers Congress, 44 percent of the congressional specialists said their biggest complaint was too much focus on scandal.

The two groups also differed significantly in how they viewed the work of the institution and ways to improve it. The "powers that be" are much more critical of Congress. Thirty percent of the editors and producers, compared with 15 percent of specialists, said that Congress "doesn't do anything well." When asked which congressional reforms they favored, editors and producers (33 percent) chose the line item veto, very popular with the public but considered unproductive by those who study the institution; only 15 percent of the specialists favored this reform. On the other hand, 51 percent of the specialists, but only 13 percent of the editors and producers, named campaign finance reform as the top proposal. One major reason for the nature and substance of coverage of Congress then becomes clearer: the group determining what that coverage will be has less knowledge, a more negative attitude, and more cynicism than those who closely follow the institution.

The hostility to Congress of the media gatekeepers does not alone explain the negative and scandal-driven coverage of the institution and its members. Broader reasons can be found in the news business itself. Readership among young people is at depressing levels; newspaper and newsmagazine circulation is on the wane; the news divisions of television networks are reeling from a lengthy period of cost-cutting coupled with competition from syndicated "public affairs" programming and entertainment-driven prime-time shows, many masquerading as news.

Under these relentless pressures, even the most prominent and prestigious news organizations have changed their product to compete in the marketplace—meaning, to compete with the tabloid-style print and electronic outlets that have been prospering. The phenomenon, coined "tabloidization," has been apparent in the news focus on rumor and scandal in all institutions, reporting far more extensive than comparable incidents in earlier eras. Minute attention has been given to the O. J. Simpson trial, to the sex lives of Sen. Charles S. Robb, D-Va., and Rep. Barney Frank, D-Mass., to the sexual harassment charges against Sen. Bob Packwood, R-Ore., or the legal woes of Illinois Democrat Dan Rostenkowski, a former member of the House.

What began as an unbalanced tendency to cover conflict within Congress has become, with the aid of negative public attitudes toward government and the financial pressures of declining circulation and viewership, irresponsible front-page coverage of unsubstantiated rumors. These stories have dominated news on politics and politicians more than at any time in modern history, not just in column inches or broadcast minutes, but in emphasis.

News organizations have also found that the high level of public hostility toward Congress makes it a particularly easy target, one that doesn't require any of the usual or customary checks and balances. If you bash Congress, even in a patently unfair fashion, who will protest? Most often, no one, except perhaps a few members, who can be dismissed as self-serving—especially if the Congress-bashing is led by one of Congress's own.

One of the best examples of this phenomenon occurred in January 1994 on CBS's highly rated (and respected) program *60 Minutes*. Morley Safer profiled freshman representative Luis Gutierrez, a Democrat from Chicago. Gutierrez was portrayed as a selfless and courageous reformist newcomer who was beaten down, ostracized, and punished by congressional leaders and insiders when he wouldn't kowtow to them and the special interests.

The story fit a contemporary version of the *Mr. Smith Goes to Washington* movie except that it was wildly distorted and basically untrue. *60 Minutes* ran the story completely on Gutierrez's word, ignoring any evidence that might cast doubt on his own self-serving version of the facts (CBS 1994). The only hint of attempted "balance" in the piece came from two harsh critics of Congress, retiring representative Tim Penny, D-Minn., and Common Cause President Fred Wertheimer.

In fact, Gutierrez was not punished for his apostasy but rewarded with good committee assignments. He was not a mover and shaker in the congressional reform movement, but was virtually invisible to his colleagues. When one prominent Republican member of the Joint Committee on the Organization of Congress heard of the piece, he asked, "Who is this guy Gutierrez? He never asked to testify before our committee, and I've never seen him when we put together reform proposals" (Ornstein 1994, 5). Other members had similar responses.

The *60 Minutes* piece exemplified smirking, unrestrained Congress-bashing by the press with the co-conspiratorial assistance of individual lawmakers. Unfortunately, it was not an aberration but a fairly typical example of the coverage of Congress on tabloid news shows such as *Hard Copy* or *Inside Edition*, not to mention *PrimeTime Live*. The decision by *60 Minutes*, the most prestigious broadcast newsmagazine and for a long time the top-rated television show in the country, to run this kind of shoddy piece is a stunning sign of the spread of tabloidization.

Not all the criticism of Congress comes from television, newspapers, or newsmagazines. Another major player in influencing public opinion of Congress is the radio talk show, which has grown sharply in the past few years in visibility and influence. Congress became a primary target of the talk shows beginning with the congressional pay raise debacle in 1988-1989. Conservative hosts played such a large role in the 1994 Republican victory that the freshman members made Rush Limbaugh (the most influential conservative host) an honorary member of their class. Speaker Gingrich, an avid listener, has given radio talk show hosts space in the Capitol for the first time ever. A Times Mirror survey conducted in 1993 revealed that radio talk show hosts, as a group, are not as sharply conservative as the Limbaugh or Gordon Liddy stereotype would suggest. But the survey established that they are very critical of Congress; seventy-three percent rated the institution unfavorably (Times Mirror 1993).

Encouraged by the hosts, radio talk show listeners are both more negative toward Congress, and more actively involved in politics, than others in the electorate. According to the Times Mirror survey, 48 percent of the general public gave Congress unfavorable ratings compared with 59 percent of regular radio listeners. And, of those respondents who said they were regular listeners, 83 percent had voted in the 1992 presidential election. Though the public has begun to chide the press for some of its coverage, voters still greatly value efforts by the media to keep our political leaders in line. A Times Mirror study conducted January 6-13, 1994, revealed that 74 percent of the public credited the print media and 71 percent credited TV news as having a good influence on the country (Times Mirror 1994a). Most interesting is that 60 percent of respondents said newspapers and 63 percent said TV news invaded people's privacy, but at the same time they see the watchdog role of the press as extremely important. Sixty-nine percent felt that the press keeps people from doing things they shouldn't, while only 18 percent felt that it kept people from doing their job. The believability of the media rated even higher than that of churches; TV received a high believability rating from 73 percent of those questioned, and newspapers received that rating from 68 percent.

Congress, on the other hand, acquired a high believability rating from only 24 percent of respondents. In a showdown between the press and Congress, Congress loses. Even if the public's criticism of the news media escalates, it is highly unlikely that it would outweigh public mistrust of Congress and provoke major change in the media's behavior.

The rage that a substantial number of members of Congress feel toward the press was documented in a compelling article by media critic Ken Auletta in *The New Yorker* (Auletta 1994, 40-47). Nevertheless, in its attempt to transmit a positive message to the people, Congress spends more than $1 million a year on the seven news media galleries in the Capitol (Elving 1994, 186). When asked about ways to improve their image, members feel the need to work *with* journalists, and often turn to them for answers.

Institutional Reforms

When Watergate and other scandals promulgated by the press began to tarnish its image, Congress sought ways to cleanse it. Unfortunately, many of these steps proved unsuccessful, even adding to the negative views of the institution, and Congress is still frustrated and at a loss over how to achieve anything near the image it once had.

The period from the late 1960s through the mid-1980s was perhaps the most sustained era of institutional reform in the history of Congress. Through changes in the majority party caucus, the Legislative Reorganization Act of 1970, the Bolling and Stevenson committees, the House Commission on Administrative Review, the Commission on the Organization of the Senate, and a myriad of additional bodies and other efforts, Congress changed its internal processes and structures, created new codes of ethics, reformed campaign finance laws, and altered budget and war-making procedures.

One of the major thrusts of all the reforms was more openness and disclosure. The reforms in each chamber were effective in the sense that they gave the public more direct information on the operations of Congress. But they also created and revealed behavior that resulted in further negative opinions. Instead of cleaning up the system, the monetary disclosures stimulated continuous derogatory stories of members' expenditures and receipts. Weaker leaders and more independent rank-and-file lawmakers reinforced the notion of an unproductive, unmanageable institution, filled with vacillating policy makers.

Congress tried again to revive public support by providing more access to congressional activities. It introduced cameras on the floor of the House in 1979 and of the Senate in 1986, which inspired the creation and then expansion of C-SPAN. While C-SPAN has performed admirably its intended job of presenting an unbiased, straightforward account of House and Senate floor action, the image conveyed has, if anything, added to the negative perceptions of Congress. Though we can now watch both chambers live and Congress has become more accessible, the legislative process itself comes across as confusing, unfocused, and unproductive. Part of the problem is that general debate—a time of pure discussion about a pending bill, without amendments or votes—has lost much of its value and influence over the years. In the House it has become a time of reading prepared statements by the floor managers and is widely considered a filler time between adoption of the rule and voting on amendments.

In an open, decentralized and democratized institution, members continuously contribute to the fractured voices of the institution and succumb to the temptation to gain leverage and political insulation by criticizing their colleagues and their chamber. Although the phenomenon of running for Congress by running against Congress was recognized nearly two decades ago (Fenno 1978, 168), it has become far more widespread, dominating campaign discourse in 1994 for challengers in both parties—and increasingly dominating the rhetoric of prominent and senior lawmakers. The harsh partisanship of recent years has been a major factor in the escalation of anti-Congress rhetoric from inside Congress. Newt Gingrich instigated much of this institutional and member bashing when he arrived in Washington in 1978. In his new position as Speaker, his success will be largely determined by that of the institution. This should deter him from his past anti-institutional rhetoric, which could, in turn, inspire others to suspend such bashing.

Just as disturbing as the pervasive anti-institutionalism is the growing tension between the chambers. The changes in House and Senate leadership in the 104th Congress leave the question of future relations wide open. Gingrich will certainly be powerful as House Speaker, but the contrasting and distinctive characteristics of this leader of the "revolutionaries" and Bob Dole, the rooted, father-figure leading the Senate, raise doubts as to whether that power will have a positive influence on interchamber relations or the institution as a whole.

We even witnessed this widespread divisiveness in the Joint Committee on the Organization of Congress, created in 1992 to work through some of the internal problems and promote a more positive image. When it came time to report committee recommendations, the House and Senate deadlocked over their differing interests. Unable to reach a consensus, the committee issued separate Senate and House recommendations.

The House recommended cutting the staff by 12 percent, setting targets on entitlement spending, establishing a pool of private citizens to rule on the validity of ethics violation charges, creating a joint Office of Compliance to enforce the application of national laws to Congress, and limiting modestly committee assignments. Though the Senate version withheld any ethics reform (pending the reports of two task forces working on that issue), it embraced much more ambitious committee reforms. It called for substantial assignment limitations per member (two major committees, one minor committee, and five subcommittees), tough waiver prohibition and centralized assignment authority, a reduction in the number of subcommittees, and elimination of joint committees.[4]

Public hostility toward Congress has not focused on internal reform as a solution, which gave lawmakers little pressure to move ahead with the Joint Committee's recommendations. Weak support from congressional leaders and indifference from many members blocked passage of any part of the Senate's reform package and nearly all of the House's.

One practice that the Joint Committee did help to initiate in the House in the 103rd Congress was Oxford-style debates—debates on the floor independent of the formal consideration of legislation. These debates, televised on C-SPAN, received positive public response. With a few modest alterations in format to emphasize ideas and de-emphasize boisterous conflict, they will become institutionalized and mark the House as a place for serious and intelligent debate on the big issues facing society. In the 104th Congress, the Senate should follow the House's lead and enact Oxford-style debating as well.

Republicans, as the new majority, have promised to produce many of the reforms on which the Democrats failed to act. House Republicans took the first promising steps on day one of the 104th Congress by passing rules to restructure committees, downsize staff, and ban proxy voting, as well as finally passing the Congressional Accountability Act. This new Republican majority has also worked to ease the tension between the majority and minority parties by giving the minority the right to offer a motion to recommit with instructions, if authorized by the minority leader, as well as more proportional representation on most committees. And changes in C-SPAN coverage to improve communication with the public are being considered.

The committee changes Speaker Gingrich instituted should be commended. Merchant Marine and Fisheries, District of Columbia, and Post Office and Civil Service were long overdue for elimination as full committees, but so were Veterans' Affairs and Small Business, committees that represent Republican interests and were kept intact for the 104th Congress. Unfortunately, this new House majority also passed measures—the opening of all committee hearings to the public and a Balanced Budget Amendment—detrimental to the institution. The Senate rejected the Balanced Budget Amendment by one vote on March 2, 1995, but Dole promised to take up the measure again before the 104th Congress adjourned. Finally, Republican leaders in the House and Senate failed to include an important item in their agenda to coincide with improved C-SPAN coverage of Congress—better education about the institution and its inner workings.

Conclusion

Too many people—journalists, interest group representatives, partisan operatives, and lawmakers themselves—have a deep vested interest in Congress-bashing to expect any change soon. Too many voters have a level of anger toward Congress, politicians, Washington, and elites generally to make any change, if it occurred, meaningful in altering public attitudes. But every attempt has to be made to alter the coverage of Congress in the press, to change the attitudes and behavior of other Washington actors who regularly bash the institution, to get Congress's own internal operations in order, and to improve Congress's public face. There have been numerous recommendations for ways to accomplish these changes, many of which were put forward in the Renewing Congress reports and in *Congress, the Press, and the Public* (Mann and Ornstein 1992, 1993, 1994a, 1994b).

Americans' attitudes toward Congress seemed to reach rock bottom in the mid-1990s. Whether they ascend during the rest of the decade depends largely on the rhetoric and actions of members of Congress, the news media's coverage of the institution, and the public's interest in gaining a better understanding of it.

Notes

1. On November 29, 1994, the Supreme Court heard arguments on a case that tests the constitutionality of term limits for members of Congress. On May 22, 1995, it ruled against the state's right to pass laws limiting congressional terms, leaving a constitutional amendment as the only option.

2. Remarks by Gary Griffith of Hearst Broadcasting during a conference sponsored by the American Enterprise Institute and the Brookings Institution on May 13, 1993. The conference, entitled "Congress, the Press, and the Public," was a part of the AEI-Brookings Renewing Congress Project. A book based on this conference as well as three reports were published in conjunction with this project. See Mann and Ornstein (1992, 1993, 1994a, 1994b).

3. Remarks made during the AEI-Brookings Conference, "Congress, the Press, and the Public," May 13, 1993.

4. The Senate report recommended that the Senate majority and minority leaders make committee assignments rather than the full Senate as stipulated in the current rules. Further, it recommended that "no waiver to the assignment limitation be granted unless a resolution amending the Senate rules naming the senators receiving the waivers is offered by both the majority and minority leaders and passed by a yea-and-nay vote."

8

IF THE GAME IS TOO HARD, CHANGE THE RULES: Congressional Budget Reform in the 1990s

James A. Thurber

The modern congressional budget process has been evolving ever since 1974, when the landmark Congressional Budget and Impoundment Control Act was enacted. From an initial focus on budgetary priority setting (1974-1985), the process shifted dramatically—to deficit control in the Gramm-Rudman-Hollings acts (1985-1990), to spending control in the 1990 Budget Enforcement Act, and most recently to reforms promised in the Republicans' "Contract with America" (unfunded mandates reform, the balanced budget amendment, and the line-item veto). Changing the rules of the budgetary game has been a dynamic issue in Congress for the past 20 years and a central part of remaking Congress in the 1990s.

As the public's anger with the institution of Congress has increased, so has members' attention to budget reform. The taxing and budget cuts taken by President George Bush and Congress in the Omnibus Budget Reconciliation Act of 1990 (OBRA 1990) and President Bill Clinton's substantial tax increases and spending cuts enacted by the Congress in the Omnibus Budget Reconciliation Act of 1993 (OBRA 1993) resulted in sizable deficit reductions in the early 1990s. The demand for budget reform, however, was not over. Dozens of proposals for changes in the budget process were considered in the 103rd Congress before the Joint Committee on the Organization of Congress (JCOC) and other committees (JCOC 1993a, 1993f). The Republican-led budget reforms in 1995, the first year of the 104th Congress, included the Balanced Budget Amendment (H.J. Res. 1), the Line-Item Veto Act (H.R. 2), and the Unfunded Mandate Reform Act (H.R. 5). In addition, congressional reformers (some Democrats as well) advocated eliminating appropriations as a separate committee jurisdiction, forbidding appropriations report language that contravenes provisions in an authorization, eliminating unauthorized appropriations without the concurrence of an authorizing committee, creating a joint budget committee, prohibiting "baseline budgeting," and establishing congressional zero-based budgeting. To control spending and further reduce deficits, reformers have attempted to set caps on mandatory spending, to embark on sunset budgeting, and to pass special bills to cut spending, such as the "A to Z spending reduction plan" introduced by Rep. Robert E. Andrews, D-N.J., and Rep. Bill Zeliff, R-N.H. They recommended that the House set aside a full week in its calendar to consider proposals to cut federal spending. Still other members of Congress were concerned about the rapid growth of entitlement programs.

Many concerns about the budget process have been expressed since 1974, but only four major reforms have passed: the Congressional Budget and Impoundment Control Act of 1974, the Balanced Budget and Emergency Deficit Control Acts of 1985 and 1987 (Gramm-Rudman-Hollings or GRH I and II), and the Budget Enforcement Act of 1990 (BEA).[1] Supporters of these acts suggested that their passage would promote more discipline in congressional budgeting, reduce deficits, control runaway spending, and make the process more timely and effective. However, in the years since the adoption of these reforms, concerns about spending, taxing, deficits, debt, and the budget process itself have not abated and the recent GOP takeover in Congress brought a new round of budget reform efforts.

Budget Reform: First Try, 1974

The most important change in the way Congress collects and spends money in the past 50 years was the Congressional Budget and Impoundment Control Act (also referred to as the Congressional Budget Act).[2] The Congressional Budget Act created standing budget committees in the House and in the Senate that are responsible for setting overall tax and spending levels. It also required Congress annually to establish levels of expenditures and revenues with prescribed procedures for arriving at those spending and income totals. The procedures include three important elements. First, a timetable was established that set deadlines for action on budget-related legislation. This timetable was intended to ensure completion of the budget plan prior to the start of each fiscal year. Second, the Congressional Budget Act required the annual adoption of concurrent budget resolutions (which do not require presidential approval). Initial concurrent budget resolutions establish targets for total budget authority, budget outlays, and revenues for the upcoming fiscal year. Then, a final "binding" resolution with ceilings on budget authority and outlays and a floor on revenues is adopted. Finally, the act instituted a reconciliation process to conform revenue, spending, and debt legislation to the levels specified in the final budget resolution (Thurber 1989, 80).

The reconciliation process is the procedure under which the budget committees may direct other committees to determine and recommend revenue and/or spending actions deemed necessary to conform authorizations and appropriations to the determinations made in the budget resolutions. The budget committees have the option of mandating that House and Senate committees report legislation that will meet budget authority, outlays, and revenue targets (Schick 1981; Tate 1981, 887-891). The reconciliation process allows the budget committees to direct one or more of the legislative committees to make changes in existing laws to achieve the desired budget reductions. The budget committees submit the recommended changes to each house without any substantive revision.

The reconciliation bill for fiscal year (FY) 1981 established an important precedent. By most interpretations of the 1974 act, reconciliation measures were to be inserted in the second concurrent "binding" resolution and applied only to appropriations. However, for FY 1981 the House and Senate included reconciliation directions for authorization and appropriations committees in the first budget resolutions. This strategy resulted in savings for fiscal years 1981 to 1985 of more than $50 billion in outlays (not budget authority) and $29 billion in additional revenues for the same period.

Reconciliation combines spending reductions and revenue increases in the same legislation. This communicates "shared sacrifice" to the American public and allows members of Congress to build a coalition to reduce the deficit. The use of reconciliation under the 1974 budget act made basic changes in the budget much easier but failed to solve the problem of large deficits.

Congress Tries Harder in 1985 and 1987: Gramm-Rudman-Hollings I and II

By the early 1980s projected budget deficits were in the $200 billion range, far more than had ever been experienced before.[3] Congress, concerned with its continuing inability to control those soaring deficits, passed more drastic measures: the Balanced Budget and Emergency Deficit Control Acts of 1985 and 1987 (otherwise known as Gramm-Rudman-Hollings I and II (GRH I and II) after Senators Phil Gramm, R-Texas, and Ernest F. Hollings, D-S.C., and former Republican senator Warren Rudman of New Hampshire. The GRH legislation revised budgetary deadlines in order to bring more discipline to congressional budgeting and focus attention on reducing the deficit.[4]

The central enforcement mechanism of GRH is a series of automatic spending cuts that occur if the federal budget does not meet, or fall within $10 billion of, the deficit targets (Penner and Abramson 1988, 97). These automatic spending cuts are referred to as *sequestration*. If Congress and the president do not enact laws to reduce the deficit to the maximum deficit amount allowed for that year then across-the-board spending cuts must be made, evenly divided between domestic and defense programs, until the target is met. In 1985 most entitlement programs (then approximately 43 percent of the budget) and interest payments (then approximately 14 percent of the budget) were "off-budget," partially or totally exempt from the potential cuts.

The 1985 GRH legislation gave the General Accounting Office (GAO) the responsibility for triggering the across-the-board cuts. In 1986 the Supreme Court declared that part of the legislation was unconstitutional because it gave the GAO, a legislative support agency, executive functions.[5] The Supreme Court's decision would have prevented the implementation of GRH, but Congress responded by passing a revised version of the act in 1987 (GRH II). GRH II altered the original GRH deficit reduction plan by directing the Office of Management and Budget (OMB), an executive agency, to issue the report that would trigger sequestration if deficit reduction targets were not met. GRH II also revised the original deficit reduction targets in accordance with more realistic economic assumptions.

The Failure of GRH

The Gramm-Rudman-Hollings legislation promised long-term progress toward lower deficits and a balanced budget, but these goals proved to be elusive and overly optimistic. The deficit never has been as low as the law requires (see Table 8-1).

Although attention to each budget year has increased, long-term budgetary goals are not considered. Since 1980 more than half of all roll-call votes in Congress have been on budget-related bills, with a high of 56 percent in the House and 71 percent in the Senate (Thurber 1991, 148). Even though GRH II revised the original deficit targets, the new targets were well out of reach as early as 1990 when Congress considered the budget of FY 1991.

However, the threat of sequestration did not have the intended effect. Comparing the projected effects of sequestration on their favored programs with the potential impact of cuts from regular legislation, policy makers simply decided that their interests were best served by delaying the passage of bills until after sequestration occurred (House Committee on the Budget 1990).

Two other factors contributed to the failure of GRH. First, sequestration could be avoided by using overly optimistic economic and technical assumptions as substitutes for actual policy changes—a common practice in recent years. Second, Congress (until 1990) evaluated the budget only once a year to ascertain whether it was meeting GRH deficit reduction targets. The result was a "snapshot" of the budgetary situation. After that evaluation, Congress was free to add new expenditures to the budget, which often increased the budget deficit. After the snapshot was taken, indicating that the deficit target had been met, legislation could be adopted that raised the deficit in the current year and following years as well (Senate Committee on Governmental Affairs 1988, 52).

In spite of their goals, GRH I and II did not curb the growth of federal spending; bring an end to the growth in uncontrollable spending; reduce the deficit; force Congress to complete budgeting on time; reorder national spending priorities; allow Congress to control fiscal policy; or eliminate the need for continuing resolutions. Clearly, something needed to be done. Congress tried again with the Omnibus Budget Reconciliation Act of 1990. In particular, hopes were focused on title XIII of the act, the Budget Enforcement Act of 1990.

New Rules: The Budget Enforcement Act of 1990

By early 1990, it was obvious to congressional budgeteers that the budget was not going to be balanced by 1993, the revised deadline. In fact, the deficit in 1993 turned out to be $255 billion. Therefore, the budgetary rules were changed again with passage of the Omnibus Budget Reconciliation Act of 1990 (OBRA 1990). The restrictions that were made in spending and taxing lowered the deficit by almost $500 billion over a five-year period (1991 through 1995). The bipartisan agreement was intended to lessen conflicts over the budget, promote negotiated

Table 8-1   Deficit Reduction Targets and Actual Deficits,
Fiscal Years 1986–1996 (billions of dollars)

Fiscal Year	1985 GRH Targets[a]	1987 GRH Targets[a]	1990 BEA Targets[a]	CBO Deficit Projections[b]	Actual Deficits
1986	172	____	____	____	221
1987	144	____	____	____	150
1988	108	144	____	____	155
1989	72	136	____	____	152
1990	36	100	____	____	195
1991	0	64	327	331	269
1992	____	28	317	425	290
1993	____	0	236	348	255
1994	____	____	102	318	203
1995	____	____	83	162	193
1996	____	____	____	176	197

Source: The 1985, 1987, and 1990 deficit reduction targets are from CBO (1990b, 8; 1990d, x). The deficit projections for 1991 to 1994 are from CBO (1991, xiii) and for 1995 and 1996 are from CBO (1994, 31). The actual deficits for 1986 to 1993 are from CBO (1994, 31). Those for 1994 to 1996 are from the Office of Management and Budget as reported in the *Washington Post*, February 7, 1995, A13.

[a] Includes Social Security, which is off-budget but is counted for purposes of Balanced Budget Act targets; excludes the Postal Service, which is also off-budget.

[b] Excludes Social Security and Postal Service.

compromises to difficult economic and political questions, solve the problems of increasing deficits, and provide political cover for unpopular election-year decisions (Yang and Mufson 1990, A4).

The reforms of the Budget Enforcement Act of 1990 further centralized power within Congress by forcing members to make "zero-sum" choices: that is, visible reductions in one program for visible increases in another, or tax cuts for some in exchange for tax increases for others. The BEA included changes in substantive law and budgetary procedures designed to bring more top-down party leadership control over the budget process and to reduce the deficit, thus increasing the centralization of budgetary decision making. In December 1990, the Congressional Budget Office estimated that the tax hikes, spending cuts, and procedural changes of the BEA summit agreement would reduce the cumulative deficit by about $496 billion for the 1991-1995 period (Congressional Budget Office 1990e, 36). The most visible change was the elimination of fixed deficit tar-

gets as established in GRH I and II, but other innovations—such as categorical se-
questers, pay-as-you-go (PAYGO) provisions on taxes and spending, and a new
enhanced role for the Office of Management and Budget (OMB)—were included
as well.[6]

Categorical Sequestration

The 1990 budget reforms changed the process of sequestration, the hallmark
of the GRH legislation. The 1990 BEA requires a specified amount of savings for
each of five years covered by a multiyear budget plan. Through FY 1993, sequestration was not linked to the total federal budget but to "ceilings" on discretionary
federal spending (spending for programs that must be appropriated each year).
The ceiling covered three discretionary spending categories: defense, domestic,
and international.[7] The BEA eliminated the acceptable $10 billion cushion be-
tween the actual deficit and the deficit target for fiscal years 1991 to 1993—the
norm under GRH.

The ceiling of each discretionary spending category is enforced by an end-of-
session sequestration applied across-the-board to all of the programs *within* that
category. (For example, if the ceiling for discretionary spending in the international category is exceeded, the end-of-session sequester applies to all programs
within the international category.) This process is referred to as "categorical sequestration." It will be triggered only if the spending limits are exceeded due to
changes in legislation (such as an extension of the benefits of a program or of the
number of people eligible to receive benefits or tax cuts). If the spending limits are
exceeded because of changes in economic conditions (or, as is the case with many
domestic programs, the number of eligible recipients increases), sequestration
would not be triggered. If more is appropriated for discretionary spending than is
allowed under the discretionary limits, automatic sequestrations will be imposed
but only on the accounts in the category in which the breach has occurred.

In FY 1994-1995, the system was supposed to return to fixed deficit targets
enforced by the same sequestration rules used prior to the 1990 act, but President
Clinton wanted to reduce the deficit further so he proposed another five-year
deficit reduction package. The goal of this plan was to reduce cumulative budget
deficits by a total of $500 billion between fiscal years 1994 and 1998. With few
changes, Congress passed the 1993 OBRA. It codified a new five-year deficit reduction plan that embraced tax increases, discretionary spending cuts, and more
stringent limitations on discretionary spending. The BEA's enforcement procedures, including the discretionary caps and the pay-as-you-go (PAYGO) process,
were extended through 1998 (see Table 8-1).

The Look-Back Requirement

The GRH legislation required Congress to evaluate the budget only once a
year to ascertain whether it was meeting the deficit targets. After that snapshot
evaluation, Congress was relatively free to add new expenditures to the budget,
often increasing the actual level of the deficit. The "look-back" requirement of the

BEA ended this freedom. Any amount added to the current year's deficit by policy changes made after the final budget snapshot must be added to the following year's deficit reduction target. This eliminates incentives for postsnapshot deficit increases and for schemes that reduce a given current year's budget deficit by shifting spending into the next fiscal year, but it reduces the flexibility of fiscal policy in case of emergencies or changing national or international situations. However, the law provides for exemptions to spending ceilings due to "emergency needs." For example, the expenditures for the Persian Gulf War were designated as an "emergency need" and were not counted against the defense spending ceiling.

Pay As You Go

The 1990 BEA and Clinton's 1993 OBRA budget called for all tax and direct spending legislation to be "deficit neutral" in each year through FY 1998. This major reform was called a pay-as-you-go (PAYGO) procedure. PAYGO cuts nonexempt entitlement spending automatically to make up for any increase in the deficit because of new legislation (for example, legislation that increases entitlement benefits or extends benefits to more people or legislation that would lead to revenue reductions).[8] This makes the budget process a zero-sum game, the most important consequence of the budget reforms of the 1990s.

The primary impact of PAYGO has been to discourage spending. According to former Congressional Budget Office (CBO) director Robert D. Reischauer, "To date, this pay-as-you-go requirement has proved to be an effective poison pill that has killed a number of legislative efforts to cut taxes and expand entitlements."[9] The difficulty of either raising taxes or cutting popular existing mandatory programs (like social security) has resulted in PAYGO effectively closing out new mandatory programs (such as Clinton's 1993 health care reforms).

Other BEA Reforms

The Budget Enforcement Act gives OMB and the president new power in the budget process. The economic and technical assumptions made by OMB, and used in estimating the president's budget proposal each January, are locked in for the purposes of the sequestration projection to be made later in the year, giving OMB and the president new power in the budget process. Congress is no longer aiming at "moving targets" as the president alters his estimating assumptions during the year.

Programs that are part of the budget (such as the savings and loan cleanup) are not counted against the category's spending limit. Social Security receipts and disbursements have been taken completely off-budget. None of these transactions is counted in estimations of the deficit or the calculations for sequestration.[10] Both the House and Senate took steps to protect the Social Security Trust Fund. They adopted rules (so-called "fire walls") that prevent transferring money from the trust fund to other government programs.[11]

House and Senate points of order against "budget busting" provisions are an important enforcement mechanism in BEA. Under the 1990 act, legislation is subject to a point of order for breaching either the budget-year levels or the sum of the five-year levels set in a budget resolution. (The five-year enforcement mechanisms apply to all budgets through 1999, after which the requirement lapses.) To prevent temporary savings and timing shifts (such as military pay delays), budget resolutions in each year through FY 1995 were for five years.

The 1990 budget pact led the House and Senate to create different procedures for the appropriators. House appropriations are allowed to proceed on May 15 even in the absence of a budget resolution. Senate committees, other than the Senate Appropriations Committee, are allowed to proceed in the absence of a new budget resolution if their bills conform to the out-year allocations in the most recent budget resolution. This establishes more spending control by appropriations committees over members and other committees, but allows the House and Senate to move bills even if the budget resolution is late.

Summary

The Budget Enforcement Act significantly changed the way Congress budgets in the 1990s. Those reforms have affected the budget process, the internal workings of Congress, and congressional-presidential budgetary powers (Thurber 1989; Thurber and Durst 1991). The act set spending caps for both budget authority and outlays in discretionary appropriations for five years. Spending limits (hard "ceilings" and informal "floors") were imposed upon defense, international, and domestic discretionary spending in fiscal years 1991 to 1993 in the BEA and extended to FY 1998 by the first Clinton budget in 1993. Appropriations bills that breach any of the three appropriation categories triggered across-the-board automatic cuts (sequestration) in programs within the breached category. Adjustments in the spending limits were permitted for several reasons: changes in inflation, revision of concepts and definitions, credit re-estimates, appropriations for emergency needs, and an estimating cushion. The discretionary caps on spending and "fire walls" between spending categories tightened controls and lessened freedom for members and committees, especially the appropriators, by not allowing funds from one category to be used to offset spending that breaks the caps in another. For example, shifts from defense to domestic were not allowed for the first three years of the agreement.

Consequences of Budget Reforms in the 1990s

The recent reforms establish more budget control, expand the power of the appropriations committees, and narrow other committees' influence. At the same time, the congressional budget process is made more accessible and accountable to the public, interest groups, and the federal executive branch by publicly revealing the tradeoffs that must be made in discretionary and entitlement program spending. With controls on the number of behind-the-scenes budget tricks that can be played, the budget process is more visible to everyone. Although the new rules could increase conflict over the budget, they were *intended* to create a more congenial budget process. The 1990 and 1993 budget agreements ensured that the president and the Congress would not fight over the size of the deficit, but they would battle over domestic discretionary spending in a controlled, zero-sum budget game.

Presidential vs. Congressional Budgetary Power

"Score keeping" is the process of accounting for the cost of authorizations and appropriations bills and determining whether they are consistent with the budget resolution. The 1990 BEA shifted this function from the Congressional Budget Office to the Office of Management and Budget, an executive branch agency. This was a major gain for the president, greatly enhancing his power, and a loss for congressional committees and party leadership. This shift of responsibility makes the budget process less complex, more open, yet more time consuming because of the conflicts over cost estimates. In 1991, however, the House Democratic Caucus revised the 1990 budget agreement by requiring the CBO and the Joint Committee on Taxation to do the scoring of spending and tax actions. President George Bush immediately objected in a press release: "This rule would change the new pay-as-you-go enforcement mechanism by overturning a specifically negotiated and agreed scoring provision. More important, if the proposed rule is adopted, the House of Representatives will have begun the 102nd Congress by undercutting the credibility of the entire budget agreement."[12] Despite these harsh words the revision held, retaining within the legislative branch the key power of score keeping. The 1990 budget agreement also required that all new revenues go toward reducing the deficit, further limiting members' options.

When members of Congress have disliked budget outcomes or procedural reforms, they have simply made more revisions in the process. When the game is too hard, they change the rules.[13] In this game power shifts back and forth. "A balance of power between the executive and the legislature, so one actor can catch the other at bad practice," Rubin argues, "is probably more sound over the long run than the weakening of one and the continual strengthening of the other" (Rubin 1990, 234).

Before the BEA reforms, Congress had significant flexibility in budget decision making, in spite of the self-imposed limitations made by the Congressional Budget Act and the GRH acts. The deficit targets of the 1990s, taking Social Security Trust Fund surpluses off budget, pay-as-you-go provisions, and categorical sequestration all decreased the ability of Congress to choose funding levels. The five-year budget agreement made new tax increases more public and painful, thus limiting new spending by Congress. The pay-as-you-go proposals especially limit the prospects for new programs, and thus the power of the authorizing committees, because they require funding for new programs to be taken from existing programs or new taxes. Domestic programs now compete with one another for funding. Military savings can no longer be used to finance them.

This zero-sum game gives more budget power to conservative members of Congress and presidents who want to limit domestic spending. It takes budgetary power away from those in Congress who want to allocate money for new programs and expand old ones. It also made it easier for the Republican leadership of the 104th Congress to cut programs and cut President Clinton's domestic spending priorities.

The reforms discouraged individual members from initiating their own "budget proposals" because cuts and revenue enhancements had to be instituted in other programs in order to save their proposals. On the other hand, the reforms raised the public's understanding of spending priorities and thus raised the specter of heavy lobbying. This intensified pressure on members and committees to protect their favorite programs and to make cuts in other programs. The pay-as-you-go, zero-sum reforms centralized budget decision making with the party leadership and the budget committees, institutions with the power to negotiate tradeoffs in the zero-sum game. Although the rigid constraints set by the 1990 BEA further reduced the autonomy of the appropriations committees, most budget participants argue that those committees were the big winners in the 1990 pact. The new budget process rules diminish the role of the House and Senate budget committees by giving more degrees of freedom to the appropriations panels. One budget expert summarized this shift: "Since the pot of money the Appropriations Committees will have to work with has already been decided, they needn't wait for a spending outline from the budget committees before divvying it up" (Yang 1991, A12).

Appropriators can determine the legislative details within the BEA constraints more easily than through the old reconciliation process and sequestration under GRH. The appropriators have more control over "back-door spending" by the authorizers in reconciliation bills. The budget process reforms of the 1990s also encouraged appropriators to favor "pain-deferral budgeting" (choice of slow-spending programs over fast-spending programs in order to reduce the projected spending for the next year). Congress (and the administration) have failed to terminate major programs (such as the space station) whose budgetary requirements are likely to escalate sharply in future years. "The camel's nose is being allowed under the tent; next year the camel's shoulders will want in, and then his hump," according to CBO's Robert Reischauer (Congressional Budget Office 1990e).

The New Budget Process: More Complex, Less Timely?

According to Irene Rubin, "closing the budget process is often considered one way to help control increases in expenditures; opening it is usually a way of increasing expenditures" (Rubin 1990, 66). The BEA attempted to do the opposite: it opened up the process and placed more controls on expenditures. More transparent budgeting revealed the tradeoffs within mandatory spending, and within each of the three discretionary spending categories, thus putting tough spending and taxing decisions in full public view.

The 1990 and 1993 budget agreements simplify the process only if members abide by the agreement. The innovations tend to work at cross-purposes when it comes to timeliness. A five-year budget agreement theoretically should make it easier to pass budget resolutions on time. If the budget resolutions are not passed on time, the appropriators may still pass money bills.

However, several other reforms of the 1990s increased the complexity and thus the potential delay in Capitol Hill budget making. Steps in the process have multiplied, as have the decision-making rules. Typically, the more complex the process, the more time it consumes. Categorical sequestration and PAYGO provisions have slowed budgeting by increasing the number of confrontations within Congress and between Congress and the president. Alternatively, confrontations increase complexity and delay in the process since more cuts (or tax increases) are required to meet the caps. Already vexing budget decisions were made more difficult because of the budget process changes of the 1990s.

In addition, the budget categories are frustratingly complicated and inconsistent. The 21 functional categories in the budget resolutions do not neatly fit the 13 separate appropriations subcommittee bills or the three categories of spending in the 1990 BEA. Appropriators are required to translate the functional allocations into appropriations allocations and report the results, which in turn must be compared to the ceilings and guidelines set out in BEA—all of which compounds the complexity and delay in the budget process.

"Contract with America" and Budget Reform

The Joint Committee on the Organization of Congress considered dozens of budget proposals, but none was adopted in the 103rd Congress (1993-1994). The 1994 elections transformed the budget reform agenda on Capitol Hill. The new Republican majority in the House and Senate brought to the top of the agenda of the 104th Congress the Balanced Budget Amendment, the line-item veto, and the unfunded mandate reform.

The first promise in the Republicans' "Contract with America" was the Balanced Budget Amendment (H.J. Res. 1), a constitutional amendment requiring the president to propose and Congress to adopt a balanced budget each fiscal year starting in FY 2002 (or for the second fiscal year following its ratification). Congress may not adopt a budget resolution in which total outlays exceed total receipts unless three-fifths of the membership of each house approves. Congress may waive these provisions for any fiscal year in which a declaration of war is in effect or the country faces "an imminent and serious military threat to national security." A majority of each chamber must pass and the president must sign a joint resolution identifying the threat. The Balanced Budget Amendment was a popular proposal with the public. A Gallup poll conducted on November 28, 1994, revealed that 77 percent of those questioned ranked the amendment either a top or a high priority for the 104th Congress. Congress had previously rejected several balanced budget amendments since the first one was introduced in 1936. The closest Congress had come to passing it was in 1986 when the Senate defeated the proposal by a single vote. During the first weeks of the 104th Congress, the Balanced Budget Amendment passed the House but stalled again in the Senate in March 1995.

The second major budget reform in the "Contract with America" was the Line-Item Veto Act (H.R. 2), which gives the president a permanent legislative line-item veto. Under this procedure, the president may strike or reduce any discretionary budget authority or eliminate any targeted tax provision in any bill. The president must prepare a separate rescissions package for each piece of legislation and must submit his proposal to Congress within 20 working calendar days after the original legislation arrives on his desk. The president's proposed rescissions take effect unless Congress passes a disapproval bill within 20 days after receiving them. The disapproval bill must pass by a two-thirds vote in both houses.

The line-item veto would confer substantial new budgetary powers to the president. Proponents of the line-item veto maintained that given large deficits, the president should have the authority to single out "unnecessary and wasteful" spending provisions in bills passed by Congress. Critics of the line-item veto argue that it cedes too much power to the executive branch to control federal spending, a responsibility clearly given to the legislative branch in the U.S. Constitution. The line-item veto was one provision of the Contract with America that found agreement between President Clinton and the Republicans.

The Unfunded Mandate Reform Act (H.R. 5) amended the 1974 Budget Act (P.L. 93-344) to restrict the imposition of unfunded requirements (mandates) by the federal government on state and local government entities. Unfunded mandates are provisions in federal legislation that impose enforceable duties on state and local governments without appropriating funds to pay for them. Unfunded mandates are included in most environmental legislation (for example, the Clear Air Act Amendments of 1990, the Clean Water Act, and the Safe Drinking Water Act), the Motor Voter Act, and the Americans with Disabilities Act.

The bill establishes a Commission on Unfunded Federal Mandates to investigate and review the impact of current unfunded state, local, and private entities. The act also requires federal agencies to assess the effects of federal regulations on state, local, tribal, and private sector entities. The Congressional Budget Office is required to prepare an impact statement assessing the cost of the proposed mandates for any legislation. The CBO statement must detail estimates of the total direct costs of compliance exceeding $100 million in the first five years. The bill repeals mandates at the beginning of any fiscal year in which no funds are provided to cover their costs, and it assigns to the budget committees the responsibility to determine the appropriate mandate funding levels.

The Balanced Budget Amendment, line-item veto, and unfunded mandate reform will all: (1) favor a more conservative agenda for federal spending, (2) increase complexity, and (3) shift power between the president and Congress. Further cutbacks in federal spending and limits on new legislation would occur as a result of these three "Contract with America" reforms. If a presidential line-item veto were adopted, it would substantially decrease congressional power to control budget outcomes. Not only would the president gain a powerful tool for actually preventing funds from being distributed in accordance with the wishes of Congress, but he would be able to use the threat of the line-item veto to negotiate and build support for his budget. Although enactment of the Balanced Budget Amendment is unlikely, it could force Congress to centralize more of its budget activities around the leadership and the budget committees. Use of the line-item veto would also centralize budgeting and be time-consuming. It would extend the budget process over a longer period of time by forcing Congress to react to presidential actions in another budgetary loop in the process. The cycle of actions and reactions (by Congress and then by the president and then by Congress again) would add another time-consuming step in an already complex process. Already complex and time-consuming decision making would be made even more difficult with the Balanced Budget Amendment and the costing requirements of the Unfunded Mandates Reform Act.

Conclusion

The budget reforms of the 1990s have not dramatically changed specific policy outcomes. But Republicans won in record numbers in 1994 because they promised to make fundamental changes in the budget process and in government policy if elected. In office, they may find it more difficult to effect changes than they expected.

The constraints of previous budget decisions, especially deficits and mandatory entitlement spending in social welfare and health care, will continue for the foreseeable future. Congress is attempting to be more honest about budget deficits by showing the "real" number for each of the next five years rather than playing budgetary tricks, but it will be nearly impossible to fix blame for the increasing deficits under the "remote control" budget process rules now in operation. The Budget Enforcement Act of 1990 diffused the target of responsibility for spending and the deficit (although the latter is dropping rapidly). Who will get the blame (or the credit) for the deficit? Not the budget committees, the tax committees, the appropriations committees, party leaders, or the president. President Clinton understood this. His fiscal year 1996 budget proposal abandoned serious deficit reduction. Clinton's FY 1996 budget invited the Republicans to show how they could balance the budget while indulging their predilections for cutting taxes and increasing defense spending. Realizing that he was not getting credit for deficit reduction, Clinton "punted the ball" to the Republicans, to pursue that politically thankless task. House Republicans' pledges of massive cuts in the growth of spending have been followed by a series of missed deadlines and internal conflict in the 104th Congress.

Budgets are political documents, and budgetary politics will continue to hold center stage in Congress. Budget and party leaders will continue to build coalitions in the formulation of the budget and to negotiate with the president about spending priorities. This was the case during divided party government under President Bush, during unified party government under President Clinton in his first two years in office, and again during divided party government under President Clinton in 1995 and 1996.

Budgeting suggests the capacity to make intentional decisions about the entire budget and its parts, as well as to achieve some balance between what is purchased by government and what is paid for. The budget reforms of the 1990s seem to limit the ability of Congress to do just that (Caiden 1991, 46). The features that make the Budget Enforcement Act and other reforms in the 1990s attractive insulate Congress from accountability and make it difficult to assign responsibility for the growth of the federal budget or the size of the deficit. The budget process has become more complex and difficult to understand. The problems of assessing the impact of spending decisions remain. The reforms of the 1990s seem to promise further abdication of power, and thus responsibility for tough budgetary decisions.

While the budgetary problems grow, lawmakers blame the process and make themselves less accountable. Instead of forcing itself to pass a budget with tough choices, Congress continues to change the rules of the budget game (the 1974 Congressional Budget Act, reconciliation in 1981, GRH I and II, BEA in 1990, and a wide variety of new "quick fixes"). The budget reforms of the 1990s encourage both the legislative and executive branches of government to make short-run decisions that will complicate federal budgeting down the road. The reforms emphasize process reform instead of long-term policy solutions (Fisher 1985, 698).

James Sasser, the former chairman of the Senate Budget Committee, was right when he said: "The problem is not the process. . . . The problem is that revenues do not match outlays" (Yang 1991, A12). As former CBO director Rudolph Penner put it, the problem is the problem. On Capitol Hill, however, members increasingly see the process as the problem. Therefore, in the 103rd and 104th Congresses they introduced the enhanced rescission and line-item veto bills, Balanced-Budget-Amendment bills, and dozens of other budget reforms.

Presidents and Congress must demonstrate that they have the leadership and political will to eliminate the budget deficit and to budget responsibly for the benefit of their various constituencies and of the country as a whole. The Budget Enforcement Act may have just been another means by which Congress and the president temporarily avoided deadlock over the budget, by delaying the time in which they must come to grip with the deficit. The primary effect of the 1990 reforms may have been to eliminate the struggle over the budget process by moving "away from deficit control and toward no-fault budgeting, where process compromises have been made to ameliorate divisions among budget participants in the White House and Congress who wanted dramatically different policies" (Doyle and McCaffery 1991, 38). That certainly changed under the budget cutting battles of the 104th Congress. Although the deficit in the early 1990s was reduced dramatically, the reforms of the 1990s reflect a breakdown in the government's capacity to make hard budget decisions (Schick 1990).

The 1974 budget act was designed to control spending and revenue priorities in the budget. Later revisions were designed to control the deficit (GRH I and II), to control total spending (BEA), and to limit new spending (BEA and 1993 OBRA). Further change in budget making will come, if at all, from the American electorate. The 1994 voters seemed to want a balanced budget and the line-item veto. Congress responded. In the past, the American electorate has failed to make this kind of commitment. Yet process reforms cannot make up for the lack of political will. Neither the American electorate nor their elected officials in the White House or on Capitol Hill have yet displayed the political firmness necessary to make revenues match outlays. It is difficult to put the common good above that of individual interests. What President Clinton's chief of staff (and former House Budget Committee chair) Leon Panetta concluded in early 1991 about Congress applies to the reforms of the 1990s: "The instincts of this institution are not to accept constraints" (Yang 1991, A12). When the budget game gets too hard, the members change the rules.

Notes

Author's Note: For their valuable observations about the congressional budget process, I would like to thank Phillip G. Joyce of the Congressional Budget Office; James V. Saturno and Edward Davis of the Government Division, Congressional Research Service, Library of Congress; and Nicholas Masters, Senior Staff, House Budget Committee. I would also like to thank the budget specialists who participated in the Roundtable on Budget Process Reform held jointly by the Joint Committee on the Organization of Congress and the Center for Congressional and Presidential Studies on April 15, 1993. (Several observations made in this chapter were first presented at the Spring Symposium of the American Association for Budget and Program Analysis [AABPA] on May 11, 1994.) Finally, I would like to thank the School of Public Affairs and the Center for Congressional and Presidential Studies at the American University for suporting the research for this analysis.

1. For a discussion of these reforms, see Thurber (1991, 145-170; 1989, 78-118); Fisher (1985); Havens (1986, 4-24); LeLoup, Graham, and Barwick (1987, 83-103); and Thelwell (1990, 190-197).

2. The Congressional Budget Office (CBO), Congress's principal source of information and analysis on the budget and on spending and revenue legislation, was established by the act. The CBO has a specific mandate to assist the House and Senate budget committees and the spending and revenue committees; secondarily, it responds to requests for information from other committees and individual members of Congress. Prior to the creation of the CBO, Congress was forced to rely on the president's budget estimates and economic forecasts and on the annual analysis of the economy and fiscal policy by the Joint Economic Committee.

3. Another measure of budget deficit problems is the imbalance of outlays and receipts as a percentage of the Gross National Product (GNP). The deficit is reducing as percentage of GNP. For example, outlays were 24.3 percent of GNP and receipts were 18.1 percent of GNP in 1983; 23.7 percent outlays to 18.4 percent revenues in 1986; and 22.2 percent outlays to 19.2 percent revenues in 1989. See Congress Budget Office (1990a, 123).

4. The new deadlines have been delayed or modified informally each year since GRH I and GRH II were passed.

5. *Bowsher v. Synar* 106 S. Ct. 3181 (July 7, 1986).

6. Detailed explanations of the OBRA 1990 and the BEA reforms can be found in Doyle and McCaffery (1991, 36-41); and Congressional Budget Office (1990e).

7. The Budget Enforcement Act of 1990, Pub. L. No. 101-508, sec. 13101, 990 U.S.C.C.A.N. (104 Stat.) 1388-574. See also Kee and Nystrom (1991, 8).

8. The Budget Enforcement Ace of 1990, Pub. L. No. 101-508, sec. 13204, 1990 U.S.C.C.A.N. (104 Stat.) 1388-616.

9. Speech to the National Tax Association, 84th Annual Conference on Taxation, Williamsburg, Virginia, November 11, 1991.

10. The Budget Enforcement Act of 1990, Pub. L. No. 101-508, sec. 13301, 1990 U.S.C.C.A.N. (104 Stat.) 1388-573.

11. See the Budget Enforcement Act of 1990, Pub. L. No. 101-508, sec. 13302 and 13303, 1990 U.S.C.C.A.N. (104 Stat.) 1388-623. See also Conference Committee Report, final draft, 101st Cong., 2nd sess. (1990) section 6, "Treatment of Social Security," 10.

12. President George Bush, press release, December 21, 1990.

13. I would like to thank James V. Saturno, Government Division, Congressional Research Service, Library of Congress for this observation.

9

CAMPAIGN FINANCE REFORM:
Recent History and Prospects After the 1994 Elections

Candice J. Nelson

The 1990s began with the debate over campaign finance reform echoing the problems that had mired the debate in the late 1980s: disagreements between Republicans and Democrats over public funding and spending limits, and disagreements between U.S. representatives and senators over sources of funding—specifically, the role of political action committees. What distinguished the early 1990s from the previous decade, however, was that a campaign finance reform bill actually passed the House and Senate and was sent to the president. President George Bush vetoed the legislation, but the election of Bill Clinton in 1992 renewed hopes for campaign finance reform.

Yet more than two years into the Clinton administration, Congress still had not reached agreement on a bill. Legislation passed both the House and Senate in 1993, but in the waning days of the 103rd Congress the House and Senate Democratic leadership, despite a last-minute compromise, were unable to draft a bill that would avoid a filibuster in the Senate. This chapter examines the tortuous path campaign finance legislation has taken since the 1980s, and speculates on the future of campaign finance reform in light of the Republican takeover of Congress following the 1994 elections.

A Brief History

The campaign finance system that governs federal elections today was written during the 1970s. The Federal Election Campaign Act of 1971, passed in January 1972, was amended three times: in 1974, 1976, and 1979. While campaign finance reform legislation did not pass the House and Senate again for a little more than a decade, efforts to change the congressional campaign finance system continued almost nonstop in the late 1970s and throughout the 1980s.[1]

The current effort to reform campaign finance laws began in December 1985, when Senators David Boren and Barry Goldwater introduced a nongermane amendment to a bill granting the consent of Congress to a low-level radioactive waste compact. The Boren-Goldwater amendment proposed to amend the Federal Election Campaign Act. Specifically, it limited the total amount of funds a congressional candidate could receive from a political action committee (PAC), lowered the individual PAC contribution limit from $5,000 to $3,000 (and raised the individual contribution limit from $1,000 to $1,500), prohibited "bundling" of contributors by PACs, and tightened the definition of independent expenditures.[2] Procedural maneuvers by then majority leader Robert Dole, R-Kan., prevented a vote on the amendment, but Senator Boren received assurances from Senator Dole that the amendment would receive consideration in the second session of the 99th Congress in 1986 (Kubiak 1994, 91-95).

Senator Boren's amendment limiting PACs passed the Senate in August 1986 by a vote of 69 to 30. However, procedural maneuvering again prevented a vote on final passage of S. 655, the bill to which the Boren amendment was attached. In November 1986, following the 1986 midterm elections, the Democratic Party regained control of the U.S. Senate, and the Senate's new majority leader, Robert C. Byrd, D-W.Va., pledged to enact "campaign finance reform to stop the money chase" (Kubiak 1994, 97).

Even before the 100th Congress was sworn in on January 6, 1987, Senators Boren and Byrd began meeting to draft a comprehensive campaign finance reform bill. Throughout the winter and spring of 1987 a Democratic leadership group, including Senators Boren, Byrd, Alan Cranston (the majority whip), George Mitchell (the chair of the Democratic Senatorial Campaign Committee during the 1986 election cycle), and Wendell Ford (the chair of the Senate Rules Committee), met to draft a campaign finance bill, S. 2. The legislation included voluntary spending limits for Senate candidates, public financing, aggregate PAC limits, and language to address PAC bundling and independent expenditures.

S. 2 was brought to the Senate floor in early June. Despite seven cloture votes during the summer and fall of 1987, and a record eighth cloture vote in early 1988, the Senate could not muster the necessary 60 votes to cut off the Republican filibuster against S. 2.

During the 101st Congress the House of Representatives, as well as the Senate, considered campaign finance reform legislation, and legislation passed both the Senate and House in August 1990. However, conferees were not appointed; consequently, a final bill was not enacted.

The 102nd Congress passed campaign finance reform legislation. As expected, President Bush vetoed the bill.

Major Reform Issues Facing Congress

Three major issues confront members of Congress as they grapple with campaign finance reform: public financing, spending limits, and the role of special interests (PACs) in congressional elections.

Defenders of political action committees argue that PACs are a way for individuals with limited financial resources to play a role in financing congressional elections. The argument is that by making contributions to a PAC (which pools many donations), individuals have more input than they would have if they gave the same amount of money directly to a candidate. (For example, a teacher earning $30,000 a year has little discretionary income—so the argument goes—to make a $500 or $1,000 contribution to a congressional candidate, but by contributing $25 to the National Education Association's PAC, the teacher can make his or her views heard in a much louder voice than by making a $25 contribution directly to the candidate.) Rep. John Lewis, D-Ga., made this argument during consideration of campaign finance reform legislation in 1994. In an op-ed article in the *Washington Post*, Lewis wrote:

> Political action committees—especially those of labor unions and ideo-logical groups such as those supporting or opposing abortion rights, gay rights or gun control—give working people and people with little means the ability to participate in the political process. Many of these people who contribute through a "checkoff," or small deductions from their paycheck each week, would effectively be denied participation in the process if it weren't for their union or company PAC. (Lewis 1994, A25)

Opponents of political action committees argue that PACs are yet another way for special interests to influence the political process. Opponents argue that because PACs can contribute five times as much money to congressional candi-dates as can individuals, members of Congress will be more receptive to PACs and the interests that they represent than to individuals.

One problem facing members of Congress as they debate further restrictions on PAC contributions is the lack of consensus. PAC contributions are a much more important source of campaign funds for House candidates than they are for Senate candidates. In 1994 House incumbents received 46 percent of their total contributions from PACs, compared with the 23 percent of contributions received by Senate incumbents.[3] Consequently, senators are more willing than representa-tives to reduce the amount of money candidates can receive from PACs, or to abolish PAC contributions altogether. House members, particularly House Demo-crats, have fought strenuously to keep PAC contribution limits at their current level. The disagreement over PAC contributions became the last serious impedi-ment to campaign finance reform in the 103rd Congress.

A second problem facing Congress is public funding of congressional elec-tions. In this case the disagreement is not between House and Senate members but between Democrats and Republicans. Democrats support public funding, while Republicans oppose it. House Republican challengers would benefit the most from public funding because they historically have been the most poorly funded type of candidate.[4] Nevertheless, Republicans consistently oppose using federal funds to support congressional elections,[5] labeling public funding "a taxpayer-funded entitlement program for politicians" (Curran 1994a, 19).

The third major problem facing Congress is the issue of spending limits in congressional elections. Again, the disagreement is between Democrats and Re-publicans, with Democrats supporting spending limits and Republicans opposing them. Democrats, particularly Senate Democrats, decry the amount of time that must be spent raising money to run a competitive Senate race in the 1990s. Republicans argue political spending should be encouraged and often make the argument that considerably more money is spent in the United States on advertising for pet food than is spent on campaign advertising.[6]

Republican opposition to public funding is based on philosophical and practical concerns. Philosophically, Republicans oppose using federal funds to finance congressional elections. Practically, Republicans (who, prior to the 1994 congressional elections had been the minority party in the House for four decades and in the Senate for all but six years since 1955) were concerned that spending limits would make it impossible for them to become the majority party. Republican candidates, particularly challengers, feared they would not be able to spend the amount of money necessary to defeat entrenched Democratic incumbents. In 1994 House Republican challengers increased their median spending by 66 percent, and one in four Republican challengers raised at least $400,000, compared with just one in ten in 1992.[7] Although increases in spending likely contributed to Republican successes in the 1994 congressional elections, the median spending for House Republican challengers in 1994 was only $114,884, compared with median spending of just over $501,155 for House Democratic incumbents.[8]

While PACs, public funding, and spending limits are the three major problems facing Congress as it grapples with campaign finance reform, two other issues also pose difficulties for members attempting to pass a bill. Reformers have attempted to impose restrictions on both soft money and bundling. Soft money refers to unrestricted contributions to state and local political parties for party-building activities, such as voter registration and get-out-the-vote drives. Soft money has become an important source of revenue for both the Democratic and Republican parties. The Democratic Party raised $30.9 million in soft money contributions during the 1992 election cycle, and the Republican Party raised even more, $47.1 million.[9] During the 1994 election cycle the Democratic National Committee (DNC) raised $43 million in soft money and the Republican National Committee (RNC) raised $43.6 million.[10]

Thus, at the same time that members of Congress were trying to write legislation to restrict soft money in federal elections, the Democratic and Republican parties were becoming increasingly dependent on soft money to fund party activities. A study by the Center for Responsive Politics in 1993 found that the majority of money raised by the Democratic and Republican parties was retained by the national party committees for payroll and other administrative costs; only 20 percent of the soft money raised by the DNC and 30 percent of the soft money raised by the RNC was transferred to state and local parties and candidates (Babcock 1993, A13).

Campaign finance reformers also faced a dilemma as they tried to grapple with the practice of bundling: one organization collects campaign contributions for candidates from individuals and then presents the contributions to the candidates in a "bundle," enabling the organization to "get credit" from the candidate for contributions often well above the maximum $10,000 PAC contribution limit. The organization that has best perfected bundling is EMILY's List, a PAC that raises money for pro-choice Democratic women candidates. In the 1993-1994 election cycle EMILY's List claimed to have contributed $8.2 million to progressive Democratic women candidates.[11] While campaign finance reformers decry bundling as a way for PACs to elude contribution limits, they are reluctant to eliminate such a ready source of campaign funds. For Democrats, particularly House Democrats, the challenge was to generally restrict bundling but still allow EMILY's List to function.

Reforms Proposed in the 103rd Congress

In 1993, with a newly elected, pro-reform, Democratic president in the White House, many were optimistic that campaign finance reform would at last become law. During the presidential campaign and in his first State of the Union Address, Bill Clinton had called for reform of the nation's federal campaign finance laws. President Clinton even introduced his own reform proposal in May 1993. It called for spending limits in House and Senate elections, further restrictions on PAC contributions, restrictions on soft money expenditures by national party committees, and a prohibition on funding by PACs, lobbyists, unions, and corporations (Donovan 1993c, 1121-1122).

Campaign finance reform legislation passed the Senate in June 1993. The legislation established spending limits in Senate general elections of between $1.2 and $5.5 million, depending on a state's population, and it limited spending in primary elections to 67 percent of the general election spending limit or $2.75 million, whichever was less. The primary and general election spending limits in the 1993 Senate bill were remarkably close to the limits contained in the 1987 campaign finance legislation; the only difference was the spending limits for the least populous states were raised from $950,000 to $1.2 million. The legislation also prohibited candidates for federal offices from accepting PAC contributions, but contained a provision that if the Supreme Court were to find the prohibition unconstitutional, the amount a PAC could contribute to a candidate would be reduced to $1,000 per candidate per election. The bill limited total PAC contributions to any one candidate to 20 percent of the spending limit or $825,000, whichever was less (Donovan 1993b, 2240).

The legislation also severely limited the use of soft money by the national party committees. Soft money could no longer be used for voter registration and generic party activities, or for any activities that promoted a federal candidate or would "significantly affect" a federal election (Donovan 1993d, 2240).

The Senate bill also banned PACs, trade associations, and lobbyists, among others, from bundling contributions (Donovan 1993d, 2241). The prohibition on bundling would apply to EMILY's List and other groups, such as WISH List, that bundle individual contributions and send them to candidates.[12]

Candidates who complied with the spending limits would be able to send two mailings to all citizens of voting age in the state at the lower, nonprofit bulk rate, and candidates would be able to buy nonpreemptible broadcast time at 50 percent of the lowest unit rate for the same time. However, in order to achieve enough votes to avoid a filibuster, the Senate dropped from the legislation provisions for public funding that were included in earlier versions of the legislation considered and passed by the Senate. The Senate bill would have provided public funding only to candidates whose opponents did not accept voluntary spending limits or to candidates who were subject to an independent expenditure campaign against them that exceeded spending of $10,000 (Donovan 1993d, 2239).

Finally, in order to encourage candidates to accept spending limits, the legislation contained a tax provision. Candidates who did not accept spending limits would have all campaign receipts taxed at an amount equal to the highest corporate tax rate (Donovan 1993d, 2240).

Five months after the Senate passed a campaign finance bill, and in the waning days of the first session of the 103rd Congress, the House passed its version of campaign finance reform. The House bill established a spending limit of $600,000 for House elections, but the spending limit would rise with inflation. Candidates who accepted the spending limit would receive $200,000 in communication vouchers, which could be used for paid media, postage, and other voter contact programs. Restrictions were placed on aggregated PAC contributions. This meant that all House candidates, whether or not they accepted spending limits, could accept no more than $200,000 from PACs. The contribution limit from individual PACs would remain at $5,000 per candidate per election.

The House bill contained provisions similar to those in the Senate bill with respect to the restrictions on the use of soft money by the national political parties. The House bill, like its Senate counterpart, placed restrictions on bundling, but it prohibited bundling only by PACs connected to a corporation, union, or other "entity" that lobbies Congress (Donovan 1993e, 3093). Consequently, groups such as EMILY's List, which make campaign contributions but do not lobby Congress, would be exempted from the bundling provisions under the House language.

Little action on campaign finance occurred in the early months of 1994, but by late spring the House and Senate leadership began meeting to try to work out a compromise between the House and Senate versions of the legislation. The leadership wanted to reach some compromise prior to appointing conferees. As the end of the session neared, Congress once again found itself in a familiar situation— mired in debate and delay over campaign finance reform.

Throughout the night of September 22 and the morning and afternoon of September 23, the Senate stayed in session, as Senate Republicans availed themselves of a little used procedural motion allowing 30 hours of debate on an issue once cloture is invoked. Under Senate rules, a bill that has passed both houses of Congress in different forms is subject to three procedural motions before the bill can be sent to a conference committee (Rosenbaum 1994a, 1). Senate Republicans, rather than trying to prevent cloture on the first motion, decided to slow Senate action by talking for 30 hours following the first of the three procedural votes. After 30 hours of continuous debate, with Republicans taking turns talking for one hour each, the first of the three motions passed, 93-0 (Rosenbaum 1994a, 1; Dewar 1994b, A1, A16).

Republicans were expected to use the same delaying tactics the following week when the second procedural vote came to the Senate floor. Instead, they were able to defeat the cloture vote. A second effort to invoke cloture also failed, and the Democratic leadership then declared campaign finance reform legislation dead for the 103rd Congress.

Political Obstacles to Reform

In 1987 and 1988, when Ronald Reagan was president, and in 1989 and 1990, when George Bush was president, pro-reform forces in the House and Senate could craft a campaign finance bill with reasonable confidence that it wouldn't be enacted. One cornerstone of all bills considered and passed during that period was public financing, and neither President Reagan nor President Bush was likely to sign a bill with such a provision.

With the election in 1992 of a president committed to campaign finance reform, members of Congress knew that they might have to run for reelection under the campaign finance revisions they passed. Consequently, the freedom to construct a bill unconstrained by enactment disappeared. As a result, members began to think even more seriously about all proposed changes in the rules.

Nowhere was this more evident than in the House of Representatives. As stated earlier, the final sticking point between the House and Senate was PAC contribution limits. After months of negotiation House Democrats finally agreed to lower the amount a candidate could accept from PACs by $1,000 in both the 1996 and 1998 election cycles, so that by 1998 the total amount of money a candidate could accept from PACs would be $6,000, rather than $10,000 (Curran 1994b, 1). In exchange for a lowered individual PAC contribution limit, House members raised the aggregate amount a House candidate could accept from PACs from one-third of the $600,000 spending limit to 40 percent of the limit (Curran 1994b, 20). However, the compromise came too late. Recalcitrant senators who had supported an outright ban on PACs refused to support the compromise and allow the campaign finance reform bill to go to a conference committee with the House.

In the late 1980s the primary area of contention seemed to be partisan, and it focused on public funding and spending limits. In the 1990s, in contrast, the primary area of contention was chamber oriented, between House members and senators, and it focused on political action committees. Public funding was all but removed from the Senate bill, and the Senate passed a bill with spending limits. Public funding and spending limits were included in the bill that passed the House, though passage in both the House and the Senate was largely along party lines.[13]

As PACs became the central point of contention in the debate over campaign finance reform in the 1990s, the depiction of the role of PACs in congressional elections began to change. In the 1980s PACs were seen as the epitome of special interests; they influenced the electoral process, and consequently the policy process, at the expense of the "public" interest. For public interest groups, such as

Common Cause, the removal of special interest money, in the form of PACs, was one of the central goals of campaign finance reform.

During the debate over campaign finance reform in 1993 and 1994, some members of Congress began to depict PACs differently. Minority candidates and women candidates began to describe PACs as the only resource for candidates like themselves, candidates who did not have ties to individuals with wealth. In his op-ed article in the *Washington Post* in July 1994, John Lewis, a fourth term African-American member of Congress, wrote: "Let there be no confusion—minorities, women, candidates from poor rural and urban districts are the beneficiaries of PACs. PACs take power and influence out of the hands of the 'country club set' and put it in the hands of the people who can't afford to write $500 or $1,000 checks. This is one of the reasons PACs were established, and this is exactly why PACs should be protected in any campaign finance legislation" (Lewis 1994, A25). A female, first-term member of Congress made a similar argument in June 1994.[14]

Although the Senate filibuster that night in September 1994 might have seemed remarkably similar to one in 1987, the debate over campaign finance reform had changed. Public funding and spending limits, while still contentious topics between Democrats and Republicans, were less important to the debate than political action committees. PACs, which Senators Boren and Goldwater had criticized as the embodiment of the evils of special interests, were now being defended as the protector of the rights of those without wealth and influence in the political system. Once defended by Republicans and denounced by Democrats, PACs were now facing abolishment by Republicans and redemption by Democrats.

The Future of Campaign Finance Reform

The defeat of campaign finance reform legislation at the end of the 103rd Congress, coupled with Republican control of the House and Senate after the 1994 elections, does not bode well for comprehensive campaign finance reform in the near future. Democratic leaders were unable to agree on legislation and get it passed when they controlled the House and Senate; it seems unlikely they will have any success in moving campaign finance reform legislation while they are in the minority. Although the Republicans proposed a broad array of reforms in their "Contract with America," campaign finance reform was not one of them. Republican House leaders said publicly that they did not plan to make campaign finance reform "an immediate priority" in the 104th Congress, and Kentucky senator Mitch McConnell, the leading Republican spokesman on campaign finance reform since 1987, said that campaign finance reform is "not on the agenda and will not be on the agenda in the Senate" (Curran 1994c, 7). If the Republican leadership does decide to address campaign finance reform, the debate will likely begin where it left off—with political action committees. Rep. Dick Armey of Texas, the House majority leader, has said he would like PAC contributions to be reduced from $5,000 per candidate per election to $1,000 per candidate per election (Curran 1994c, 7).

In his State of the Union Address in 1995, President Clinton reaffirmed his support for campaign finance reform. However, given his lack of serious advocacy of the issue in the Democratic-controlled and reform-friendly 103rd Congress, it is difficult to imagine President Clinton pushing hard for campaign finance reform in the Republican-dominated 104th Congress.

The present system of campaign finance is likely to continue, at least for a while. Campaign spending for the 1993-1994 election cycle was $724 million, an increase of 6 percent over the 1991-1992 election cycle, despite the fact that fewer candidates ran in 1994 than ran in 1992.[15]

While overall costs will continue to rise, some challengers and open seat candidates will continue to be underfunded. Challengers will continue to be outspent by incumbents. More spending does not guarantee success, as eight-term House incumbent Mike Synar found out; in 1994 Synar was defeated, 51 percent to 49 percent, by a 71-year-old retired school principal who spent less than $17,000 (Burger 1994, 1, 26). Usually, however, incumbents prevail. Challengers' inability to raise enough money to get out a campaign message and become competitive means incumbents will continue to enjoy the high reelection rate that has characterized congressional elections in the 1980s and early 1990s.

Although House incumbents who seek reelection have been just as successful in the 1990s as they were in the 1980s, retirements have ensured turnover in Congress. With 110 House freshmen elected in 1992 and 86 House freshmen elected in 1994, almost half the House of Representatives in the 104th Congress had served in Congress for two years or less.

Campaign receipts continued to rise in the 1994 election cycle, but PAC contributions to congressional candidates held fairly constant. PACs contributed $178.8 million to congressional candidates in 1994 compared with $178.6 million in 1992.[16] There was some speculation early in 1994 that PACs, in anticipation of further restrictions on their activities, were beginning to look for ways to influence congressional elections other than through direct contributions to candidates. However, with the defeat of campaign finance reform in September 1994, PACs stepped up their direct campaign contributions to candidates late in the election cycle. It is reasonable to expect that PAC contributions will continue to rise in the 1996 election cycle, and that Republicans, now in the majority, will see increased contributions from corporate and trade PACs.

The consequences of stability in the campaign finance system are numerous. Soft money will continue to flow into the Democratic and Republican parties, enabling wealthy individuals to ignore the $25,000 per year aggregate limit on individual contributions. EMILY's List, WISH List, and other PACs will continue to bundle campaign contributions, thus skirting the PAC contribution limit. Wealthy candidates (such as Michael Huffington, a first-term member of the House who spent almost $30 million in 1994 in an unsuccessful run for a U.S. Senate seat) will continue to spend millions of their own money to run for Congress. Candidates will continue to spend large segments of their time raising money, and underfunded candidates will continue to run uncompetitive races. Finally, the press and the public will continue to be concerned about how campaign money is collected and used.

It is difficult to know what the consequences would have been if the campaign finance legislation had not been defeated in 1994. The costs of congressional elections probably would have stabilized and in some races actually declined. Reductions in communications costs would have enabled all candidates to spend more money communicating with potential voters, but challengers, who don't have the resources of incumbency, probably would have been most advantaged. Further restrictions on PAC contributions, or an outright ban, might have caused some PACs to disband, but the larger PACs might have turned to independent expenditures as a way to influence elections. Special interest money, still a factor in congressional elections, might have been harder to trace. Party-building activities of the political parties might have been hurt if their access to soft money had been curtailed.

While supporters and opponents of campaign finance reform might differ in their evaluation of the current system and prediction of the future, the debate at the beginning of the 104th Congress seemed all but academic. Action was unlikely for two reasons. The first was the lack of consensus on Capitol Hill—among House and Senate members, among Democrats and Republicans, and within the parties. The second reason was President Clinton's failure to follow up his reform oratory with steady pressure on Congress to change the system. A Republican-controlled 104th Congress, with no commitment to campaign finance reform, makes passage of a comprehensive campaign reform bill in the 1990s seem remote at best.

Notes

1. For a chronology of campaign finance reform bills introduced in the House and Senate between 1977 and 1985, see the *Congressional Record,* December 2, 1985, 33626.

2. Ibid., S33613.

3. Calculated from Federal Election Commission (FEC) data contained in "1994 Congressional Spending Sets Record," Federal Election Commission press release, December 22, 1994, 4. Data represent campaign finance reports filed with the Federal Election Commission through November 28, 1994.

4. In 1992 House Democratic incumbents collectively raised 2.3 times as much money as House Republican challengers. Democratic incumbents raised over $126 million, while Republican challengers raised $53.9 million. "1992 Congressional Election Spending Jumps 52% to $678 Million," Federal Election Commission press release, March 4, 1993, 4. In 1994, despite increases in spending by House Republican challengers, House Democratic incumbents collectively raised 2.7 times as much money as House Republican challengers. Democratic incumbents raised over $137 million, while Republican challengers raised $51 million. "1994 Congressional Spending Sets Record," Federal Election Commission press release, December 22, 1994, 4.

5. This issue became particularly difficult for Senator Dole in 1987. At the time Dole was seeking his party's presidential nomination and accepting federal matching funds. At the same time, he was urging Republicans in the Senate to refuse to allow debate on S. 2, in part because it would have provided federal funds for congressional candidates.

6. *Congressional Record,* June 9, 1987, S7548.

7. FEC press release, December 22, 1994, 2.

8. Calculated from "1994 Congressional Fundraising Climbs to New High," Federal Election Commission press release, April 28, 1995, 11.

9. Federal Election Commission, *Record,* January 1995, 7.

10. Ibid; data represent soft money receipts through October 19, 1994.

11. EMILY's List, *Notes from Emily,* December 1994, 6.

12. WISH List was formed in 1991 to contribute contributions to pro-choice Republican women candidates (Nelson 1994, 190).

13. S. 3 passed the House by a 255-175 vote, with 22 Republicans voting for it and 151 voting against; 232 Democrats voted for the bill and only 24 voted against. *Congressional Quarterly Weekly Report,* November 27, 1993, 3288. In the Senate the bill passed by a 60-38 vote, with 7 Republicans voting for the bill and 38 against it; Democrats supported the bill, 53-3. *Congressional Quarterly Weekly Report,* December 18, 1993, 3452.

14. Rep. Leslie Byrne, D-Va., personal conversation with the author, June 10, 1994. Representative Byrne was one of 16 House freshmen defeated for reelection in 1994.

15. FEC press release, April 28, 1995, 1.

16. Ibid.

10

LOBBY REFORM: Curing the Mischiefs of Factions?

Ronald G. Shaiko

S hortly after ten o'clock on the morning of Thursday, October 6, 1994, on the floor of the U.S. Senate, the Lobbying Disclosure Act of 1994 was pronounced dead by a failed cloture vote of 52-46.[1] Following the vote, Sen. Carl Levin, D-Mich., the chief Senate architect of the lobby reform bill, sounded the death knell: "It seems a Republican-led filibuster has killed the toughest lobbying and gift ban law that Congress has been able to consider in decades" (quoted in Dewar 1994c, A1). This statement is certainly a far cry from the optimistic pronouncement made by Senator Levin less than two months earlier and echoed by his counterpart lobby reform champion in the House, Rep. John Bryant, D-Texas: "There's no rug big enough [to sweep it under]—happily" (quoted in Love 1994a, 6). The activities of this intervening period as well as the lobby reform work undertaken throughout the entire 103rd Congress (1993-1994) provide some clear insights into the flaws in the process of institutional reform in the U.S. Congress.

The latest round of proposed lobby reform was precipitated by the campaign rhetoric of presidential candidate Bill Clinton. Upon his election, President Clinton wasted little time taking up the lobby reform challenge. Following the initial legislative activity of the first session of the 103rd Congress, Clinton sought to reenergize the Congress in its efforts to pass legislation to curb the influences of special interests in Washington. Adopting the positions of earlier Democratic presidents, Clinton used the reformist political rhetoric of Woodrow Wilson but cultivated the insider political relationships of John F. Kennedy. President Wilson was the first twentieth-century president to challenge the power structure of organized corporate and business interests in Washington: "The masters of the government are the combined capitalists and manufacturers. It is written over every intimate page of the records of Congress; it is written all through the history of conferences at the White House. . . . The government is a foster child of special interests. It is not allowed to have a will of its own" (quoted in Birnbaum, 1992, 75).

President Kennedy also spoke out against the undue influence of special interests, but he maintained close relationships with powerful Washington lobbyists, including Clark Clifford. When asked about the propriety of such relationships, Kennedy quipped, "You don't hear Clark [Clifford] clamoring. All he asked was that we advertise his law firm on the back of the dollar bills" (quoted in Birnbaum 1992, 79). Like Kennedy, President Clinton has surrounded himself, both formally and informally, with powerful individuals whose political influence in Washington predates his ascendancy to the White House. Arguably, Clinton's Clark Clifford is Vernon Jordan. Characterized in journalistic accounts as "Clinton's Mr. Inside, [Jordan] is everything that America loves to hate about Washington: a lawyer-lobbyist, a rainmaker, an influence peddler. He sits on 11 corporate boards. . . . He is a managing partner in one of the most politically aggressive law and lobbying firms in Washington, Akin, Gump, Strauss, Hauer & Feld. He makes between $1 million and $2 million a year" (Williams 1993, 173-174).

Yet another indication of the inextricable linkage between organized interests and the Clinton administration is identified in the funding of the 1992 presidential campaign. The Clinton campaign was the beneficiary of an estimated $40 million in "soft money" funneled through state and local political parties; these federally unregulated funds are collected from a variety of big dollar donors, the vast majority of which are linked to organized interests. The Clinton campaign, however, was not alone in utilizing this form of fund raising; the Bush campaign benefited from $25 million raised through "soft money" contributions (Arterton 1993, 83; see also Chapter 9 in this volume for a more detailed account of the use of "soft money" in campaign financing).

Despite these ties to Washington power brokers and organized interests, Clinton targeted the perceptibly pervasive problem of special interest influence. In his 1994 State of the Union Address, the president challenged the Congress to clean up the system of interest group influence:

> Facing up to special interests will require courage. It will require critical questions about the way we finance our campaigns and how lobbyists peddle their influence. The work of change will never get easier until we limit the influence of well financed interests who profit from the current system.

The basic premise of this statement and virtually all of the contemporary political commentary is that there are clearly defined boundaries between the government on one side and organized interests and the general public on the other. This pluralistic view of the relationships between government and society, while theoretically attractive as well as instructive in describing the macro-level phenomenon of interest group influence, is not representative of the ongoing interactions between elected representatives in Congress, their staffs, appointed officials in the executive branch, career bureaucrats, and the myriad of organized interests in the political system. As a result, previous formulations have been rather ineffective in remedying the perceived problems of interest group influence. Since the efforts at lobby reform in the 103rd Congress failed, the following analysis focuses on the key components of the House (H.R. 823) and Senate (S. 349) bills, the resultant conference report, and the degree to which any of the major targets of lobby reform would, indeed, clarify and codify the relationships between government and organized interests in the real world of Washington politics. Key components of the lobby reform legislation include disclosure and registration, reporting requirements, executive branch lobbying, grassroots lobbying, coalition building, and the ban on gifts from lobbyists. Prior to the analysis of the Lobbying Disclosure Act of 1994, however, it is necessary to outline the scope of lobby registration requirements currently employed by the federal government to regulate the lobbying industry.

Lobby Regulation and the First Amendment

Whenever one discusses the relationship between organized interests, the citizens they represent, and the federal government, one must remain cognizant of the constitutional protection guaranteed to citizens and their representatives under the First Amendment "to petition the Government for a redress of grievances." Currently, there are five legislative mandates that govern the activities of interest group lobbying, none of which has been interpreted to infringe upon the First Amendment rights of petitioners. These acts include the Foreign Agents Registration Act (FARA) of 1938 (22 U.S.C. 611 et seq.), the Federal Regulation of Lobbying Act of 1946 (2 U.S.C. 261-270), the "1976 lobby law," [2] the 1989 Byrd Amendment (31 U.S.C. 1352), and Section 112 of the Housing and Urban Development (HUD) Reform Act of 1989 (42 U.S.C. 3537b). In addition there are two recent actions taken by the Clinton administration and the Internal Revenue Service to regulate further the lobbying industry: Executive Order 12834 and Section 13222 of Title XIII of the 1993 Omnibus Budget Reconciliation Act (OBRA).

The Foreign Agents Registration Act of 1938

FARA, or the McCormack Act as it is also known, was promulgated in order to regulate the influence of foreign actors in the American political system. Originally directed at the activities of Nazi propagandists in the late 1930s, the act and its amendments were later applied to the broad class of foreign commercial and business interests attempting to influence U.S. policies. President Jimmy Carter's brother, Billy, ran afoul of FARA regulations in his dealings with Libyan interests in 1980. Many current observers view the McCormack Act rather critically. Richard Sachs of the Congressional Research Service (CRS) identifies three specific weaknesses with FARA:

> (1) two exemptions that apply, first to lawyers appearing in formal or informal proceedings before U.S. courts or agencies, and second, to activities on behalf of a foreign-owned company in the United States that further the bona fide commercial, industrial, or financial interests of the U.S. subsidiary; (2) extensive but vague and confusing disclosure requirements; and (3) administrative difficulties. (Sachs 1994a, 5)

The Federal Regulation of Lobbying Act of 1946

The 1946 lobby act was largely an afterthought, quickly drafted and attached to the Legislative Reorganization Act of 1946. This four-page addendum has long survived, although not without modification, as the basic regulatory instrument through which Congress oversees the lobbying industry. Due to its brevity and rather haphazard authorship, key sections of the act, particularly the operational definition of a lobbyist in Section 307, were challenged in federal court. Section 307 required lobby registration of any individual "who by himself, or through any agent, or employee or other persons in any manner, solicits, collects, or receives money or any thing of value to be used *principally* to aid ... the passage or defeat of any legislation by Congress" (emphasis added).

The court challenge focused on the extent to which a citizen could petition the government on behalf of clients for fees without such actions being construed as lobbying. In 1954 the Supreme Court of the United States addressed this question in *U.S. v. Harris* (347 U.S. 612). In an attempt to clarify the vague statute passed by Congress, the Court ruled that the act covered only those persons whose "principal purpose" is to influence legislation. The Court further limited the activities that constituted lobbying to include only "direct communications with congressmen" on pending or proposed legislation.

As a result of poor legislative drafting and the subsequent Supreme Court clarifications, the 1946 act contains numerous loopholes that remain today. Political scientists Ronald J. Hrebenar and Ruth K. Scott have identified eight major weaknesses in the 1946 lobbying regulations:

> (1) Many lobbyists refuse to register since they claim that lobbying is not their "principal purpose"; (2) Others do not register because they use their own financial resources to lobby and therefore they do not "solicit, collect, or receive" money for lobbying; (3) No grassroots or indirect lobbying is covered in the Act; (4) The Supreme Court's decision that only direct contacts with Congress must be reported excluded such activities as testifying before congressional committees and also the preparation of that testimony; (5) The Act excludes lobbying of the congressional staff of the individual representative or the professional staffs of the committees; (6) The law covers only congressional lobbying and thus lobbying of the White House, the various executive departments, regulatory agencies, the courts, or any other governmental organization is exempt; (7) The decision on what to report under the financial reporting provisions is basically left up to the lobbyist to determine; and (8) Investigation and enforcement of the provisions of the Act are almost nonexistent in recent years. (Hrebenar and Scott 1990, 247-248)

The 1976 Lobby Law and the Nonprofit Sector

The nonprofit sector in the United States is granted special status by the federal government. Organizations designated Internal Revenue Service Code 501(c)(3), the vast majority of nonprofit entities, receive tax-exemption and are beneficiaries of governmental subsidies that facilitate organizational maintenance (Shaiko 1991, 109-129). The tradeoff for such entities is a limitation on the amount of lobbying they can conduct. The 1976 legislation states that "no substantial part" of the organizational activities may involve attempting to influence the outcome of legislation. This language has been interpreted to mean that spending ceilings will be based on percentages of the organizational budgets, beginning with 20 percent of the first $500,000 and ending with 5 percent of expenditures over $1.5 million.

For nonprofit organizations the meaningfulness of the lobby law lies not in the spending ceilings but in the activities *not* included as lobbying under the IRS Code. Bob Smucker, vice president for government relations at Independent Sector, the umbrella organization representing the nonprofit sector, identifies five broad activities that do not constitute lobbying for nonprofits:

> (1) Communications to members of an organization that discuss legislation but do not urge action by the members; (2) Making available the results of "nonpartisan analysis, study or research" on a legislative issue that presents a sufficiently full and fair exposition of the pertinent facts to enable an audience to form an independent opinion; (3) Responding to written requests from a legislative body (not just a single legislator) for technical advice on pending legislation; (4) So-called self-defense activity—that is, lobbying legislators on matters that may affect the organization's own existence, powers, exempt status, and similar matters; and (5) Discussion of broad social, economic, and similar policy issues whose resolution would require legislation, as long as there is no discussion of specific legislative measures. (Smucker 1991, 68-69)

Unlike previous provisions, the nonprofit sector regulation by the IRS includes limitations on grassroots lobbying. Communications that do urge direct action by members on legislative issues are included as lobbying activities. Such expenditures are limited to one-quarter of the organization's overall spending ceiling. In the late 1960s the Sierra Club lost its 501(c)(3) status due to its extensive grassroots lobbying efforts (Berry 1977, 48-49).

The 1989 Byrd Amendment and the HUD Reform Act

These two provisions attempt to regulate federal spending on lobbying activities. Government contractors, prior to extensive congressional investigations, were making a practice of incorporating lobbying expenses into their government contract budgets. These acts attempt to end such expenditures.[3] These acts, however, have not escaped negative scrutiny. Again, Richard Sachs of CRS finds weaknesses in these legislative initiatives: "Criticized for vagueness and inconsistencies, both measures have combined to create a patchwork of disclosure statutes that have failed to provide for informed identification of lobbyists and their activities and, further, have frustrated those seeking to comply with the statutes' requirements (Sachs 1994a, 5).

Executive Order 12834

Executive Order 12834, issued by President Clinton on January 20, 1993 (58 F.R. 5911 et seq.), further limits the postemployment lobbying activities of executive branch political appointees. Prior to this action, the postemployment activities of government (legislative and executive) employees were regulated by the Ethics in Government Act of 1978, amended by the 1989 Ethics Reform Act (18

U.S.C. 207). The general guidelines set forth in the ethics legislation prohibit former executive branch employees from contacting the federal government on matters in which the employees were personally and directly involved; this ban is for life. In addition, such executive branch employees are banned for two years from contacting government officials on matters that were within each employee's jurisdiction. All senior employees in both the legislative and executive branches may not make contact with their former employers, their staffs, or their agencies on behalf of another person or interest for one year. Former members of Congress, cabinet secretaries, and senior White House officials, likewise, are banned from contacting their former departments, offices, or institutions for one year. Additional restrictions on working for foreign entities are placed on those officials in both branches who deal with trade or treaty negotiations.

The Clinton executive order increased the contact ban on certain senior political appointees from one year to five years. It also placed a lifetime ban on former senior officials in the executive branch on working as a foreign agent on behalf of a foreign government or foreign political party. Interestingly, the ban does not include working for foreign corporations.

Section 13222 of Title XIII of the 1993 OBRA

As a means of generating additional revenues, the Clinton White House proposed in its 1993 Omnibus Budget Reconciliation Act the elimination of tax deductibility for lobbying expenses by corporations and related business associations. Since 1962, under Section 162(e) of the Internal Revenue Code, such entities were permitted to deduct costs associated with lobbying activities. As of January 1, 1994, as a result of the passage of the 1993 OBRA, organizations may no longer claim lobbying expenses as tax deductions. An estimated $500 million over five years will be generated from the elimination of the tax deductibility of lobbying expenses (Sachs 1994b, 11).[4]

As one might expect, corporations and associations did not respond well to this initiative. Along with a host of individual companies, two umbrella organizations representing the lobbying profession—the American League of Lobbyists (ALL) and the American Society of Association Executives (ASAE)—having lost the legislative battle, attempted to lobby the Internal Revenue Service rulemaking process in order to clarify the legislative intent of Section 13222. Although they filed formal comments on the proposed regulation section (1.162-29) with the IRS, the adversely impacted organizations have accepted the inevitability of the deduction elimination, even while waiting for permanent IRS regulations to be issued. In fact, the ASAE, in conjunction with Gnossos Software, Inc., was marketing a new software package, "LOBBY TAX," for use in compliance with the new law as early as July of 1994.

Conclusion

This checkered collection of statutes and regulations constitutes the current lobby registration and disclosure requirements in force. At their best, they represent marginally instructive guideposts from which benevolent professional lobbyists may fashion their quarterly filing reports, should they desire to file such reports. Clearly, much has changed in the relationships between organized interests and the federal government in Washington since the passage of FARA and the 1946 act. Unfortunately, the U.S. Congress has been institutionally incapable of providing coherent lobby reform in the intervening half-century. The efforts undertaken during the 103rd Congress to remedy this situation, while ending in failure, are commendable, if not totally in step with the realities of lobbying in the 1990s.

The Lobbying Disclosure Act and the Real World

The earliest incarnation of the Lobbying Disclosure Act of 1994 dates back to 1991, when Senator Levin held hearings in the Senate Governmental Affairs Subcommittee on Oversight of Government Management. The hearings were precipitated by the Wedtech affair. In June of the following year, the full committee reported out a lobby disclosure bill, but no action was taken during the remainder of the 102nd Congress. At the opening of the 103rd Congress, Levin introduced S. 349, a bill fashioned after the initiative that died the year earlier.

Senate Action: S. 349

In comparatively short order, S. 349 made its way through committee and was passed overwhelmingly on May 6, 1993, by a vote of 95-2. The version that passed sought to reorganize the aforementioned legislative corpus into a manageable, coherent lobby disclosure law. Substantively, it covered only full-time professional lobbyists.[5] The definition of lobbying was expanded to include interactions with members of Congress, their staffs (personal and committee), executive branch officials (including White House officials), and senior agency and military officials (SES and Schedule C employees).

S. 349 also created a new registration and disclosure entity, the Office of Lobbying Registration and Public Disclosure. Under the Senate bill, this office would exist within the Department of Justice, although it would have no audit or investigatory authority. Compliance issues were to be managed through informal resolution processes, but fines could be assessed, ranging from up to $10,000 for minor noncompliance to $200,000 for significant noncompliance. Semiannual reporting would replace the quarterly filings under the 1946 act rules. Grassroots lobbying was included as a lobbying activity, but the language basically mirrored the nonprofit language regarding reporting mechanisms. FARA regulations would be subsumed under the new reporting requirements. The characterization of coalitions was also addressed in the Senate bill; coalition members that contributed more than $5,000 toward the lobbying effort and that had a significant role or financial stake would be included (Kuntz 1994, 1016-1022).

The Senate bill came to the floor without comment on treatment of gifts from lobbyists. Sen. Paul Wellstone, D-Minn., however, offered an amendment that would require lobbyists to disclose the gifts given to members of Congress if the value of any meals, entertainment, or travel amounted to more than $20. The amendment passed by voice vote.

House Action: H.R. 823

Lobby reform in the House did not have its genesis in the 102nd Congress. Rep. John Bryant, D-Texas, first introduced H.R. 823 in January 1993. The road to passage began with the first committee hearing on March 31, at which time the topic of gift disclosure was introduced by representatives from several public interest groups, including Common Cause. Originally, there were no gift ban requirements in H.R. 823; however, as a result of the hearing, the gift ban language became a key feature of the bill. This addition had a chilling effect on the legislation. Beyond the committee ranks, a growing number of members disliked the disproportionate focus on gift disclosure and away from lobby reform. H.R. 823 remained in limbo until shortly before the Thanksgiving break in 1993.

On November 22, the Subcommittee on Administrative Law and Governmental Relations, chaired by Representative Bryant, reported out H.R. 823 with an amendment in the nature of a substitute that included an outright ban on all gifts from lobbyists to members of Congress. Perhaps more significantly, H.R. 823 as reported contained substantial disclosure requirements relating to grassroots lobbying, including information regarding any grassroots lobbying efforts that the organization might be planning. Lobbyists would also be required to include any information about any individual or organization that had been retained to conduct grassroots lobbying on behalf of the registered lobbyist or the client of the lobbyist. The semi-annual reports required in the House version would also include disclosure of grassroots activities. The first session of the 103rd Congress ended without further consideration of H.R. 823.

During the first three months of the second session, debate continued on the gift ban as well as on the disclosure requirements. Despite the serious misgivings of members of both parties, but particularly Republicans, the House took up H.R. 823 on March 24, 1994. The text of H.R. 823 was substituted for the Senate-passed language of S. 349 and was adopted by a significant margin of 315-110 under suspension of the rules. As a result of the differing language, a conference committee was formed. House conferees included Representatives Bryant; Dan Glickman, D-Kan.; Mike Synar, D-Okla.; Hamilton Fish, Pa. R-N.Y.; and George Gekas, R-Pa.[6] Conferees representing the Senate included Levin; John Glenn, D-Ohio; Daniel Akaka, D-Hawaii; Bill Cohen, R-Maine; and Ted Stevens, R-Alaska. As the conference took shape, the Senate passed S. 1935, a stricter version of the House gift ban and disclosure legislation, sponsored by Sen. Frank R. Lautenberg, D-N.J.

Conference Committee Action and Final Floor Votes

The major points of contention in the conference were the gift ban provisions and grassroots lobbying disclosure. A compromise was reached on the gift ban that provided leeway for interpretation to be determined within each chamber. On the grassroots disclosure provisions the Senate conferees accepted the stronger

House language. The report of the Conference Committee was sent to each chamber for final consideration.

The House was the first to address the conference report of the Lobbying Disclosure Act of 1994 on September 29, 1994. Unfortunately for those who had sought to pass the final version and send it to the White House in short order, the damage had been done by the time the bill reached the floor for the final vote that day. A crucial mistake was made in the Rules Committee. Under normal House procedures, before a controversial bill may be considered for final passage, it must receive from the Rules Committee a rule governing the length of debate as well as the opportunity for amendments. Traditionally, there is a three-day layover rule for conference reports returning to the House. This gives members an opportunity to analyze the new legislative language. The three-day rule may be waived by a simple majority vote by the Rules Committee. At the time, with a 9-4 Democratic majority on the committee, it was usually easy to waive the layover rule.

The conference report was approved by the conferees on Monday, September 26. The Rules Committee took up the report on the afternoon of the following day. When the committee was called to order, only eight committee members were present, four Democrats and four Republicans. After much discussion Democrat Anthony C. Beilenson of California tipped the scales in favor of the Republicans: "Let's not argue about waiving the three-day rule. There's no reason we can't wait until Thursday if it makes people happy" (quoted in Love 1994b, 3).

This short delay in the legislative process was crucial for implementing the opposition strategies to kill the lobby reform bill. Republican floor leaders Tom DeLay of Texas and Ernest Jim Istook, Jr., of Oklahoma, aided by then minority whip Newt Gingrich of Georgia, quickly mobilized a grassroots opposition campaign targeted not only at members of the House but, more importantly, at senators (Weisskopf 1994, A1, A4). In substance, the bulk of the opposition campaign focused on the perceived intrusiveness of the grassroots lobbying provisions. Inside Congress, the gift ban provision caused many members to view the entire lobby reform package in a much less favorable light.

The external opposition campaign brought together a collection of politically strange bedfellows. For example, the conservative Christian Coalition joined forces with the liberal American Civil Liberties Union under the guise of the Free Speech Coalition.[7] The many grassroots organizations against the reform bill argued that its reporting requirements would force them to expose their memberships to direct public scrutiny, in violation of First Amendment rights. By activating their electronic networks, the organizations, within hours, flooded House and Senate offices with telephone calls and faxes and later with letters and mailgrams.

By the time the conference report reached the floor on Thursday for a final vote, House Republicans and Democrats had begun to hear from their constituents about the grassroots provisions in the lobby reform package. Despite the deluge of calls received in opposition to the bill, many members of the House, including a significant number of Republicans, had already voted for the earlier version that contained virtually identical grassroots language.

Although an attempt was made to defeat the bill on the preceding procedural motion, the rule passed 216-205, only after the Democratic leadership held open the vote on the motion for several minutes beyond the 15-minute period. The vote on final passage was a comfortable 306-112, although the debate prior to the vote was quite intense, with several key Republicans leading the charge. Perhaps the most telling comments on the floor were registered by the retiring minority leader, Robert Michel of Illinois. Regarding the gift ban, he concluded, "This is not self-reform. This is self-flagellation, a practice which may have a fascinating attraction for some, but I consider it degrading and debasing, and what is more important, not really reform" (Michel 1994, H10269).

The rumblings in the House were but an early sign of the groundswell of public opposition to be felt in the Senate. The grassroots provision that was adopted by the conference was not widely appreciated by a large number of senators, both Democrat and Republican. Regardless of the validity of the claims being made by their mobilized constituents, many senators either were unable to support the provision that was being perceived widely as too intrusive or now had the needed political cover to oppose the reform package in its entirety.[8] With a sufficient number of senators in place for a prolonged filibuster, the Republican opposition, led by Kentucky senator Mitch McConnell, upheld the cloture vote on October 6, 1994, by a vote of 52-46, thereby ending any hope of lobby reform in the 103rd Congress.

Prospects for the 104th Congress

The new Republican-controlled 104th Congress did not place lobby reform on its list of top priority items to consider during the first session. It was not included as a component of the "Contract with America," nor was it seriously discussed by either the House or Senate leadership, although Senate Majority Leader Robert Dole rhetorically stated that the Senate would deal with lobby reform at some point in the 104th Congress.

Early in the first session, the initial trial balloon relating to lobbying was floated by Sen. Paul Wellstone, D-Minn. Wellstone offered an amendment to the first piece of legislation signed into law in the 104th Congress, the Congressional Accountability Act of 1995. His amendment would have barred a lobbyist or a political action committee controlled by a lobbyist from contributing funds to any member of Congress with whom the lobbyist had made a lobbying contact during the preceding 12 months. The amendment failed overwhelmingly, by a vote of 74-17. Less than three weeks later President Clinton, in his 1995 State of the Union Address, echoed his own words uttered a year earlier:

> As the new Congress opened its doors, lobbyists were still doing business as usual—the gifts, the trips, all the things that people are concerned about haven't stopped. . . . I ask you to just stop taking the lobbyist perks. Just stop. We don't have to wait for legislation to pass to send a message to the American people that things are really changing.

Unfortunately for President Clinton, his rhetoric became entangled with his own political reality. The president's legal defense fund, set up by his political allies to help defray legal costs associated with the Whitewater affair and the Paula Jones sexual harassment case, had received more than $600,000 in contributions—largely from the inner circle of the Washington/Hollywood/New York Democratic network, including a number of lobbyists. As a result, rather than stepping up the political battle, Clinton was forced to respond to the comments of Majority Leader Dole, who called his challenge a "cheap shot," saying, "When we have lobbyists contributing to the president's legal defense fund, I think he'd be a little careful about bringing it up" (quoted in Marcus 1995, A1). Clinton responded the following day by stating that the fund would no longer accept contributions from lobbyists. The end result was that the issue of lobby reform was removed from the top priority list of the Clinton agenda, at least for the short term.

Prospects for movement on lobby reform in the House were not terribly optimistic. The House Judiciary Committee's newly named Subcommittee on the Constitution, chaired by sophomore Republican Charles Canady of Florida, has jurisdiction over all "Contract with America" items that involve constitutional changes. In the early stages of the 104th Congress, the new subcommittee staff was overwhelmed with many more pressing issues, such as the Balanced Budget Amendment and term limits. According to subcommittee staff director Kathryn Hazeem, lobby reform is "up in the air." She added that the subcommittee may take up lobby reform later in 1995. One must remember that the floor leaders in the 103rd Congress who opposed lobby reform, Representatives DeLay and Gingrich, now hold positions as majority whip and Speaker of the House, respectively.

On the Senate side the initial failure of the Wellstone amendment provided an indicator of the willingness of the chamber to address the issue. As in the 103rd Congress, Sen. Mitch McConnell, R-Ky., remains the leader of the opposition forces. Sen. William Cohen, R-Maine, who replaced Senator Levin as the subcommittee chair of jurisdiction, introduced S. 101 in the 104th Congress. This bill is very similar to S. 349, which failed in the 103rd Congress. Peter Levine, Senator Levin's chief subcommittee aide during the 103rd Congress, was retained for several months by Cohen as staff counsel on the Senate Governmental Affairs Committee's Subcommittee on Oversight of Government Management. Levine, while "pushing for commitment" to S. 101 to address lobby reform by the subcommittee, is not optimistic that the pro-reform rhetoric of Majority Leader Dole will be matched by any substantive action on the part of the Republican majority.

Postmortem: Recommended Modifications
in Future Lobby Reform Legislation

Lobby reform failed in the 103rd Congress, and its prospects for passage in the first session of the 104th Congress were not great. This leaves the complex relationship between organized interests and the federal government largely unregulated. Although there were some clear shortcomings in the legislation, the lobby reform package that was ironically lobbied to death in the 103rd Congress would have provided greater public disclosure of lobbyists and would have included regulation of lobbying activities directed at the executive branch.

Upon closer analysis, the disparate organized interests that derailed the lobby reform legislation are not as strange allies as one might think. There was, in fact, a clear common denominator among all of the grassroots groups that opposed the conference report—they were all nonprofits. Utilizing the largely fallacious argument regarding infringements on the rights of organization members in grassroots lobbying efforts, the nonprofit sector stood to suffer most significantly from many of the changes in the reform package unrelated to grassroots activities.

Remember that under current statutes, all nonprofit entities are regulated by the IRS, not the Congress. As such, they are limited in the amount of lobbying of Congress (including grassroots activities) they may conduct. The proposed legislation did not address the overall limits on lobbying by nonprofits, but it included executive branch activities, thereby having a chilling effect on the abilities of nonprofit organizations to lobby as they had under IRS regulations. More than one nonprofit leader has expressed "quiet delight" in the demise of lobby reform in the 103rd Congress.

Apart from this opposition, as well as the partisan Republican opposition driven by ideological and political considerations, Congress missed the opportunity to address two of the dominant techniques of organized influence in the 1990s: grassroots lobbying and coalition building.

Grassroots Lobbying

First, on the grassroots lobbying provision, the architects of the conference report should have been more pragmatic regarding their decision to adopt the stronger language of the House version. The adoption of such language should have been accompanied by a proactive educational effort, particularly in the Senate. Knowing that the House language would generate negative responses from the nonprofits, members of the Conference Committee should have sought out the nonprofit leaders and addressed the issues of grassroots regulation prior to releasing the conference report. In addition, committee members should have educated their colleagues regarding the potential difficulties with the conference language.

How quickly members of both houses forgot the deluge of mail earlier in 1994 from home schoolers, irate over two lines in the 960-page Elementary and Secondary Education Act. The entire education bill was held up when hundreds of thousands of home school advocates became alarmed by the omission, in two places, of the word "public" before the word "school." Congress had never intended to include home schooling in the certification process mentioned in the act; however the perceived threat to this organized constituency was sufficient to make virtually every member of Congress aware of its needs. Unfortunately, the response from most members and their staffs was "I hear you and I will protect you," rather than "you are not fully informed on this matter; let me try to explain the bill to you so you will understand our intent." [9]

If members of Congress are going to make the difficult policy decisions, then it is incumbent upon them to challenge their constituents on the basis of the real substance of the legislation, and not be whiplashed by an orchestrated constituency mobilization. These tactics are effective because members of Congress are not willing to take stands and challenge their constituents. At some point members of Congress ought to activate their educational role and give their constituent servant role a rest.

Thomas Jefferson once wrote, "I know of no safe depository of the ultimate powers of the society but the people themselves; and if we think them not enlightened enough to exercise their control with a wholesome discretion, the remedy is not to take it from them but to inform their discretion" (quoted in Fulbright 1979, 719). Woodrow Wilson went even further: "This informing function of Congress should be preferred to even its legislative function. Unless [Congress informs the citizenry] the country must remain in embarrassing, crippling ignorance of the very affairs which is most important that it should understand and direct" (quoted in Frantzich 1986, 6).

Many of the orchestrated grassroots campaigns that reach the halls of Congress give credence to the old adage that "a little knowledge is a dangerous thing." In this instance, despite the groundswell of grassroots opposition, the House version was the better choice. But it should not have been chosen by the conferees if the institutional will did not exist to uphold the bill in both chambers.

Coalition Activities

Regarding the conference report language on coalitions and coalition building, Section 103(2) states: "In the case of a coalition or association that employs or retains other persons to conduct lobbying activities, the client is (A) the coalition or association and not its individual members when the lobbying activities are conducted on behalf of its membership and financed by the coalition's or association's dues and assessments." It is further stipulated that individual members, when lobbying apart from the coalition, must also be registered as separate entities.

Later, in Section 104(B)(3), indirect reference to coalition building is made. This section stipulates that registration of the "client" (coalition) will include the "name, address, and principal place of business of any organization (coalition member), other than the client, that (A) contributes more than $5,000 toward the lobbying activities of the registrant in a semiannual period *and* (B) participates significantly in the planning, supervision, or control of such lobbying activities."

Even for the largest and most enduring coalitions, it is less than clear that these new reporting requirements would shed any additional light on the component organizations often veiled under well-meaning, high-minded rubrics. Coalitions such as the Consumers Foundation, the Coalition for Health Insurance Choices, and the National Wetlands Coalition, even under the proposed definitions, would not be identified with Sears, Woolworth's, and Walgreen's in the first instance, the Health Insurance Association of America in the second, and a group of oil drillers, land developers, and natural gas companies in the last (Shephard 1994, 2).

Two additional examples derived from the ongoing telecommunications debate demonstrate the weaknesses of the proposed legislation regarding the activities of coalitions. For coalitions that include member organizations, each supporting the coalition through dues, the coalition is the entity of record, not the constituent member organizations. During the ongoing debate over the multi-billion-dollar future of telecommunications in the United States, two coalitions have been heavily involved in lobbying activities, including grassroots efforts: the MFJ Task Force (named after the Modification of Final Judgment by federal Judge Harold Greene that resulted in the divestiture of AT&T) and the Competitive Long Distance Coalition (CLDC). The proposed act would provide the public with the following information: The MFJ Task Force receives lobbying representation from Epstein, Becker and Green, PC; Jeanne Campbell; Daniel Crane; and Wunder Diefenderfer Cannon and Thelan, with combined expenditures of $45,000 for 1994. Conversely, the Competitive Long Distance Coalition receives lobbying representation from Randall Harvey Erben; Raffaelli Spees Springer and Smith; O'Neill and Athy, PC; and Mintz Levin Cohn Ferris Grovsky and Popeo, with expenditures of $19,500.[10]

Aside from seriously underreporting expenses related to lobbying, given the campaigns being waged, one fails to learn that the MFJ Task Force is comprised of the regional Bell operating companies (RBOCs) and that the CLDC includes AT&T, Sprint, MCI, and 400 telecommunications companies.[11] The problem of identifying the constituent parts of a coalition was specifically addressed in the Senate, albeit unsatisfactorily. Senate staff relied on a First Amendment argument and cited *NAACP v. Alabama* (357 U.S. 449, 1958) as relevant case law. In this case the state of Alabama sought to gain access to individual names of NAACP members, having outlawed the organization in question. The Supreme Court, in denying the state access to NAACP membership lists, ruled: "It is beyond debate that freedom to engage in associations for the advancement of beliefs and ideas is an inseparable aspect of the 'liberty' assured by the Due Process Clause of the Fourteenth Amendment, which embraces freedom of speech." Clearly, information regarding organizations (not members) as component parts of a coalition poses no such constitutional invasion. A similar First Amendment argument was put forth by the nonprofits as it relates to identifying entities involved in grassroots mobilization efforts.

Caucuses

One final weakness lies in what is omitted from the Lobbying Disclosure Act of 1994. While broad attempts were made to regulate the influence of external interests, only a single mention was made in the entire lobby reform debate in the 103rd Congress regarding the growing number of internal interest groups on the Hill—caucuses. Today more than 140 caucuses exist in the U.S. Congress; in the 103rd Congress alone more than 20 caucuses were created. Interestingly, the creators of many of these new caucuses were veteran legislators. For example, Representatives Floyd D. Spence, R-S.C., and John P. Murtha, D-Pa., each with more than 20 years of service in the House, created the Congressional Defense Caucus in 1993. Members of Congress decry the influence of organized interests, yet an increasing number facilitate the life work of a wide variety of interests, many times right in their own offices. The caucuses provide internal representation to a vast array of economic, social, ethnic, and ideological interests. Only Rep. George Gekas provided some recognition of the special relationships that exist in Congress between members and the variety of organized interests represented through caucuses. In his motion to recommit the conference report with instructions, Representative Gekas asked that those working for the off-campus institutes and think-tanks of the sanctioned legislative service organizations (LSOs) be required to register as lobbyists. The elimination of (LSO) status for caucuses in the 104th Congress does not directly address the relationships alluded to by Representative Gekas, but it is an appropriate first step.

These caucus-member relationships are hardly of a pluralist nature. In these contexts, organized interests and elected representatives are singing from the same hymnal. These micro-corporatist relationships are becoming increasingly prevalent, and they are certainly not limited to congressional-interest group alliances. One may easily identify such relationships in the executive branch as well as those involving actors and interests in both branches. These relationships will become increasingly dominant in the years to come.

Recasting the Relationships between Organized Interests and Government

William Greider, in his recent book *Who Will Tell the People: The Betrayal of American Democracy,* labels the increasingly blurred relationship between the private sector and government as "deep lobbying" (Greider 1992, 43). The example of deep lobbying he presents is the Superfund Coalition. Following the creation of Superfund in 1986, major corporate entities (such as General Electric, Dow, Du Pont, Union Carbide, Monsanto, and AT&T), insurance interests (such as Aetna, Cigna, and Hartford), as well as several national environmental organizations came together to sponsor authoritative analyses of the Superfund implementation process and to recommend possible improvements. Eventually developing a close working relationship with the Environmental Protection Agency, the coalition achieved a level of prominence in the policy debate unmatched by other policy actors. Greider concludes: "It is another dimension of mock democracy—a system that has all the trappings of free and open political discourse but is shaped and guided at a very deep level by the resources of the most powerful interests" (Greider 1992, 43).

What appears to be "mock democracy" for Greider would be easily accepted, in Japan for example, as a valid component of government planning that incorporates the input of industry and other policy resources. On a wide variety of policy fronts, government officials and organized interests in the United States are beginning to understand the utility of public-private partnerships. In particular, the energy sector in the United States has forged close working relationships with Congress and the Clinton administration, especially when their interests coincide on foreign policy matters. When the interests of the U.S. government in dealing with Russia, as manifest in the ongoing Gore-Chernomrydin negotiations on oil and gas, coincide with the interests of major American oil and oil-related companies such as Texaco, Mobil, Enron, and McDermott, is it not mutually beneficial that these two policy actors in the international domain act in concert? If the answer is yes, then the next question, from a lobby reform perspective, is: who is lobbying whom? Future reforms should acknowledge the disintegration of the pluralist model that easily identifies the "we" and the "they" and concentrate on regulating the "us" in the relationships between government and organized interests in the next century.

At an even more basic level, however, the daily interactions that take place between lobbyists, members of Congress, and executive branch officials must be presented to the American public in an honest and forthright manner. The political demagoguery from officials of all political stripes, emanating from both ends of Pennsylvania Avenue as well as from the media, does little to inform the citizenry about the constant interactions between interest representatives and public officials.

Jonathan Rauch, in *Demosclerosis: The Silent Killer of American Government,* while presenting a rather negative view of the impact of lobbying on American society, makes an argument quite different from Greider's. Rather than asserting that the American political system is becoming an increasingly closed mock democracy, Rauch argues that the proliferation of organized interests has led to a hyperpluralistic policy-making process. This process is so jammed with interests that the American system of governance has the equivalent of hardening of the arteries (or demosclerosis). Within Rauch's argument is the kernel of truth that is clearly overlooked by the lobbying demagogues: "We have met the special interests, and they are us" (Rauch 1994, 12).

Those who wield the "special interest" sword in the battle over lobby reform are rarely quick to attach the names of specific organizations to their blanket indictments. Since the right to petition government for a redress of grievances is constitutionally protected, the responsibility for discerning the credibility of the messages delivered by organized interests lies not with those organized to petition government, but with the elected representatives and government officials. James Madison, in attempting to create an open system of political representation that would not restrict or inhibit organized interests (or factions), argued that structural or institutional safeguards as well as the collective responsibility of elected officials would be the cures to the "mischiefs of factions." In *Federalist* No. 10 Madison delineates the role of elected representatives:

> [By] the delegation of the government . . . to a small number of citizens elected by the rest . . . the effect is . . . to refine and enlarge the public views by passing them through the medium of a chosen body of citizens, whose wisdom may best discern the true interest of their country, and whose patriotism and love of justice will be least likely to sacrifice it to temporary and partial considerations. (*Federalist* 1788:82)

The real world relationships between lobbyists and government officials are largely symbiotic and are based on information sharing, but the ultimate arbiter of truth is the elected representative or executive branch official, to the degree that these officials are able to judge the credibility of the information provided. The late Jesse Unruh, political architect of the modern California legislature, argued that lobbyists "have influence in inverse ratio to legislative competence. . . . The information that a lobbyist presents may or may not be prejudiced in favor of his client, but if it is the only information the legislature has, no one can really be sure" (quoted in Muir 1982, 136). It is the informational relationship that should be more widely documented and incorporated into the lobby reform debate. Today these lobbyist-legislator interactions are more important than ever before, given recent cutbacks in committee staffs and the relative lack of Washington political experience of the majority of House members elected since 1990. To recast the famous words of Jesse Unruh: if information (rather than money) is the mother's milk of politics, then lobbyists are the nursemaids.

Notes

Author's Note: I would like to thank the following individuals for their insights into the lobby reform debate: Nan Aron and Carol Seifert of the Alliance for Justice; Bob Smucker of the Independent Sector; Brian Pallasch of the American Society of Association Executives; Wright Andrews, president, and Howard Marlowe, former president, of the American League of Lobbyists; Richard Sachs of the Congressional Research Service; Peter Levine on the Senate Governmental Affairs staff; Kathryn Hazeem on the House Judiciary staff; and the participants at the Conference on Congressional Change, where an earlier version of this chapter was presented. Special thanks to Rep. Curt Weldon, R-Pa., who allowed me, as an APSA Congressional Fellow in 1993-1994, to experience firsthand the real world of lobbying on the Hill.

1. Because the Lobbying Disclosure Act involved changes in the internal rules of the Senate, a supermajority of 67 votes would have been necessary to break the filibuster.

2. Section 1307 of P.L. 94-455, the 1976 lobby law, clarifies and expands lobbying by tax-exempt nonprofit organizations under Section 501 (c) (3) of the Internal Revenue Service Code. After 14 years of negotiations between the nonprofit sector and the IRS, new 1990 regulations further codified the lobbying rights of nonprofit organizations.

3. Government contractors are not the only ones whose lobbying is regulated. The lobbying activities of quasi-governmental entities, such as public utilities, are regulated by the Public Utility Holding Company Act of 1935.

4. One may recall that the elimination of the tax deductibility of lobbying expenses was proposed as a funding mechanism in various campaign finance reform proposals.

5. The nonprofit sector fought strongly against many of the provisions in early drafts of the legislation. In a letter to all members of Congress co-signed by Bob Smucker of the Independent Sector and Nan Aron, executive director of the Alliance for Justice, and more than 300 organizations, the nonprofit sector position was presented. High priority issues included leaving the nonprofit sector under IRS regulations (which was not included in either the Senate or House versions) and raising the reporting threshold from $2,500 to $5,000 for each six-month period (which was included in the Senate bill and incorporated

in the subsequent conference report). The higher threshold exempted many of the non-profits from being considered as full-time lobbying operations.

6. In 1994 Hamilton Fish retired, and Dan Glickman and Mike Synar were not re-elected to Congress.

7. The Free Speech Coalition includes a number of conservative and liberal public interest groups. In addition, it was funded by several for-profit direct marketing firms, including Richard Viguerie and Associates; Craver, Mathews Smith & Co.; Target Market Search, Inc.; and Moore Response Marketing Services.

8. In an effort to appease those opposed to the grassroots provision, Majority Leader George Mitchell, D-Maine, offered up a unanimous consent resolution that would have stricken the grass roots language from the bill. Senators Malcolm Wallop, R-Wyo., and Don Nickles, R-Okla., objected to the unanimous consent, thereby preventing consideration.

9. Such orchestrated mobilizations have legislative costs apart from skewing the policy debate. The home school campaign was so intense that the Capitol Hill switchboard was forced to shut down. House offices reportedly received more than 1,000 calls on average during a two-day period; staff response time, including mailings, amounted to several thousand staff-hours dealing with this constituency.

10. The organizations and lobbying costs are cited in reports to the Clerk of the House that were filed by the MFJ Task Force and the Competitive Long Distance Coalition. These reports are required under current legislative mandates.

11. Each of these coalitions has spawned even larger coalitions. The Alliance for Competitive Competition contains the RBOCs, the United States Telephone Association (USTA), and the Communications Workers of America (CWA), the major telecommunications union. The Unity Coalition includes the AT&T, Sprint, and MCI telecommunications companies and a vast array of manufacturing, long distance, and information services companies.

11

RENEWING CONGRESS:
A Report from the Front Lines

Thomas E. Mann

The dramatic Republican sweep of the 1994 midterm elections set in motion the most substantial shakeup of Capitol Hill in decades. After 40 consecutive years in the minority, a status that with only two exceptions (1947-1948 and 1953-1954) extended all the way back to 1930, House Republicans used their new majority to put in place far-reaching changes in party and House rules and practices. A congressional reform agenda that was widely pronounced dead at the end of the 103rd Congress sprang to life following the election returns. The pace and extent of change in the Senate lagged behind that of the House, not surprisingly given its recent experience with Republican control and its highly individualistic nature. But even the Senate was obliged to cut back its staff, pass the House measure that applied federal workplace laws to the Congress, and consider proposals for internal reform.

This surprising turn in the road to congressional reform put a very different light on the Renewing Congress Project, a joint undertaking of the American Enterprise Institute and the Brookings Institution. Norman Ornstein and I launched the project in early 1992 to assist a fledgling effort inside Congress to revise its organization and procedures. While there is ample precedent for the participation of congressional scholars in reform activities, both as staff members and as outside consultants, the Renewing Congress Project was unique in its form and in its ambition. Consequently, recounting our three-year experience with this effort may be of value.

Origins

Readers will readily recall the context in which this reform effort was launched. Congress was under siege, its legitimacy threatened by a public distemper toward politicians in general and toward the legislative branch in particular. A healthy skepticism that had long characterized public attitudes toward Congress had degenerated into corrosive cynicism. A populist critique of Congress—that its members were career politicians out of touch with ordinary Americans, consumed with maintaining their lavish perquisites of office, and inattentive to pressing national needs—gained widespread currency in the wake of public revelations about the House Bank and Post Office. In the public's mind, reform meant punishment:

limiting the terms members could serve, giving the president a line-item veto, reducing Congress's authority over fiscal policy through a balanced budget amendment, slashing congressional staff, and scaling back the perks and privileges of office.

Congress seemed hopelessly unprepared to respond to this critique. Its leaders were defensive and reactive, generally doing too little too late to quench the public appetite for punishment or to ward off new waves of Congress-bashing. What was lacking, unlike earlier periods of ambitious reform, was any countervailing view inside Congress as to what was broke and needed fixing. While individual members promoted their own pet reforms, there was little agreement within the majority party of either house on the appropriate focus of a reform agenda. Republicans in the House were inclined to embrace and amplify the public critique, since it served their larger objective of undermining confidence in an institution they had not controlled for four decades.

The Renewing Congress Project had its genesis in a meeting that Ornstein and I had with four members of Congress—Representatives Lee H. Hamilton and Bill Gradison and Senators David L. Boren and Pete V. Domenici—who were attempting to fill the reform agenda vacuum by creating a new Joint Committee on the Organization of Congress.[1] We discussed what difficulties they encountered in persuading the leadership and their colleagues to agree to this reform initiative and how an outside effort by congressional scholars might both increase external pressure on Congress to act favorably on the resolution and begin the research essential to effective diagnosis and prescription. The four co-sponsors agreed to prepare a letter requesting the two of us and our research institutes to initiate such an independent assessment, a letter which together with a strong personal endorsement by Hamilton allowed us to approach the Carnegie Corporation and eventually put together a consortium of eight foundations to underwrite our Renewing Congress Project.

While our project began in close association with the effort by Hamilton and his colleagues to create a 1946-style Joint Committee on the Organization of Congress, we understood that public discontent with Congress had little to do with its shortcomings of organization and procedure. Traumatic national events and mediocre economic performance had led to a general deterioration of trust in government. Struggles to grapple with huge budget deficits reinforced an image of gridlock. A growing ideological polarization between the parties, largely a result of changes in their coalitional bases, produced a much more confrontational stance in the House by the "permanent minority" and an ensuing partisanship that discredited the institution in the eyes of the public. And the wave of well-publicized scandals that rocked Capitol Hill in recent years deepened public distrust of the ethics of those elected to Congress.

Although the most serious problems confronting Congress were largely a result of outside forces, we believed the legislature could profit from a thoughtful self-examination and institutional renewal. The challenge was to channel the public hostility associated with the populist critique of Congress toward serving the republican needs of the institution. This entailed shifting the focus of reform from punitive to constructive measures and evaluating individual proposals within a broader conceptual framework that clarified the appropriate place of Congress in the American political system. Decisive steps by Congress to address institutional shortcomings might not satiate a rapacious public and press hell-bent on punishment, but they would begin a process of renewal that might eventually win back the respect if not affection of those members of the attentive public whose support constituted a bedrock of legitimacy.

Activities

The Renewing Congress Project was formally launched in the spring of 1992. An advisory committee was constituted and under its guidance an agenda of activities and reports identified.[2] Throughout the spring and summer of 1992, the project co-directors (Mann and Ornstein) met with current and former members of Congress and staff to get their views on reform. Roundtable discussions with members of the House and Senate were held, with transcripts available on a not-for-attribution basis. In June we held our first major conference, "What's Wrong With Congress?", where congressional scholars from around the country gathered to put the current reform efforts into a broader context and to identify those aspects of Congress most in need of reform. Papers were commissioned before and after the conference.[3] A working group on budget process reform was established. During this period we testified in support of the resolution to set up a new Joint Committee on the Organization of Congress and met informally with congressional leaders to urge its timely adoption. In August, with members desperate for some measure of reform with which to face their surly electorates, the resolution was finally adopted.

The major focus of the project throughout the late summer and fall of 1992 was on producing *Renewing Congress: A First Report* (Mann and Ornstein 1992). This report was aimed not at the Joint Committee, which was expected to begin its work in 1993, but rather at the House party caucuses whose organizational meetings were scheduled to be held several weeks after the election. Anticipating a large freshman class elected on a platform of cleaning up the mess in Congress, we thought it important that a comprehensive case for constructive reform be available as soon as the new members arrived in Washington. In addition, since most of the consequential reforms in recent decades were achieved through changes in party rules and practices, the organizational meeting of the House Democratic Caucus provided a great opportunity for a fast start on the reform agenda.

The recommendations in the *First Report* and the actions taken in response to them are summarized below. Here I simply note that the report, which was released at the National Press Club in a briefing covered by C-SPAN and reported by major news outlets, received substantial attention from members of Congress. It was used by several groups of members pursuing changes in party rules, including the Democratic Study Group Task Force on Reform and the freshman class of

1993. We actively promoted our recommendations in meetings with members and staff and in discussions with the press.

During this initial stage and throughout the project, we found a market in Congress and in the press for our analysis and recommendations. Members and staff on both sides of the aisle took our efforts seriously and engaged us in discussions and negotiations before and after the release of our reports. Conditions were ripe for the active engagement of congressional scholars in the reform process (Mann, Ornstein, and Pinkus 1993).

Once the 103rd Congress convened, we turned our attention to the work of the Joint Committee. In three hours of testimony before the Joint Committee on February 16, 1993, Ornstein and I discussed the range of issues facing its members and suggested a strategy of reform. We returned on April 20 to elaborate our ideas for committee reform, arguing that reducing assignments and consolidating committees and subcommittees were needed to reduce fragmentation and improve the quality of deliberation in Congress. A revision and extension of the testimony prepared for these two hearings was published as *Renewing Congress: A Second Report* (Mann and Ornstein 1993) and released to the public on June 21 at a briefing on Capitol Hill. This report also received considerable attention in Congress and in the press, and the co-directors pressed their recommendations in a variety of settings, including meetings with members and staff of the Joint Committee and a memorable session with House committee chairmen, during the summer and fall of 1993.

When the Joint Committee issued its final report in December, we reviewed its contents and prepared an analysis of its recommendations, which was released at a March 1, 1994, press briefing as *Renewing Congress: A Progress Report* (Mann and Ornstein 1994a). Specific suggestions were made for strengthening the measures approved by the Joint Committee. In the months that followed we used every available opportunity—testimony at congressional hearings, meetings with the leadership in both houses, and various public forums—to press the case for institutional reform.

During 1993 and 1994 the project worked to advance institutional reform on several other fronts. We met with Representatives Christopher Shays, R-Conn., and Dick Swett, D-N.H., to discuss how best to make Congress subject to the workplace laws it applies to others.[4] The idea for a congressional office of compliance, included in the Shays-Swett proposal, the Joint Committee recommendations, and the final legislation approved by Congress, came out of that meeting. We also continued to promote Oxford Union-style debates, which were finally inaugurated in the House on March 16, 1994. Finally, we assembled approximately 50 journalists, congressional specialists, and media and public opinion scholars to examine how media coverage shapes public attitudes toward and public understanding of Congress. The proceedings of that conference, together with a set of recommendations for the press and the Congress, were published as *Congress, the Press, and the Public* (Mann and Ornstein 1994b) in the fall of 1994.

Analysis and Recommendations

The recommendations proffered by the Renewing Congress Project flowed from a conception of Congress as a deliberative body whose primary challenge is to balance its representational and policy-making responsibilities. Congress must give voice to the full range of views that exist in our sprawling, diverse country as well as come to independent judgment on important issues of public policy. We took our cue from James Madison, who argued in *Federalist No. 10* for the need to "refine and enlarge the public views by passing them through the medium of a chosen body of citizens, whose wisdom may best discern the true interest of their country and whose patriotism and love of justice will be least likely to sacrifice it to temporary or partial considerations."

Madison and his colleagues explicitly rejected direct or plebiscitary forms of democracy that placed a premium on registering immediate public preferences and temporary majorities. Instead they opted for their own brand of deliberative democracy, in which separated institutions and ambitious politicians competing for shared powers produce wiser policy attentive to the broader public interest. The implications for Congress are clear. Where a genuine consensus exists in the country, or a least the makings of a durable majority sentiment to pursue a course of action, Congress should be structured to articulate, deliberate, and act upon that sentiment, enabling the voices of majorities to ring louder than the extremes. Where the public is divided, Congress should work to form a consensus rather than hardening those differences and perpetuating conflict and deadlock.

From this perspective the object of reform is not to punish Congress but to strengthen it, by taking steps to bolster its capacity to carry out the essential tasks outlined by the framers. A stronger Congress would give the majority the tools it needs to set an institutional agenda and to act on it, to express its collective voice when it can do so. And a stronger Congress would have a much improved deliberative capacity—an enhanced ability, in other words, to study and debate alternatives, to process and communicate information, both for considering legislation and, more broadly, for educating members and the public alike.

While we believed that the populist critique of Congress was ill informed and distorted and that its reform agenda (term limits, balanced budget amendment, line-item veto, and deep, across-the-board cuts in staff) would do much more harm than good, we also agreed that the contemporary Congress had serious problems that needed attending. These included:

• A pattern, especially prevalent in the Senate, of catering to the interests of individual members at the expense of collective responsibility.

• A frenetic schedule (of committee hearings and markups; floor votes; fund raising; meetings with constituents, lobbyists, and staff; and weekly trips back home) that crowds out reflection on public policy matters and meaningful deliberation among colleagues and encourages a hypersensitivity to constituent and interest group demands.

• Institutions for debate that put a premium on cheap shots and devalue discussions that could either develop agreements or help the public choose among competing positions.

• Weak coordination of committee activity and untimely floor action that detracts from the quality of the legislative product and diminishes the public's appreciation of it.

• An intense and destructive partisanship, especially in the House, born of the entrenched majority status of the House Democrats at that time, the frustration of Republicans, the legacy of battles between the executive and Congress, and the use of procedure and symbolism to embarrass the opposition in a quest for partisan advantage.

• Lax and self-serving management of congressional operations and support services and a process of campaign finance that together contributed to a crisis of legitimacy.

• The demise of any principled defense of Congress as the bedrock of American democracy, as an institution in which members have a shared stake, in spite of their different individual and partisan interests.

First Report

The first report of the Renewing Congress Project was designed to inform new and returning members of the 103rd Congress as they grappled with congressional reform questions in the organizing meetings of the House Democratic Caucus and Republican Conference. It offered a series of concrete recommendations to strengthen the ability of Congress to set an agenda and act upon it, increase the quality of deliberation and debate, improve the relations between the parties, reform the campaign finance system, and clean up the support system in Congress.

Setting and Executing an Agenda in Congress. The thrust of our recommendations was to strengthen the capacity and incentives of the majority party leadership to set legislative priorities, schedule timely action, and monitor implementation by committees. Specific proposals called for establishing a majority agenda committee, organizing the House before new members are sworn in, ending the automatic renomination of committee chairs, and giving the Speaker the power to declare a chairmanship vacant at any time during a Congress.

Improving the Quality of Deliberation and Debate. Here our recommendations focused on the committee system, scheduling, and floor debate. We urged the House to move toward a system of committees of roughly equal breadth and workload. At the same time the House should try to reduce the size of committees and the number of subcommittees, limit further the number of committee and subcommittee assignments each member may hold, phase out the select committees, encourage some rotation of committee membership, greatly restrict proxy voting, limit multiple referrals, and strengthen the Speaker's ability to improve the conference committee process. Proposals were also offered to provide more control and predictability in legislative scheduling and to create Oxford Union-style debates in the chambers.

Enhancing the Role of the Minority. Efforts to strengthen the ability of the majority party to set an agenda and act upon it in a timely manner should be balanced by steps to ensure that the minority party has the resources and opportunities it needs to play its appropriate role. At a minimum this requires one-third minority staffing on all House committees and guaranteeing the minority's right to a motion to recommit with instructions.

Reforming Campaign Finance. No effort to reform Congress and revitalize its role in national policy making can possibly succeed without a fundamental restructuring of the campaign finance system. The present system puts challengers at a distinct disadvantage, relies excessively on "interested money," and forces politicians to devote too much time and attention to fund raising. We offered a series of principles and guidelines for crafting a new system that would distribute resources more equitably among candidates, alter the mix of contributions to candidates, and more promptly and accurately disclose all campaign contributions.

Cleaning Up the Support System. Public perceptions of bloated congressional staffs, lavish perks and privileges, and exemptions from the laws that apply to everyone else are responsible for much of the hostility toward Congress. Although often the criticism is based on misinformation, constructive steps can be taken to cut, redeploy, and professionalize staff; prevent abuses of the franking privilege; and apply federal workplace laws to Congress.

Second Report

The second report released by the Renewing Congress Project extended the analysis to the broad set of institutional issues under review by the Joint Committee on the Organization of Congress. Unlike the first report, it dealt explicitly with the Senate as well as with the relations between Congress and the executive, the courts, and the public. But our perspective on strengthening Congress rather than punishing it, on judging the institution by the standards developed by the framers, remained the same. Here, too, our recommendations to create more opportunities for genuine deliberation, encourage bargaining, focus attention on major, long-term problems, and upgrade the professionalism within Congress were designed to strengthen its comparative advantages.

Ethics and the Public Reputation of Congress. Even though Congress's crisis of legitimacy is much more than a public relations problem, effective communication of the role of Congress in our constitutional system must be part of the solution. Improving public understanding of Congress requires changes in the way leaders and rank-and-file members explain their institution to the public as well as changes in the pattern of media coverage of Congress. Specific recommendations (elaborated in Mann and Ornstein 1994b) include restructuring floor debate, adding commentary and interviews to the C-SPAN coverage of the chambers, creating an institutional voice for Congress, and enriching the experience of citizens who visit the Capitol. As part of its effort to restore its institutional integrity, Congress should reform its ethics process to involve private citizens whose experience and knowledge about professional ethics and the workings of Congress qualify them to decide whether charges of unethical conduct have merit and should be brought to the Congress for resolution. In addition, as recommended in the first report, Congress should reform its campaign finance system and create an independent agency within the legislative branch, an Office of Congressional Compliance, to ensure that Congress lives by the workplace laws it writes for others.

The Committee System. Proposals for committee reform should be judged in terms of how well they advance the institution's broader responsibilities: representation, deliberation, and collective decision making. Our report developed a strategy of committee reform consisting of four major elements. First, the sizes of committees, the total number of slots for committees and subcommittees, and the assignments held by each member should be reduced. Second, the number of committees should be reduced, and committee jurisdictions consolidated and partially realigned to highlight important emerging policy areas and to create a better balance in the workload and attractiveness among standing committees. Third, coordinating mechanisms to deal with pressing national policy problems that inherently cut across committee boundaries should be strengthened. Fourth, new committee procedures should be devised to increase attendance, to improve the quality of information gathering and deliberation, and to strike an appropriate balance between majority and minority rights and responsibilities. As part of that effort, the allocation of staff resources among and within committees should be rationalized and centralized.

The Budget Process. Frustrated by the decade-long persistence of huge deficits and the complexity and duplication of the three-ring budget, authorization, and appropriations process, many critics have increasingly turned to radical proposals to simplify the process or to shift substantial powers from Congress to the president. We believe most of these proposals, many of which enjoy broad popular support, could seriously harm the institution and the policy-making process. Consequently, we have recommended a series of small changes to the existing system, built on the experience of the last several years under Gramm-Rudman and the Budget Enforcement Act, rather than a wholesale rebuilding of it. These include incentives for the president to submit honest proposals for reducing the deficit and for Congress to respond to them in a timely and explicit fashion (for example, expedited rescission authority, using the sequester as a fallback position rather than a threat, and independent scorekeeping rules); steps to reduce the tensions between authorizing and appropriating committees; and measures to simplify the process, including multiyear authorizations and biennial budget resolutions.

Floor Procedures. Each chamber of the Congress has a comparative advantage. The House, a majoritarian institution, puts a premium on the timely, orderly consideration and disposition of legislative business. The Senate, which likes to think of itself as the world's greatest deliberative body, favors debate and deliberation over resolution of questions put before it. Unfortunately, in recent years each chamber has moved beyond its comparative advantage to the point at which important values are being sacrificed. Under the Democrats, House leaders used restrictive rules to routinely deny the minority an opportunity to amend legislation on the floor. The Senate, on the other hand, fell prey to the capricious use of holds by individual senators to delay consideration of legislation and the routine use of filibusters to frustrate majority rule.

In the House we recommended that the minority be guaranteed the right to offer a motion to recommit with instructions, if offered by the minority leader, and that the majority allow other avenues for amendments to be offered as part of the normal amending process. In the Senate steps should be taken to sharply restrict the use of holds by individual senators (for example, by limiting debate on the motion to proceed) and to require public identification of any senator placing a hold on a nomination or piece of legislation. In addition, the Senate should return the filibuster to its classic model—with senators required to engage in continuous debate, day and night, while all other business gets put on hold; the Senate should also consider adopting a sliding scale for cloture votes: 60 votes to cut off debate initially; 55 votes after a week of debate; and a simple majority two weeks after the initial cloture vote.

Staffing. In the face of persistent demands for drastic, across-the-board cuts in congressional staff—based on the erroneous belief that staff growth continued unabated through the past decade—we called for a modest downsizing. This would be achieved by consolidating the committee system, reforming administrative systems and legislative services, and improving management of personal offices.

Accomplishments in the 103rd Congress

Our effort—and more importantly the larger reform initiative—produced a meager harvest in the 103rd Congress. When weighed against the high expectations, relatively little was accomplished. The clear verdict of the public was that the reform movement launched by the 1992 elections had flopped.

The Renewing Congress Project was not without some small victories. A number of recommendations in our first report were embraced by the House Democratic Caucus: formation of a Speaker's Working Group on policy development, reduction in the number of subcommittees, stricter limits on committee and subcommittee assignments, new measures designed to make committee chairmen accountable to the Caucus, and early organization of the House. Unfortunately, then Speaker Thomas S. Foley made little use of the new Caucus group designed to help set priorities, schedule legislation, and monitor implementation of the majority agenda. And the other changes were widely viewed as inadequate, especially by many freshmen Democrats who had campaigned on a platform of congressional reform.

In a move bolstered by a recommendation in our first report, the full House surprised the leadership of both parties by eliminating all select committees. And the bipartisan House leadership eventually began to experiment with our proposal for Oxford Union-style debates.

Other recommendations were included in legislative proposals but failed to be enacted into law. For example, the Congressional Accountability Act sponsored by Representatives Chris Shays and Dick Swett (which incorporated our idea for implementation within the legislative branch) was not scheduled for House floor debate until late 1994 and fell victim to an end-of-session stall in the Senate. In addition, the final recommendations of the Joint Committee on the Organization of Congress, which echoed many of our recommendations, never saw the light of day during the 103rd Congress. (See Chapter 5.)

Although the Renewing Congress Project had been a fascinating and rewarding personal experience for Ornstein and myself, I was forced to conclude at the end of the 103rd Congress that we failed in our larger objectives. Congressional leaders were never persuaded that early, decisive action on internal reforms, including campaign finance, would reduce the public's appetite for more punitive measures. Speaker Foley and other leaders thought this strategy would produce minimal benefits at the very high cost of exacerbating divisions among Democratic members at a time when unity within the majority party was essential to the success of President Bill Clinton's legislative program. The appetite for reform among Democratic members was minimal. Some felt the issues being addressed by the Joint Committee were largely irrelevant to the public standing of Congress and to its ability to operate effectively; they preferred acting through the Democratic Caucus. They also were deeply suspicious of bipartisan approaches to reform in such a highly charged partisan atmosphere. Others, including senior legislators and many members of the Black Caucus, felt personally threatened by possible committee reforms. The legacy of the Bolling Committee weighed heavily on Foley and other members who had lived through that largely unsuccessful effort in the early 1970s to update committee jurisdictions. Many Democrats preferred venting their anger at renegade party members, the Senate, and the press to building a coalition on behalf of a broad-based reform package.

It is by no means certain that an aggressive campaign by the president and Democratic congressional leadership early in the 103rd Congress to adopt campaign finance, lobbying, and internal reform would have been successful—in winning approval for the measures in both houses and in curbing public demands for more punitive measures. Formidable obstacles within the Congress made passage of serious measures doubtful; and the public anger at Congress was driven by powerful forces not easily diminished by procedural changes. But surely the failure to act reinforced the populist critique of Congress and fueled public demands for measures (like term limits) that would cut the institution and its entrenched and self-serving members back to size. Reform and renewal of Congress would have to await a change in party control.

The 1994 Elections and the New Market for Reform

That change in party control of Congress set in motion a series of changes in Washington that were unimaginable during the 103rd Congress. The market for congressional reform was transformed by the freshness of the new majority, the high proportion of junior members in the Republican Conference, and commitments made in the "Contract with America."

From our perspective, the change in party control of the House constituted the most significant element of institutional renewal. The public perception of change, intensified by the extraordinary media coverage given to Speaker Newt Gingrich of Georgia and his new Republican majority, provided much-needed breathing room for an institution under siege. And for the first time in decades, Republicans had a clear stake in the institution, promising a cease-fire in the war being waged against Congress from within.

The organizational and procedural changes adopted in 1995 at the beginning of the 104th Congress were in several important respects consistent with the general thrust of the Renewing Congress recommendations. The first piece of legislation considered and approved by the new Republican Congress was the Congressional Accountability Act, which applied federal labor laws to Congress and established an Office of Compliance within the legislative branch to implement them.

Even earlier, House Republicans moved to centralize authority in the Speaker, thereby improving their ability to set an agenda and act upon it in a timely fashion. This was accomplished partly through the Republican Conference, by reconstituting the committee on committees and giving the Speaker substantially more control over it. Gingrich acted quickly and decisively on this new authority by personally choosing the individuals to be nominated as committee chairmen. He skipped over the most senior Republican on three committees. This sent a clear signal that chairmen would be expected to be responsive to the party leadership. Gingrich also took an active role in restructuring subcommittees and designating their chairmen, and he formed leadership teams to closely monitor the implementation of the "Contract with America."

Gingrich's power was further enhanced through changes in House rules—term limits on committee chairmen, elimination of simultaneous referral of legislation to more than one committee, a restructured administrative system, and the replacement of the House Administration Committee with a leadership-appointed Committee on House Oversight. In the case of the latter two changes, both of which we supported, it remains to be seen whether this new leadership authority will be used to professionalize the administration of the House or to install a Republican patronage system.

Another set of rules changes, designed to improve the quality of deliberation in the House, closely mirrors our recommendations. These include strict limits on committee and subcommittee assignments, the elimination of three standing committees, a reduction in the number of subcommittees, and a modest shift of jurisdiction out of the Commerce Committee. In some cases the committee changes went well beyond our proposals: proxy voting in committees was eliminated rather than restricted (which is already proving problematic for Republican chairmen); committee staff were reduced by one-third, largely across-the-board, instead of the more modest, targeted reductions we suggested. In other cases the rules changes were less ambitious than we had hoped: the Small Business and Veterans' Affairs Committees, representing narrow constituencies important to the Republican Party, were retained; in the face of intense opposition from Republican members and outside interests, other proposals for jurisdictional realignment among committees were shelved.

However much we welcome these moves to centralize power in the party leadership and consolidate the committee system, we are wary of other changes embraced by the new Republican majority that do little to enhance Congress's capacity for deliberation. The requirement that a three-fifths majority pass any increase in income-tax rates enshrines a current policy preference in the rules and sets an unfortunate supermajority precedent in a majoritarian institution. Changes designed to make the House more open and accessible to citizens, while for the most part individually unobjectionable, are likely to exacerbate the tendency of the contemporary Congress to be hypersensitive to outside pressure. Most importantly, the new Republican majority, with its distinctive populist edge, remains at least nominally committed to term limits, a balanced budget amendment, and a line-item veto—punitive measures that if adopted are almost certain to weaken Congress.

The reform possibilities created by the 1994 elections have yet to be fully exploited. The Senate, hoping to match the ambition of the House, is moving to adopt a number of the recommendations of the Joint Committee on the Organization of Congress. On the crucial matter of unlimited debate, however, the Senate seems unlikely to rein in holds and filibusters. The full Congress has before it a number of difficult reform issues, including campaign finance, lobbying, the ethics process, personal office staffing, and the frank.

From the perspective of our Renewing Congress Project, the biggest challenge is helping Congress maintain its capacity for deliberation in an increasingly plebiscitary world. Although we take satisfaction from the substantial achievements of this round of congressional reform and are heartened by the openness of the system to contributions by congressional scholars, pressures to bypass Congress and deliberative democracy will intensify as the communications revolution proceeds apace. Until citizens understand the role for Congress designed by the framers, they will remain more disposed to punish Congress than to strengthen it. Improving public understanding of Congress may well be the most critical task facing those of us working toward genuine renewal of the first branch of government.

Notes

1. Bill Gradison resigned from the House in 1993. David Boren resigned from the Senate in 1994.

2. The members of the Advisory Committee were Richard F. Fenno, Jr., Charles O. Jones, Nelson W. Polsby, Cokie Roberts, and Catherine E. Rudder.

3. Many colleagues made important substantive contributions to the project. In addition to members of the Advisory Committee, we relied heavily on Matt Pinkus, Joe White, Robert Katzmann, Steven Smith, Roger Davidson, and Lawrence Hansen in drafting our two major reports. A listing of the work products of the Renewing Congress Project, including published materials, congressional testimony, and unpublished papers and documents, is available from the Governmental Studies Program, Brookings Institution.

4. Dick Swett was defeated for reelection in 1994.

12

WIELDING THE NEW BROOM: What It Swept Away, What It Left in Place

Roger H. Davidson

Already the 1994 elections are regarded as a turning point in American politics. Commentators quickly employed such terms as "earthquake" and "revolution" to dramatize what had happened. Scholars, no less intrigued but slower to pass judgment, debate whether a partisan realignment has occurred or is in progress.

That we are passing a major political milestone cannot be denied. The preceding chapters attest to the significance of the 1994 elections and their aftermath. The party fortunes of nearly two generations were upended; the public policy agenda has been transformed, and along with it the institution of Congress. Issues that had been kept hidden or subordinated suddenly came tumbling from the closet: downsizing the federal establishment, devolution of power to states and localities, welfare reform, budget stringency, and a regulatory ceasefire. Facing a struggling presidency, the resurgent Republicans on Capitol Hill confidently took command over policy initiation, media attention, and public expectations. Inside Congress, party leaders flexed their muscles, activity levels soared, and innovative procedures were explored and tested. Most notably, a House Speakership stronger than any seen in nearly a century captured the imagination and attention of the pundits and public alike.

What shall we conclude about the events we have witnessed: the popular unrest of the 1990s and the partisan turnover of 1994? This is no simple task. It is far easier to assess past events than to understand developments that are still unfolding. As the distinguished journalist Walter Lippman once remarked about the Russian Revolution, "The hardest thing to report is chaos, even if it is evolving chaos." Still, the evidence brought together in this volume suggests several important conclusons about the so-called earthquake of 1994.

Change and Continuity

Despite the publicity surrounding the 1994 vote itself, we are unquestionably faced with something that spans more than a single election. As the chapters in this book make clear, Congress has undergone a period of upheaval that intensified throughout the 1980s and reached crisis stage by the early 1990s. Readers of these essays are by now very familiar with the ways in which this crisis revealed itself on Capitol Hill: among them, variable leadership, dysfunctional committees, partisan strife, interchamber tensions, increasingly redundant procedures, and scandals both large and small—all played out against a melancholy backdrop of public distrust and scorn. Historically, this era rivals other such periods of political upheaval and change: the Progressive uprisings around 1910, the post-World War II turnover and reorganization of the mid-1940s, and the liberal reformism associated with the 1974 "Watergate" elections but spanning a much wider time frame.

Institutional attributes and trends demonstrate impressive continuity, even during periods of outward upheaval. The 1994 "earthquake," if it can be called that, was no isolated event but part of an extended period of tremors and aftershocks. (The geophysical metaphor is not inapt: surface events are only the palpable manifestations of long-term, underlying tectonic movements.) The reinvigorated House Speakership owed much to the personality and cohesive cohorts of Georgia Republican Newt Gingrich, but, as Barbara Sinclair reminds us, today's strong Speakership actually dates from the 1970s, when Democratic reformers fought to counteract the conservative "old bulls" who controlled many of the committees. Nor were the Republican plans for reforming Congress concocted overnight; they were incubated mainly within the House Republican Conference during a decade-long partisan struggle against an entrenched, sometimes overbearing Democratic majority. Even the celebrated "Contract with America" was a platform culled from the conservatives' accumulated wish-list, much of which had been bottled up in committees under Democratic rule. And although the duration of this present reform era cannot be known, it does not seem to have run its course. Nearly every essay in this volume attests to the continuity and connectedness of these events—past, present, and impending.

The stability of our governmental institutions is a function of constitutional design and historical precedent. Separated branches of government, including the bicameral legislature, rarely experience change at precisely the same moment or at exactly the same rate. Diverse constituencies, staggered elections, and overlapping terms of office generate inertia as well as responsiveness. So do long-standing internal arrangements, which on Capitol Hill include partisan leadership hierarchies, division of labor through the committee system, and norms of reciprocity among individuals and between chambers. Such attributes cannot halt change, but at the very least they absorb and cushion it.

Continuity pervades even when an institution changes in significant ways. Although the pace of change accelerated in the early 1990s, Congress—like all living institutions—shifts and adapts all the time. The 1993 Joint Committee on the Organization of Congress, only the third such joint effort (the others convened in 1945 and 1965), built upon a rich post-World War II history of congressional self-examination and structural and procedural adjustment, most of it incremental and hardly noticed by outsiders. Much of the territory traversed by the 1993 panel, as participants C. Lawrence Evans and Walter J. Oleszek explain, had already been mapped out by 1970s reformers, especially in the House and Senate committee realignment efforts (of 1973-1974 and 1976-1977, respectively). Although initially judged a failure because few of its recommendations were acted upon, the 1993 Joint Committee left two invaluable legacies. First, its hearings and reports provided a detailed historical record of Congress's operational characteristics and defects. Second, it served as a forum for drafting, debating, and revising a series of reform proposals that could be achieved once the votes became available to pass them. Accordingly, the House Republicans who had served on the Joint Committee drafted the relevant portions of the "Contract with America" and subsequently provided specific language to be inserted into Republican Conference or House rules.

Congressional committees, examined by reform panels in the 1970s and becoming increasingly dysfunctional in the 1980s, were naturally targeted by reformers of the 1990s. Committee reform was a core theme of the Joint Committee's hearings, studies, and reports; members and staff alike named it the Hill's most urgent issue. As a result both chambers, especially the House of Representatives, overhauled their committee systems. Although the 103rd Congress rejected most reorganization proposals, including those from the Joint Committee, several nontrivial innovations were adopted by the House: it reduced subcommittees and members' assignments, axed four nonlegislative select committees, and permitted the public naming of discharge petition signers (see Chapter 3). The new House majority continued the reform process in the 104th Congress, eliminating three committees, dropping more subcommittees and members' assignments, and altering certain procedures. (For instance, proxy voting and "rolling quorums" were forbidden wholesale.) But because of the same forces that had long stymied reform under Democratic rule, these Republicans shrank from more thoroughgoing revision, such as realignment of committee jurisdictions. Over on the opposite side of the Capitol, senators took steps to trim committee spending and limit subcommittees but resisted major structural reforms or staff reductions.

House and Senate floor procedures likewise exhibit few major departures but numerous incremental adjustments. As described by Sarah A. Binder and Steven S. Smith, the two chambers had settled into distinctive but divergent patterns in the postreform era. Always a haven for minority views, the Senate is characterized by extremely lax floor rules that seem virtually impossible to overturn. In contrast, majority party rule dominates House floor proceedings so completely as to stifle legitimate albeit time-consuming debate and amending activity—not only by the minority party, but by minority factions within the ruling party. Although the 104th Congress brought many changes, these left untouched the divergent biases underlying the two chambers' procedures. The Republicans, in fact, strengthened the House's majoritarian character (perhaps to excess); the Senate continued its individualistic (and seemingly irreversible) ways.

What changed was the identity of those favored or disadvantaged by the rules of the respective chambers. In the Senate it had been Majority Leader George J. Mitchell, D-Maine, who in 1993 proposed modest restrictions on filibusters, whereas under GOP rule complaints came most often from the more militant supporters of the majority party's agenda—especially younger conservatives who had "graduated" from the more partisan House. Over on the House side the triumphant Republicans forgot most (though not all) of their bitterest grievances against majority rules, whereas the Democrats, unused to minority status, loudly protested what they now considered heavy-handed exploitation of those rules.

Congress's modern-day obsession with budgetary issues has spawned a veritable museum of novel structures and procedures. Yet ever since the new era began with the Congressional Budget and Impoundment Control Act of 1974, budgetary politics has involved a recurrent quest for procedural solutions to substantive policy problems (see Chapter 8). These procedural solutions—from the 1974 act through Gramm-Rudman-Hollings I and II (1985 and 1987), the Budget Enforcement Act of 1990, and the Omnibus Budget Reconciliation Act of 1993—have had only limited success. All have aided members in avoiding individual blame for budget decisions; all have encouraged accounting tricks to magnify reported savings and hide real costs. Three long-term trends have continued: (1) toward a zero-sum game that pits budgetary commitments against one another and tends to favor existing programs over new ones; (2) toward centralized, top-down controls designed to limit deliberations and discourage interventions; and (3) toward greater complexity—a system now accessible mainly to budget-making specialists.

Continuity also marks two seemingly urgent issues of political ethics: campaign finance and lobby reform. As for campaign funding, no issue better exemplifies the venerable maxim that "where you stand depends on where you sit." Whether Republican or Democrat, whether a senator or representative, one's stance on these questions can be predicted from one's sources of funding. The 1994 elections, Candice J. Nelson contends, may actually diminish the likelihood of new campaign finance legislation in the short run. Traditionally successful in overall partisan fund raising, the now-majority Republicans will be in no hurry to rein in political action committees: they are set for a bonanza from PACs, which in the past favored incumbent Democrats. In any case Republicans would prefer to postpone campaign reform to win a better deal from a hoped-for GOP president. Meanwhile, Bill Clinton's veto pen protects Democrats from any punitive measures concocted by congressional Republicans. Nor will such an impasse necessarily be unpopular. Nelson suggests that, contrary to the assumptions of many politicians and analysts, the public really cares very little about the issue. So the long-term stalemate surrounding campaign funding shows little sign of ending.

Even more than campaign finance, the issue of lobbying regulation is insulated against fundamental change. Here the major constraint is no mundane matter of political interests, but nothing less than the cherished First Amendment guarantees of free speech, assembly, and petition. Two growing trends in contemporary lobbying, as described by Ronald G. Shaiko, exacerbate the problems of regulating lobbying activities. One is the rise of grassroots lobbying, in which interest groups supplement their face-to-face contacts with lawmakers by mobilizing their constituencies through internal communications and the mass media—processes explicitly protected by the First Amendment. Even such seemingly innocent proposals as disclosure of grassroots lobbyists can ignite fierce opposition, as reformers discovered. The second trend is the practice of building complex coalitions of groups on particular issues. How can all the constituent groups be identified, and their contributions tallied? The common element of both trends is the intermingling of lobbyists, group members, and sympathetic citizens. Lobbying, in other words, is a matter of "us," not just "we versus they." Under such circumstances, lobbying "reform" is an elusive goal indeed.

The Gains and Losses of Change

Redeeming its promises of the "Contract with America," the new Republican regime not only dramatically changed structures and procedures, but also altered the substantive policy agenda and accelerated the pace of legislative action. This impressive transformation was brought about by a vigorous party leadership, a willingness on the part of rank-and-file members to be led, and a distinctive policy agenda itemized in the Contract. The House led the way, but the Senate was not unaffected.

The Republican takeover was on balance a healthy occurrence. (This statement is made from an institutional perspective, not necessarily a partisan one.) The Democrats' unprecedented 40-year reign over the House of Representatives had fostered a certain arrogance of power that clung to outmoded arrangements and disdained the minority party's concerns. (For a variety of reasons, the disparities of power were never as severe in the Senate.) Committees and subcommittees were too numerous and too large; their jurisdictions were outdated and overlapping. Committee staffs had become bloated. Administrative structures were disorganized and wasteful. Procedures governing House floor debate were too restrictive. The Republicans' new broom swept away many (but by no means all) of these cobwebs.

The 104th Congress was fast out of the starting gate, breaking all productivity records for the previous 50 years or more. It spent more time on the job, held more hearings and markups, and produced more legislation than at any time since the fabled first 100 days of the New Deal Congress in 1933. As Table 12-1 shows, this Congress far outdistanced its predecessors by whatever measures one chooses—days and hours in session, committee meetings, floor votes, and measures reported or passed. Watching the legislative process was no longer like watching sausage being made, as the old adage had it. Now it was like watching Charlie Chaplin frantically catching cream pies off a high-speed conveyor belt.

The scope and speed of lawmaking during this period were indeed unprecedented. Committees reported, and the House debated, a host of far-reaching measures—among others, congressional reform, line-item veto, restrictions on unfunded mandates, tort reforms, cuts in federal programs, restrictions on United Nations command of U.S. troops, private property rights, and constitutional amendments requiring term limits and a balanced budget. The slower Senate hastened to consider selected parts of the Contract—passing restrictions on unfunded mandates and a version of the line-item veto, although rejecting the Balanced Budget Amendment by a single vote.

Table 12-1   House Activity During the First 100 Days,
97th–104th Congresses, First Sessions, 1981–1995

Measure of House Activity	Average 97th–102nd (1981–1991)	103rd (1993)	104th (1995)
Hours in session	128.6	208	531
Days in session	42	39	58
Measures reported	38	51	101
Measures passed	81	91	124
Number of votes	43.5	135	302

Source: Compilation by Faye M. Bullock, Congressional Research Service.

The breakneck speed of lawmaking was not accomplished without serious institutional costs, especially in the House. Powerful leadership and efficient scheduling, laudable goals in the abstract, were achieved at the expense of thorough committee hearings, detailed markup sessions, or even adequate floor debate. Hearings were abbreviated and in some cases dispensed with altogether. Markups were often chaotic races against the clock. House Democrats predictably complained that their rights were being trampled in the haste to gain action on the Contract items. On several occasions, committee meetings erupted into combat after the majority invoked procedural shortcuts in order to hasten action. Harsh words were exchanged in several committees, to the detriment of long-term working relationships. All in all, the already weakened system of standing committees was subjected to further indignities.

Haste made waste in substantive matters as well. Novel enactments were insufficiently researched and carelessly drafted. Committee products were rewritten in the Rules Committee and even on the House floor. The architects of restructuring the federal school lunch program were embarrassed at one point to discover they had overlooked a huge category of beneficiaries—children of employees stationed at military bases. Other challenges (for example, rewriting tort liability law) were simply so intricate that they defied the capacity of lawmakers to resolve the issues in the time available. Committee expertise and deliberation had been sacrificed to the goal of quick disposition of key Contract measures.

The experience of the 104th Congress illustrated the costs as well as the benefits of reform. First, insurgents risk overreacting to combat the old regime's defects. In this case, the long-term trend toward party direction was accelerated to override the seeming slowness and unresponsiveness of the standing committees. But the swing to top-down partisan management may have proved too severe: in order to meet strict deadlines for floor debates, committees had to short-circuit their procedures and subordinate their expertise and command of the details of legislation. On top of this, some of the reforms had unexpected effects—for example, stricter rules regarding committee voting (no proxies or "rolling quorums" allowed) hampered committee leaders in obtaining timely votes on Contract items.

The victorious Republicans, interestingly, borrowed from presidential rhetoric—the 100 days—to focus their efforts in the early weeks of 1995. It was as if GOP strategists had heeded the advice normally given to incoming presidents to "hit the ground running." But transporting such metaphors from the Oval Office to the committee rooms of Capitol Hill was probably a mistake. Presidents are urged to seize the legislative initiative in order to propose an action agenda and to focus public and congressional attention on a limited number of priority issues. But writing laws to address those issues takes far more time. Detailed provisions must be drafted and their effects upon diverse constituencies weighed. It is this deliberative process for which congressional committees are especially well suited—a process that was shortchanged in the push to show quick results.

Turnover, The Old-Fashioned Way

Aside from the partisan shift, the sheer influx of new members is the most potent legacy of the 1994 elections. When the new Congress convened in January 1995, more than half the representatives and nearly a third of the senators had arrived in the 1990s. Back-to-back electoral turnovers of 25 and 20 percent made the House significantly younger and more junior than it was when the 1990s begun. This followed an interlude of relatively low turnover (1984 through 1990) that brought only 162 newcomers to the House—an average of 9 percent per election (compared with a normal rate of 15 percent or more). The Senate, of course, changes more slowly, but its turnover rates in the 1990s were quite respectable. Future historians will surely regard the 1990s as a notable example of a generational changing of the guard on Capitol Hill comparable to the arrival of New Dealers in the early 1930s and of World War II veterans in the late 1940s.

Perhaps the greatest public service performed by the 1994 voters was to mute the hue and cry for mandated term limits. The term-limits movement, to be sure, resonates with an angry and disaffected citizenry. When the House took up the issue in March 1995, the public favored a constitutional amendment limiting members' terms, 72 percent to 24 percent.[1] But the drive for term limits is far from being an authentic grassroots movement.

Primarily organized and funded by a national organization based in the nation's capital, the term-limits effort was conceived by its originators as a weapon of partisan warfare whose central purpose was to dislodge the seemingly permanent Democratic majorities on Capitol Hill. Reasoning that senators and representatives (a majority of whom were Democrats) had exploited the benefits of incumbency to perpetuate themselves in office, conservative strategists seized upon term limits as a way of forcing members to retire and giving challengers (a majority of whom were Republicans) a better shot at winning the open-seat contests that would result. Although the logic of their argument was open to question, there is little doubt that the movement's leaders viewed term limits as a way to smash the "Democratic establishment." Portraying incumbents as out-of-touch, privileged, and self-perpetuating was a coded method of denouncing the Democrats' strangle-hold control of Congress. Such rhetoric, although built upon weak empirical evidence, was well tailored for a restless electorate skeptical of both major parties and probably resistent to more blatant partisan attacks.

The 1994 elections undermined the partisan appeal of term limits. As standard bearers for an ascendant majority party, Republican officeholders now reaped the very same advantages of incumbency that once flowed disproportionately to Democrats—not only the perquisites of office, but the attention of the media and the largesse of political action committees. As it turned out, Republicans were badly divided on the question, despite its prominence in the celebrated Contract. When it reached the House floor on March 30, 1995, a proposed constitutional amendment limiting all members to 12 years of service gained a 227-204 margin but fell far short of the needed two-thirds.[2] Many eminent Republicans, no less than their Democratic counterparts, found little to like about term limits. And although many junior members had vowed not only to support term limits but to retire voluntarily after a few years, who knows how many will willingly do so when the time comes? Even GOP Conference chairman John A. Boehner, who bowed to constituents' views and voted for term limits, conceded they "are not needed or necessary. I feel that voters have the opportunity to limit the careers of their representatives every two years when they cast their votes in November" (Sheffner 1995, 22).

Indeed, the 1994 outcome validates the healthy effects of the electoral marketplace on legislative bodies. First, such an election conveyed a crisp message from the electorate that could hardly have been duplicated under term limits. The ins were out, the outs were in. Republicans could, and did, claim a popular "mandate" for their programs; at the very least, they were handed a singular opportunity to prove what they could do. True, voters do not often speak with such clarity, but their messages would be muddled indeed if turnover were mandated for, say, about one-third (according to the most radical term-limit scheme) to one-sixth of the legislators.

Second, and even more important from an institutional perspective, the 1994 electoral aftermath confirmed the need for experienced senior members as well as newcomers. As the Founders recognized, the incentive of reelection is the best way to ensure responsible public officials. Moreover, what T. V. Smith (1940) called "the legislative way of life" must be learned through disciplined observation, experience, and study of parliamentary procedures and complex policy issues. The Founders, most of whom were veterans of legislative assemblies, understood this. "A few of the members," wrote the author of *Federalist* No. 53, "as happens in all such assemblies, will possess superior talents; will, by frequent reelections, become members of long standing; will be thoroughly masters of the public business, and perhaps not willing to avail themselves of those advantages. The greater the proportion of new members, and the less the information of the bulk of the members, the more apt will they be to fall into the snares that may be laid for them" (*Federalist* 1788, 346). Whatever their skills and enthusiasms, newly elected officeholders are rarely "masters of the public business." It takes two or three terms for attentive members to accumulate the necessary skills.

Legislatures, like other organizations, work best when they blend experienced seniors and new blood—sometimes featuring mentor-learner relationships, always with the possibility of creative intergenerational friction. Exhibit A is surely the 104th Congress, which required seasoned leaders in order to effect the Republican takeover. In the Senate, the 26-year career of GOP leader Robert Dole (Kan.) was average for the new majority's core leadership. In the House, veterans framed the party's policy and institutional agenda and guided that agenda into enactment. On hand to guide the newcomers were Speaker Gingrich (9 terms) and Majority Leader Dick Armey of Texas (6 terms); procedural experts such as Robert S. Walker of Pennsylvania (10 terms), Gerald B. H. Solomon of New York (9 terms), and David Dreier of California (8 terms); and policy specialists such as Henry J. Hyde of Illinois (11 terms) and Robert L. Livingston of Louisiana (10 terms). Hardly any of these Republican leaders would have been eligible to serve under even the most generous of term-limit plans.

Veterans provide not only expertise and institutional memory, but also a reform agenda that change-oriented newcomers can support yet could not possibly have conceived on their own. This happened during past reform eras. Post-World War II modernizing reforms embodied in the 1946 Legislative Reorganization Act—aimed at streamlining committees, professionalizing staff, and centralizing budget making—were in large part borrowed from scholarly canons of public administration honed by experiences from the New Deal and World War II. In adopting committee and caucus reforms, the 1974 "Watergate class" followed a script developed over a period of years by liberal Democrats, chiefly in the Democratic Study Group (DSG), and awaiting only the votes to pass them. So it was with the reforms of the 1990s. It was symbolic that when the newly elected Republicans arrived in the nation's capital, they were given lapel pins proclaiming them "Majority Makers."

Lawmaking, like other serious and complex enterprises, is a learned activity. For able, dedicated, and adaptable officeholders, extended careers need not be excessive; for incompetent time-servers, even two years is an awfully long time. Congress has been sustained and even ennobled by such careerists as Hubert Humphrey, Robert Michel, Lee H. Hamilton, Richard Lugar, and Henry J. Hyde—to name just a few. To forbid their constituents from rewarding their good service and ensuring seasoned representation would infringe upon citizen sovereignty. The one precedent at the federal level is of doubtful value. On the heels of the four-term tenure of Franklin D. Roosevelt, the Republican 80th Congress in 1947 approved a two-term limit for presidents, ratified in 1951 as the Twenty-Second Amendment. However, most students of the presidency conclude that "the amendment has been notable more for limiting presidents in their second term than for restraining presumably eager presidents from seeking a third" (DiClerico 1995, 1997).

The claims made for term limitations have received astonishingly little challenge. All too willing to believe the worst about Congress, the public by wide margins embraced this deceptively simple populist solution as a cure-all for many of the things they found fault with in the institution. However, until the dramatic House debate of March 1995, the doubts about term limits long harbored by many elected officials, scholars, and thoughtful critics were rarely aired. (Part of the blame must rest with Democrats who controlled Congress until then and who blocked extensive hearings and other deliberations.) Proponents claimed that this reform would break up the arrogant establishment of Capitol Hill careerists, raising turnover and bringing in waves of newcomers who would be closer to voters' desires; that it would offset incumbents' built-in advantages and promote competitive elections; and that by limiting seniority it would democratize the distribution of power within Congress. Most serious students of legislatures question whether the core defect—low turnover of members—was anything more than a passing phenomenon; most of them doubt that term limits could ameliorate the other problems that are cited (see Malbin and Benjamin 1992; Fowler 1992; Kazee 1994, 181-184). Even more important, term-limit schemes promise a new set of problematic results, some of which could adversely affect Congress's organizational integrity and health in the future.

Term limitations would weaken Congress as an institution, perhaps by design but most certainly by result. The most drastic scheme would limit House members to six years. Such perpetual turnover would destabilize the working arrangements of the House and increase the proportions of amateurs and lame ducks. It would certainly reduce the quality of Congress's lawmaking and representational functions. Moreover, it would lower the legislative branch's defenses against the even more permanent elements of the Washington community—the bureaucracy, interest groups, the media, and congressional staffs. Rather than enhancing the institution's responsiveness, term limits would undermine the basic functions of Congress: deliberation, representation, oversight, and education.

What About America's Contract with Congress?

The bottom line of congressional performance lies, as always, in the attitudes and judgments of the American public. It is no secret that the public's healthy ambivalence toward Congress has deteriorated into a pervasive mood of anger and distrust. In 33 Gallup polls taken between 1974 and 1995, an average of 29.6 percent of the respondents rated Congress's performance favorably (Cook 1995). Over the past decade disapproval levels rose as fewer people ventured no opinion about Congress. This sour mood was a major ingredient of the 1992 and 1994 elections (Ladd 1995, 31-40). Although citizens sometimes targeted specific politicians, policies, structures, or scandals, they were critical of virtually all public institutions and harbored doubts about the effectiveness of government and even the present and future well-being of the nation. (Present economic woes and fears for the future no doubt account for much of this unrest.) For the time being, it seemed as if Americans had abandoned their traditional pride and optimism in their country, its political institutions, and its future prospects.

If the 1994 elections achieved nothing else, they should have reminded the American people that Congress is subject to the rule of the ballot box, and that it is not necessarily the isolated, entrenched, privileged bastion it has been reputed to be. The hordes of reform-minded newcomers made it clear that a multitude of changes would occur, and events over the six months following the elections redeemed their promises. Notwithstanding the underlying continuities and the Republicans' unwillingness to undertake certain drastic reforms, there could be no doubt that significant changes were taking place. The essays in this book leave no doubt that these changes are real and probably lasting.

These events seemed, at least temporarily, to assuage the public's ill feelings. Fifty-five percent of citizens interviewed after the elections said they expected Congress and not President Clinton to take the lead in governing; only 30 percent expected the president to take the lead (Morin 1994, A6). Just what action the public expected of Congress was hazy: only 24 percent of the 1994 voters were acquainted with the highly publicized "Contract with America," for example.

As the Republicans' 100-day deadline expired, a raft of opinion surveys found positive assessments (Morin and Edsall 1995; Wines 1995). Modest majorities of citizens endorsed Congress's record over the first months of 1995. According to a *USA Today*-CNN survey conducted by the Gallup organization in early April 1995, 52 percent judged the Republicans' performance "a success," and 53 percent thought the party's proposals could move the country in the right direction (Benedetto 1995). Another survey showed the public's overall assessment was noticeably less negative than before the elections (see Table 12-2). "Only" 57 percent disapproved of Congress's performance, whereas 37 percent approved. (The comparable figures for October 1994 were 21 and 72 percent, respectively.)

Yet the public's cynicism and pessimism toward Congress and individual lawmakers seemed to be unabated. Although people tended to approve of what the Republicans were doing, they doubted whether real changes were taking place. According to a *Washington Post*-ABC News survey, two-thirds of all respondents believed that Congress had accomplished little or nothing at all in its first three months; only one-third saw significant accomplishments.[3] It was as if the noteworthy events following the partisan turnover had been unheeded or disbelieved by the great mass of the public.

The public's continuing anger about politics and government, in fact, gives every evidence of being disconnected from concrete information about what is really going on. To be sure, citizens seemed to be aware that a partisan turnover had occurred, and that the Republicans now controlled Congress. But their knowledge of what else had transpired was meager. When asked after three months of GOP rule about their reaction to the "Contract with America," nearly half the respondents (47 percent) claimed not to have heard about it (Benedetto 1995, 8A). (Of the 44 percent who voiced an opinion, 73 percent generally endorsed the Contract and 27 percent opposed it.) By a two-to-one margin, people thought that congressional Republicans were pursuing politics as usual rather than real change. And by similar margins, citizens claimed that nei-

Table 12-2   Public Support of Congress and Their Own
Representatives, October 1994 and April 1995

	Congress		Own Representative	
Choice	October 1994	April 1995	October 1994	April 1995
Approve	21%	37%	51%	65%
Disapprove	72	57	38	25
No opinion	8	6	11	9

Source: ABC News-*Washington Post* survey. The questions were: "Do you approve or disapprove of the way Congress is doing its job?" and "Do you approve or disapprove of the way your own representative to the House is handling his or her job?" Cited in *National Journal,* April 22, 1995, 1002.

ther the Republicans nor the Democrats were doing "what you want done in Washington."

Citizens' befuddlement over events in the nation's capital was not abated by the messages they received from the mass media. The Republican takeover of Congress met with a Greek chorus of lamentations from reporters and commentators. Tracking nearly 750 front-page news stories and editorials during March 1995, the Center for Media and Public Affairs found that coverage of the GOP Congress was 66 percent negative on the editorial pages and 60 percent negative in news stories (Kondracke 1995). Such negativism was nothing new: "Congress bashing" has become a common theme of media treatment of Capitol Hill, as Norman J. Ornstein and Amy L. Schenkenberg demonstrate. Nor is the press's negativism satisfactorily explained by partisan or ideological animus (the so-called leftist bias seen by Speaker Gingrich and other conservatives). Antagonistic coverage of Congress long predates the GOP takeover; the Democratic Clinton administration also was the target of unprecedented and unrelenting critical reporting and commentary. The inescapable conclusion is that negativism trumps ideology or analysis every time as a dominant media theme (Patterson 1994). For journalists, the 1994 elections brought no revolution but just more of the same.

The public's reactions to the events detailed in this book have a familiar ring. Citizens are unusually restive and upset about the way things are going; they are vulnerable to the negative messages they receive from the media and from various elites. For their part, communicators choose to portray government and politics in disparaging terms. Belittling Congress and other public institutions is an all-too-easy sport enjoyed by many people who ought to know better—news reporters and commentators, editorial writers, talk show hosts, and even politicians striving to gain or keep public office. The typical targets of their editorial one-liners—bungling bureaucrats, high-living lawmakers, powerful lobbyists—are calculated to win applause from receptive audiences, votes from restless citizens, or robust readership or listenership ratings.

"Running against Congress," and other public institutions for that matter, is a venerable American habit, almost as old as the Republic itself. Healthy skepticism about officeholders has marked political commentary from the days of humorists Mark Twain and Will Rogers to Mark Russell and David Letterman. But one-liners rarely comprise accurate assessments of public institutions or officeholders. The unrelenting negativism of public discourse about U.S. government and politics has diluted citizens' sense of loyalty and common purpose.

We end on a personal note. From the viewpoint of political scientists who study national politics and public institutions such as Congress, this extreme negativism is wrong not because it is unhealthy or divisive, but because it is empirically—factually—inaccurate. It is not that scholars have somehow been taken in by the objects of their research. Conscientious students, those who have closely examined political institutions and processes, are intimately acquainted with the shortcomings they have observed. As for Congress, the essays in this volume have addressed its leading elements—leadership, committees, procedures, floor deliberations, and the like—and explained how they are being affected by the politics of change in the 1990s. Defects and malfunctions, some of them quite serious, have been analyzed.

Interestingly enough, the malfunctions discussed in the foregoing essays are rarely those that are singled out by the noisiest critics of the institution. Nor do they, by any stretch of reasoning, justify the kind of broadscale condemnation often expressed or implied when Congress is discussed in public. The most vocal critics typically exaggerate their case: all lawmakers are venal and self-serving, all bureaucrats are bumbling, all government programs are failures. They ignore the manifest dedication and sacrifices of officeholders, the diligence of public employees, the accomplishments of federal programs. They fail to acknowledge or appreciate the purposes or benefits of traditional ways of doing things.

Most importantly, many of the loudest critics seriously underestimate the responsiveness of our governmental institutions and their persistent tendency to adapt to citizens' demands. One of the most astounding myths promulgated by many journalists and commentators, and believed by all too many citizens, is that Capitol Hill is an island somehow unconnected to the rest of the North American continent. Nothing could be further from the truth. As one editorialist, by no means an apologist for the institution, expressed it:

> The U.S. Congress is probably the most attentive, responsive parliamentary body in the western world. Members go home every week. They do a zillion town meetings and call-in shows. And, just to be sure they got the message right, they imbibe polls with their morning coffee.
>
> It shows. Over the past decade the politicians have done exactly what the people have demanded: Cut taxes, raise entitlements, borrow the rest. (Krauthammer 1992, A27)

Officeholders, in other words, are acutely aware of what is on the voters' minds and all too eager to respond.

This should come as no surprise. Congress is, after all, a representative institution—"a mirror in which the American people can see themselves," as one member put it years ago. It conducts most of its business in public. It hears voices from many quarters: from constituents, from lobbyists, from reporters, from experts of all kinds, even sometimes from scholars. Its membership constantly replaces itself—sometimes too slowly but sometimes very rapidly indeed, as in the 1990s. However one judges its members, their reactions to the scandals of the early 1990s betrayed no unawareness of, or insensitivity to, the general public's sentiments. And when the voters spoke distinctly in the 1992 elections, and then raised their voices two years later, the impact on Capitol Hill was palpable.

In this volume we have examined and explained these changes. The innovations themselves manifested underlying historical continuities, and they fell short of what many had demanded. Nevertheless, the changes are profound and significant. We can only guess whether they will help to restore some of the institution's credibility. But for now, it is our responsibility as citizens to understand what has taken place, and why.

Notes

1. *National Journal,* Opinion Outlook, April 22, 1995, 1002.

2. A majority of Republicans at all seniority levels voted for term limits, just as a majority of Democrats in all categories voted nay. But seniority was also a factor: huge majorities of nonfreshman Democrats, and a sizable minority of Republicans with 12 or more years seniority, voted against the proposal.

3. The question was: "Overall, how much do you think Congress has accomplished in the past three months?" Responses were: "a great deal" (7 percent), "a good amount" (26 percent), "not too much" (53 percent), "nothing at all" (13 percent), with 1 percent undecided. See Morin and Edsall (1995, A21).

REFERENCES

ABC News/*Washington Post.* 1994a. Survey conducted April 9.
———. 1994b. Survey conducted June 23-26.
American Talk Issues. 1994. "Steps for Democracy: The Many Versus the Few." Survey No. 24. March 25.
Andrews, Edmund L. 1994. "A Folksy Legislator with Power over Industries." *New York Times,* December 20, D1, 11.
Arnold, R. Douglas. 1990. *The Logic of Congressional Action.* New Haven, Conn.: Yale University Press.
Arterton, F. Christopher. 1993. "Campaign '92: Strategies and Tactics of the Candidates." In *The Election of 1992,* ed. Gerald M. Pomper et al., 74-109. Chatham, N.J.: Chatham House Publishers.
Asher, Herbert B., and Herb F. Weisberg. 1978. "Voting Change in Congress: Some Dynamic Perspectives on an Evolutionary Process." *American Journal of Political Science* 22:391-425.
Asher, Herbert, and Mike Barr. 1994. "Popular Support for Congress and Its Members." In *Congress, the Press, and the Public,* ed. Thomas E. Mann and Norman J. Ornstein, 15-43. Washington, D.C.: American Enterprise Institute and the Brookings Institution. September.
Auletta, Ken. 1994. "Free Speech." *The New Yorker,* September 12.
Babcock, Charles. 1993. "Soft Money: Where It Went." *Washington Post,* August 10.
Baumgartner, Frank R., et al. 1994. "Committee Jurisdictions in Congress, 1980-1991." Paper delivered at the annual meeting of the American Political Science Association, New York City, September 1-4.
Benedetto, Richard. 1995. "GOP: Good Marks for One Hundred Days." *USA Today,* March 31, 1A, 8A.
Benjamin, Gerald, and Michael J. Malbin, eds. 1992. *Limiting Legislative Terms.* Washington, D.C.: CQ Press.
Berry, Jeffrey M. 1977. *Lobbying for the People.* Princeton, N.J.: Princeton University Press.
Beth, Richard S. 1990. "The Discharge Rule in the House of Representatives: Procedure, History, and Statistics." *CRS Report for Congress,* March 2.
———. 1993. "The Motion to Proceed to Consider a Measure in the Senate, 1979-1992." *CRS Report for Congress,* September 27.

Binder, Sarah A. forthcoming a. "Partisanship and Procedural Choice: Institutional Change in the Early Congress, 1789-1823." *Journal of Politics.*

———. forthcoming b. "The Partisan Basis of Procedural Choice: Allocating Parliamentary Rights in the House, 1789-1991." *American Political Science Review.*

Birnbaum, Jeffrey H. 1992. "Lobbyists: Why the Bad Rap?" *The American Enterprise* 3 (November/December): 70-79.

Bowman, Karlyn, and Everett Carll Ladd. 1994. "Public Opinion Toward Congress: A Historical Look." In *Congress, the Press, and the Public,* ed. Thomas E. Mann and Norman J. Ornstein, 45-58. Washington, D.C.: American Enterprise Institute and the Brookings Institution.

Brady, David W. 1988. *Critical Elections and Congressional Policy Making.* Stanford, Calif.: Stanford University Press.

Brady, David W., and Barbara Sinclair. 1984. "Building Majorities for Policy Changes in the House of Representatives." *Journal of Politics* 46:1033-1060.

Brownson, Ann. 1994. *Congressional Staff Directory 1994/1,* Congressional Staff Directory, Ltd.

Burger, Timothy J. 1994. "Synar Defeat by Underdog Rocks House." *Roll Call,* September 22.

Caiden, Naomi. 1991. "Do Politicians Listen to Experts? The Budget Enforcement Act of 1990 and the Capacity to Budget." *Public Budgeting and Finance* 10 (Spring).

Carney, Eliza Newlin. 1994. "Dead Ended." *National Journal,* July 23, 1733-1737.

CBS. 1994. *60 Minutes.* February 6.

CBS News/*New York Times.* 1994. Poll conducted October 29-November 1.

Center for Responsive Politics. 1986. "*Not for the Short Winded*": *Congressional Reform, 1961-1986.* Washington, D.C.

Clymer, Adam. 1992. "The Gridlock Congress." *New York Times,* October 11, 1, 30.

Cohen, Richard E. 1990. "Crumbling Committees." *National Journal,* August 4, 1876-1881.

———. 1993a. "Dismal Reviews for Sen. Boren's Show." *National Journal,* May 29, 1308.

———. 1993b. "Running Up Against the 'Byrd Rule'." *National Journal,* September 4, 2151.

Congressional Budget Office (CBO). 1990a. *The Economic and Budget Outlook: Fiscal Years 1991-1995.* January.

———. 1990b. *An Analysis of the President's Budgetary Proposals for Fiscal Year 1991.* March.

———. 1990c. *Pay-As-You-Go Budgeting.* Staff memorandum. March.

———. 1990d. *The Economic and Budget Outlook: An Update.* July.

———. 1990e. *The 1990 Budget Agreement: An Interim Assessment.* December.

———. 1991. *The Economic and Budget Outlook: An Update.* August.

———. 1994. *The Economic and Budget Outlook: An Update.* August.

Congressional Quarterly. 1987. *The Washington Lobby.* 5th ed. Washington, D.C.

———. 1994. *Congressional Quarterly Weekly Report.* Index, January-March.

———. various years. *Congressional Quarterly Almanac.* Washington, D.C.

Congressional Research Service. Library of Congress. 1992. *Congressional Reorganization: Options for Change.* September.

Connelly, William, and John Pitney. 1994. *Congress' Permanent Majority? Republicans in the U.S. House.* Lanham, Md.: Rowman and Littlefield.

Cook, Charles E. 1995. "Voters Sense Less Gridlock, Increase Congress Approval." *Roll Call,* February 9, 8.

Cooper, Kenneth J. 1993a. "House Begins Trimming Thicket of Subcommittees." *Washington Post,* January 13, A19.

———. 1993b. "Four House Select Committees Expire as Symbols of Reform." *Washington Post,* April 1, A14.

———. 1993c. "A Different Breed of 'Cardinal'." *Washington Post,* September 21, A29.

———. 1994. "GOP Vows Quick Action to Change Housekeeping." *Washington Post,* November 15, A1.

Curran, Tim. 1994a. "Campaign Reform Is Drag for Senate." *Roll Call,* September 26.

———. 1994b. "The House Surrenders on PACs." *Roll Call,* September 29.

———. 1994c. "House Pickups at Fifty-Two After GOP Blow Out." *Roll Call,* November 10.

———. 1994d. "Campaign Finance Reform Now Ranks Low on Republican Agenda for 104th Congress." *Roll Call,* December 1.

Davidson, Roger H. 1981. "Two Avenues of Change: House and Senate Committee Reorganization." *In Congress Reconsidered.* 2nd ed., ed. Lawrence C. Dodd and Bruce I. Oppenheimer, 107-133. Washington, D.C.: CQ Press.

———. 1988. "New Centralization on Capitol Hill." *Review of Politics* 10: 345-364.

———. 1989. "Multiple Referral of Legislation in the U.S. Senate." *Legislative Studies Quarterly* 14 (August): 375-392.

———. 1990. "The Advent of the Modern Congress: The Legislative Reorganization Act of 1946." *Legislative Studies Quarterly* 15 (August): 357-373.

———. ed. 1992. *The Postreform Congress.* New York: St. Martin's Press.

———. 1994. "The Speaker and Institutional Change." In *The Speaker: Leadership in the U.S. House of Representatives,* ed. Ronald M. Peters, Jr., 157-177. Washington, D.C.: CQ Press.

———. 1995. "Congress After 1994: Political Tides and Institutional Change." *The Brookings Review* 13 (Spring): 26-29.

Davidson, Roger H., and Walter J. Oleszek. 1977. *Congress against Itself.* Bloomington, Ind.: Indiana University Press.

———. 1984. "Changing the Guard in the U.S. Senate." *Legislative Studies Quarterly* 9 (November): 635-663.

———. 1990. *Congress and Its Members.* 3rd. ed. Washington, D.C.: CQ Press.

Davidson, Roger H., Walter J. Oleszek, and Thomas Kephart. 1988. "One Bill, Many Committees: Multiple Referrals in the House of Representatives." *Legislative Studies Quarterly* 13 (February): 3-28.

Democratic Study Group (DSG). 1992. "Democratic Caucus Strengthens Leadership, Streamlines House." *DSG Special Report,* December 11.

———. 1994. "A Look at the Senate Filibuster." *DSG Special Report,* June 13.

Dewar, Helen. 1994a. "Ex-Senators Urge Restraint on Filibusters." *Washington Post,* June 23.

———. 1994b. "Delay Tactics Grind Senate into Gridlock." *Washington Post,* September 24.

———. 1994c. "New Lobbyist Curbs Unlikely as Congress Struggles to Close." *Washington Post,* October 7, A1.

DiClerico, Robert E. 1995. "Twenty-Second Amendment." In *The Encyclopedia of the United States Congress,* ed. Roger H. Davidson, Donald C. Bacon, and Morton H. Keller, vol. 4: 1996-1997. New York: Simon and Schuster.

Dion, George Douglas. 1991. Removing the obstructions: minority rights and the politics of procedural change in the 19th century House of Representatives. Ph.D. diss., University of Michigan.

Donovan, Beth. 1992. "Busy Democrats Skirt Fights to Get House in Order." *Congressional Quarterly Weekly Report,* December 12, 3777-3780.

Donovan, Beth. 1993a. "Freshmen Show Little Unity in Shaping Reform Agenda." *Congressional Quarterly Weekly Report,* March 27, 728.

———. 1993b. "Fractures in Freshman Class Weaken Impact on House." *Congressional Quarterly Weekly Report,* April 3, 807-810.

———. 1993c. "Clinton Offers Details of Plan: Big Test Is GOP Senate Unity." *Congressional Quarterly Weekly Report,* May 8.

———. 1993d. "Campaign Finance Provisions." *Congressional Quarterly Weekly Report,* August 14.

———. 1993e. "House Will Vote on Limits Nearing $1 Million in '96." *Congressional Quarterly Weekly Report,* November 13.

Donovan, Beth, with Thomas H. Moore. 1994. "Freshmen Toed Party Line But Helped Cut Spending." *Congressional Quarterly Weekly Report,* January 14, 55-57.

Doyle, Richard, and Jerry McCaffery. 1991. "The Budget Enforcement Act of 1990: The Path to No Fault Budgeting." *Public Budgeting and Finance* 10 (Spring).

Elving, Ronald D. 1994. "Bright Lights, Wider Windows: Presenting Congress in the 1990s." In *Congress, the Press, and the Public,* ed. Thomas E. Mann and Norman J. Ornstein. Washington, D.C.: American Enterprise Institute and the Brookings Institution.

Federalist, 1788, Modern Library edition, n.d. New York: The Modern Library.

Federal News Service. 1994. Verbatim transcript of GOP "Contract with America" event, West Front, U.S. Capitol. September 27.

Fenno, Richard F., Jr. 1978. *Home Style: House Members in Their Districts.* Boston: Little, Brown.

Fink, Evelyn C., and Brian D. Humes. 1992. "Electoral Forces and Institutional Change in the United States House of Representatives, 1860-1894." Paper delivered at annual meeting of Midwest Political Science Association, April.

Fisher, Louis. 1985. "Ten Years of the Budget Act: Still Searching for Controls." *Public Budgeting and Finance* 5 (Autumn).

Foerstel, Karen. 1992. "Democrats Ratify Sweeping Changes in Rules of House." *Roll Call,* December 10, 1, 14.

———. 1993. "Rules Will Soon Open, Says Foley." *Roll Call,* April 26, 22.

———. 1994a. "Among Roadblocks to Reform: House, Senate Depart on Key Points That Affect Them Both." *Roll Call,* February 3, 7.

———. 1994b. "Hamilton Warns of a 'Blood-Bath' Over Panel Cuts." *Roll Call,* February 10.

———. 1994c. "Byrd Rule War Erupts Once Again." *Roll Call,* February 24, 1.

———. 1994d. "Sen. Ted Stevens Threatens to Filibuster Reform Bill—Over Reforms for Filibuster." *Roll Call,* June 20, 3.

———. 1994e. "Crowded Calendar Can Save August Vacation." *Roll Call,* July 14, 1.

Fowler, Linda. 1992. "A Comment on Competition and Careers." In *Limiting Legislative Terms,* ed. Gerald Benjamin and Michael J. Malbin, 181-185. Washington, D.C.: CQ Press.

Frantzich, Stephen E. 1986. *Write Your Congressman: Constituent Communications and Representation.* New York: Praeger Publishers.

Fulbright, J. William. 1979. "The Legislator as Educator." *Foreign Affairs* 57 (Spring): 719-732.

Galloway, George B., and Sidney Wise. 1976. *History of the House of Representatives.* New York: Crowell.

Gold, Martin. 1981. *Senate Procedure and Practice.* Unpublished manual.

Greider, William. 1992. *Who Will Tell the People? The Betrayal of American Democracy.* New York: Simon and Schuster.

Havens, Harry. 1986. "Gramm-Rudman-Hollings: Origins and Implementation." *Public Budgeting and Finance* 6 (Autumn): 4-24.

Hook, Janet. 1992. "Extensive Reform Proposals Cook on the Front Burner." *Congressional Quarterly Weekly Report,* June 6, 1579-1585.

———. 1994a. "Voters' Hostility Is Shaping the Business of Congress." *Congressional Quarterly Weekly Report,* April 2, 785-789.

———. 1994b. "Fervor for Reform Wanes Amid Internal Misgivings." *Congressional Quarterly Weekly Report,* May 21, 1274-1275.

Hook, Janet, and David S. Cloud. 1994. "A Republican-Designed House Won't Please All Occupants." *Congressional Quarterly Weekly Report,* December 3, 3430-3435.

Hosansky, David. 1994. "GOP Bid to Reform Committees Faces Intraparty Skepticism." *Congressional Quarterly Weekly Report,* November 19, 3324-3325.

House Committee on the Budget. 1990. *The Fiscal Year 1991 Budget.* February 2. Committee print.

House Committee on Rules. 1992. *Roundtable Discussion on the Motion to Recommit.* Washington, D.C.: U.S. Government Printing Office.

———. 1993. Subcommittee on Rules of the House. *Discharge Petition Disclosure: Hearings.* September 14. Committee print.

Hrebenar, Ronald J., and Ruth K. Scott. 1990. *Interest Group Politics in America.* 2nd ed. Englewood Cliffs, N.J.: Prentice-Hall.

Jacoby, Mary. 1993. "In a Shocker, House Kills Narcotics Panel, Takes Aim at Three Other Selects." *Roll Call,* January 28, 1, 17.

———. 1994a. "Black Caucus Rejects House Reform Proposal to Cut Subcommittees, Restrict Assignments." *Roll Call,* January 20, 3, 10.

———. 1994b. "Boll Weevils Won't Automatically Join GOP to Kill Rules." *Roll Call,* April 14, 3.

———. 1994c. "FROGs Claim Success on Opening Up House Rules." *Roll Call,* July 7.

———. 1994d. "Sabo Bill Would Kill Byrd Rule for Good." *Roll Call,* July 25, 12.

———. 1994e. "House Democrats This Year Scuttled Plans to Abolish Discharge Petitions." *Roll Call,* October 24.

———. 1994f. " 'Chairman' Solomon Says He Plans to Grant Open Rules on 75 Percent of Bills Next Year." *Roll Call,* November 28, 18.

Joint Committee on the Organization of Congress (JCOC). 1993a. *Background Materials: Supplemental Information Provided to Members of the Joint Committee on the Organization of Congress.* S. Rept. 103-55. Washington, D.C.: U.S. Government Printing Office.

———. 1993b. *Business Meetings on Congressional Reform Legislation.* S. Hrg. 103-320. Washington, D.C.: U.S. Government Printing Office.

———. 1993c. *Committee Structure: Hearings.* S. Hrg. 103-74. *Floor Deliberations and Scheduling: Hearings.* S. Hrg. 103-119. Washington, D.C.: U.S. Government Printing Office.

———. 1993d. *Open Days for Members and Outside Groups.* S. Hrg. 103-128. Washington, D.C.: U.S. Government Printing Office.

———. 1993e. *Operations of the Congress: Hearings.* S. Hrg. 103-26. Washington, D.C.: U.S. Government Printing Office.

———. 1993f. *Organization of Congress: Final Report.* H. Rept. 103-413/ S. Rept. 103-215. Washington, D.C.: U.S. Government Printing Office. 3 vols.

Jones, Bryan D., Frank R. Baumgartner, and Jeffrey C. Talbert. 1993. "The Destruction of Issue Monopolies in Congress." *American Political Science Review* 87 (September): 657-671.

Kahn, Gabriel. 1995. "GOP's Next Step in Reforming House." *Roll Call,* January 23, A44-A45.

———. 1995b. "Bill Clinger's 100-Day Adventure." *Roll Call,* April 3, 3.

Kazee, Thomas A. 1994. "Ambition and Candidacy: Running as a Strategic Calculation." In *Who Runs for Congress? Ambition, Context, and Candidate Emergence,* ed. Thomas A. Kazee, 165-184. Washington, D.C.: CQ Press.

Kee, James Edwin, and Scott V. Nystrom. 1991. "The 1990 Budget Package: Redefining the Debate." *Public Budgeting and Finance* 10 (Spring).

Kenworthy, Tom. 1994. "Washington State May Silence the Speaker." *Washington Post,* October 8, A1.

King, David C. 1994. "The Nature of Congressional Committee Jurisdictions." *American Political Science Review* 88 (March): 48-62.

Kondracke, Morton M. 1995. "Is Newt Paranoid About Media Bias? New Study Says No." *Roll Call*, April 20, 6.

Krauss, Clifford. 1993. "House Rejects Drastic Cuts in Spending by Committees." *New York Times*, March 30, A20.

Krauthammer, Charles. 1992. "The Perot Delusion: It's More Wishful Thinking from a Decadent Electorate." *Washington Post*, May 1, A27.

Kravitz, Walter. 1990. "The Advent of the Modern Congress: The Legislative Reorganization Act of 1970." *Legislative Studies Quarterly* 15 (August): 375-399.

Kubiak, Greg. 1994. *The Gilded Dome.* Norman, Okla.: The University of Oklahoma Press.

Kuntz, Phil. 1994. "Lobbying and Gifts Bills Compared." *Congressional Quarterly Weekly Report*, April 23, 1016-1022.

Ladd, Everett C. 1990. "Public Opinion and the 'Congress Problem'." *Public Interest* 100:57-67.

———. ed. 1995. *America at the Polls 1994.* Storrs, Conn.: Roper Center, University of Connecticut.

LeLoup, Lance T., Barbara Luck Graham, and Stacy Barwick. 1987. "Deficit Politics and Constitutional Government: The Impact of Gramm-Rudman-Hollings." *Public Budgeting and Finance* 7 (Spring): 83-103.

Lewis, John. 1994. "In Defense of PACs." *Washington Post*, July 1.

Lichter, S. Robert, and David R. Amundson. 1994. "Less News Is Worse News: Television News Coverage of Congress, 1972-1992." In *Congress, the Press, and the Public*, ed. Thomas E. Mann and Norman J. Ornstein. Washington, D.C.: American Enterprise Institute and the Brookings Institution.

Love, Alice A. 1994a. "Hefty Reform Agenda Stilled Until September." *Roll Call*, August 18, 6.

———. 1994b. "Lobby, Gift Reform Slated for House Vote Today After Rules Panel Bungles Timing of Floor Action." *Roll Call*, September 29, 3, 18.

———. 1994c. "Hill Reform in Graveyard." *Roll Call*, October 6, 15.

Malbin, Michael J., and Gerald Benjamin. 1992. "Legislatures After Term Limits." In *Limiting Legislative Terms*, ed. Gerald Benjamin and Michael J. Malbin, 209-221. Washington, D.C.: CQ Press.

Mann, Thomas E., and Norman J. Ornstein. 1992. *Renewing Congress: A First Report.* Washington, D.C.: American Enterprise Institute and the Brookings Institution. November.

———. 1993. *Renewing Congress: A Second Report.* Washington, D.C.: American Enterprise Institute and the Brookings Institution. June.

———. 1994a. *Renewing Congress: A Progress Report.* Washington, D.C.: American Enterprise Institute and the Brookings Institution. March.

———. eds. 1994b. *Congress, the Press, and the Public.* Washington, D.C.: American Enterprise Institute and the Brookings Institution. September.

Mann, Thomas E., Norman J. Ornstein, and Matthew Pinkus. 1993. "Renewing

Congress: A Role for the Scholarly Community." *Extension of Remarks.* Legislative Studies Section Newsletter. American Political Science Association.

Marcus, Ruth. 1995. "Clinton Legal Fund Bars Donations by Lobbyists." *Washington Post,* January 26, A1, A7.

Maskell, Jack H. 1994. *Legislative Ethics in Democratic Countries: Comparative Analysis of Financial Standards.* Washington, D.C.: Congressional Research Service. April 14.

Mayhew, David R. 1991. *Divided We Govern: Party Control, Lawmaking, and Investigations, 1946-1990.* New Haven, Conn.: Yale University Press.

Merida, Kevin. 1993. "Reform of Congress May Be a Case of 'Not in My Back Yard.'" *Washington Post,* October 21.

———. 1994. "'Polishing Congress' Tarnished Image." *Washington Post,* January 25, A1.

Michel, Robert H. 1987. "The Minority Leader Replies." *Washington Post,* December 29, A14.

———. 1994. *Congressional Record,* September 29, H10269.

Morin, Richard. 1994. "Voters Repeat Their Simple Message About Government: Less is Better." *Washington Post,* November 13, A1, A6.

Morin, Richard, and Thomas B. Edsall. 1995. "Despite Change on Hill, Public Remains Critical." *Washington Post,* April 7, A1, A21.

Muir, William K. 1982. *Legislature: California's School of Politics.* Chicago: University of Chicago Press.

Nelson, Candice J. 1994. "Women's PACs in the Year of the Woman." In *The Year of the Woman: Myths and Realities,* ed. Elizabeth Adell Cook, Sue Thomas, and Clyde Wilcox. Boulder, Colo.: Westview Press.

Nyhan, Paul. 1995. "Cuts in Committee Spending Approved by House Panel." *Congressional Quarterly Weekly Report,* March 11, 735.

Oppenheimer, Bruce I. 1981. "The Changing Relationship Between the House Leadership and the Committee on Rules." In *Understanding Congressional Leadership,* ed. F. H. Mackaman, 207-225. Washington, D.C.: CQ Press.

———. 1985. "Changing Time Constraints on Congress: Historical Perspectives on the Use of Cloture." In *Congress Reconsidered,* 3rd ed., ed. Lawrence C. Dodd and Bruce I. Oppenheimer, 393-413. Washington, D.C.: CQ Press.

Ornstein, Norman J. 1994. "Who's Worse: '60 Minutes' or Rep. Gutierrez?" *Roll Call,* February 14, 5.

———. 1995. "Why GOP's Open Rule Pledge Was Doomed to Fail." *Roll Call,* February 20, 16-17.

Ornstein, Norman J., Thomas E. Mann, Michael J. Malbin. 1994. *Vital Statistics on Congress, 1993-1994.* Washington, D.C.: CQ Press.

Parris, Judith H. 1979. "The Senate Reorganizes Its Committees, 1977." *Political Science Quarterly* 94 (Summer): 319-337.

Patterson, Thomas E. 1994. *Out of Order.* New York: Vintage Books.

Peabody, Robert L. 1963. "The Enlarged Rules Committee." In *New Perspectives on the House of Representatives,* ed. Robert L. Peabody and Nelson W. Polsby, 129-164. New York: Rand-McNally.

Penner, Rudolph G., and Alan J. Abramson. 1988. *Broken Purse Strings: Congressional Budgeting, 1974-1988.* Washington, D.C.: Urban Institute Press.

Pinkus, Matthew. 1993. Statement on September 14. Hearing on H. Res. 134, Discharge Petition Disclosure. Subcommittee on Rules of the House, Committee on Rules. Washington, D.C.: U.S. Government Printing Office.

Polsby, Nelson W. 1968. "The Institutionalization of the House of Representatives." *American Political Science Review* 62 (March): 144-168.

Price, David E. 1992. *The Congressional Experience: A View from the Hill.* Boulder, Colo.: Westview Press.

Rauch, Jonathan. 1994. *Demosclerosis: The Silent Killer of American Government.* New York: Random House.

Rieselbach, Leroy N. 1994. *Congressional Reform: The Changing Modern Congress.* Washington, D.C.: CQ Press.

Rohde, David W. 1988. "Variations in Partisanship in the House of Representatives: Southern Democrats, Realignment and Agenda Change." Paper presented at the annual meeting of the American Political Science Association. Washington, D.C.

———. 1991. *Parties and Leaders in the Postreform House.* Chicago: University of Chicago Press.

Rohde, David W., and Kenneth A. Shepsle. 1978. "Thinking About Legislative Reform." In *Legislative Reform: The Policy Impact,* ed. Leroy N. Rieselbach. Lexington, Mass.: Lexington Books.

Roman, Nancy E. 1994. "Dingell Panel Cuts Would Anger Heir to Chairmanship." *Washington Times,* November 16, A3.

Rosenbaum, David E. 1994a. "With Eyes on Elections, Senate Finds an Impasse." *New York Times,* September 24.

———. 1994b. "Strong Speaker, Strong House? One Doesn't Necessarily Follow the Other." *New York Times,* December 4.

Rubin, Irene S. 1990. *The Politics of Public Budgeting: Getting and Spending, Borrowing and Balancing.* Chatham, N.J.: Chatham House.

Sabato, Larry J. 1991. *Feeding Frenzy: How Attack Journalism Has Transformed American Politics.* New York: Free Press.

Sachs, Richard C. 1994a. "Regulating Interest Groups and Lobbyists: 103rd Congress Proposals." *CRS Issue Brief,* No. IB93111, updated August 18.

———. 1994b. "Regulating Interest Groups and Lobbyists: 103rd Congress Proposals." *CRS Issue Brief,* No. IB93111, updated November 3.

Sammon, Richard. 1994a. "Focus of 'Reform' Effort Shifts to Ending Hill's Exemptions." *Congressional Quarterly Weekly Report,* July 9, 1855-1856.

———. 1994b. "No 'Reform' Breakthroughs as Clock Ticks." *Congressional Quarterly Weekly Report,* September 24, 2659-2660.

Schick, Allen. 1981. *Reconciliation and the Congressional Budget Process.* Washington, D.C.: American Enterprise Institute.

———. 1990. *The Capacity to Budget.* Washington, D.C.: Urban Institute.

Schneider, Judy. 1995. "Committee System: Rules Changes in the House, 104th Congress." *CRS Report,* January 24, 95-187.

Seelye, Katharine Q. 1994. "Lawmakers Take Sour View as Session Totters to Close." *New York Times,* October 1, 1, 8.

Senate Committee on Governmental Affairs. 1988. "Proposed Budget Reforms: A Critical Analysis." In *Proposed Budget Reform: A Critical Analysis,* prepared by Allen Schick. Washington, D.C.: Congressional Research Service and the Library of Congress. April.

Shaiko, Ronald G. 1991. "More Bang for the Buck: The New Era of Full-Service Public Interest Organizations." In *Interest Group Politics,* 3rd ed., ed. Allan J. Cigler and Burdett A. Loomis, 109-129. Washington, D.C.: CQ Press.

Sheffner, Benjamin. 1995. "Despite Boehner, Limits Lack Votes." *Roll Call,* March 23, 1, 22.

Shephard, Scott. 1994. "Grass Roots or Astroturf? Lobbying Groups Disguise Motives with Orwellian Names." *Washington Times,* December 10, A2.

Sheppard, Burton D. 1985. *Rethinking Congressional Reform: The Reform Roots of the Special Interest Congress.* Cambridge: Shenkman Books.

Shuman, Howard E. 1988. *Politics and the Budget: The Struggle Between the President and the Congress.* 3rd ed. Englewood Cliffs, N.J.: Prentice-Hall.

———. 1992. *Politics and the Budget: The Struggle Between the President and the Congress.* 2nd ed. Englewood Cliffs, N.J.: Prentice Hall.

Simpson, Glenn R. 1993. "Blacks Pushing Hard to Save Africa Panel." *Roll Call,* January 7, 1, 28.

Sinclair, Barbara. 1982. *Congressional Realignment: 1925-1978.* Austin, Texas: University of Texas Press.

———. 1983. *Majority Leadership in the U.S. House.* Baltimore, Md.: Johns Hopkins University Press.

———. 1989. *The Transformation of the U.S. Senate.* Baltimore, Md.: Johns Hopkins University Press.

———. 1992. "The Emergence of Strong Leadership in the 1980s House of Representatives." *Journal of Politics* 54 (August): 657-684.

———. 1993. "Are Special Rules Leadership Tools? House Special Rules and the Institutional Design Controversy." Paper presented at the annual meeting of the American Political Science Association, Washington, D.C., September 1-3.

———. 1994a. "House Special Rules and the Institutional Design Controversy." *Legislative Studies Quarterly* 19 (November): 477-494.

———. 1994b. "Regular Order? New Legislative Processes in the Contemporary Congress." Paper presented at the annual meeting of the American Political Science Asociation, New York City, September 1-4.

———. 1995. *Legislators, Leaders and Lawmaking: The U.S. House of Representatives in the Postreform Era.* Baltimore, Md.: Johns Hopkins University Press.

Smith, Steven S. 1989. *Call to Order: Floor Politics in the House and Senate.* Washington, D.C.: Brookings Institution.

Smith, Thomas Vernor. 1940. *The Legislative Way of Life.* Chicago: University of Chicago Press.

Smucker, Bob. 1991. *The Nonprofit Lobbying Guide.* San Francisco: Jossey-Bass Publishers.

Statistical Abstract of the United States, 1994. 114th ed. U.S. Department of Commerce, Economics and Statistics Administration, Bureau of the Census. Washington, D.C.: U.S. Government Printing Office.

Tate, Dale. 1981. "Reconciliation Breeds Tumult as Committees Tackle Cuts: Revolutionary Budget Tool." *Congressional Quarterly Weekly Report,* May 23, 887-891.

Thelwell, Raphael. 1990. "Gramm-Rudman-Hollings Four Years Later: A Dangerous Illusion." *Public Administration Review* 50 (March/April): 190-197.

Thurber, James A. 1989. "Budget Continuity and Change: An Assessment of the Congressional Budget Process." In *Studies in Modern American Politics,* ed. D. K. Adams, 78-118. Manchester, England: Manchester University Press.

———. ed. 1991. *Divided Democracy: Cooperation and Conflict Between the President and Congress.* Washington, D.C.: CQ Press.

Thurber, James A., and Samantha Durst. 1991. "Delay, Deadlock, and Deficits: Evaluating Congressional Budget Reform." In *Federal Budget and Financial Management Reform,* ed. Thomas D. Lynch. Westport, Conn.: Greenwood Press.

Thurber, James A., ed.. 1992. "New Rules for an Old Game: Zero-Sum Budgeting in the Postreform Congress." In *The Postreform Congress,* ed. Roger H. Davidson, 257-278. New York: St. Martin's Press.

Thurber, James A., and Samantha Durst. 1993. "The 1990 Budget Enforcement Act: The Decline of Congressional Accountability." In *Congress Reconsidered.* 5th ed., ed. Lawrence C. Dodd and Bruce I. Oppenheimer. Washington, D.C.: CQ Press.

Time/CNN. 1995. Survey No. 24. Conducted January 5.

Times Mirror Center for the People and the Press. 1992. Survey October 7-29. Conducted for the Renewing Congress Project of the American Enterprise Institute and the Brookings Institution conference "Congress, the Press, and the Public," May 13, 1993.

———. 1993. Survey May 25-June 11. Published in "The Vocal Minority in American Politics," Times Mirror Center, July 16.

———. 1994a. Survey January 6-13. "Mixed Messages About Press Freedom on Both Sides of Atlantic."

———. 1994b. Survey July 12-27 and September 9-11. Published in *The New Political Landscape,* Times Mirror Center, October 1994.

Towell, Pat. 1994. "GOP's Drive for a More Open House Reflects Pragmatism and Resentment." *Congressional Quarterly Weekly Report,* November 19, 3320-3321.

Weiss, C. H., ed. 1992. *Organizations for Policy Analysis: Helping Government Think.* Beverley Hills, Calif.: Sage Publications.

Weisskopf, Michael. 1994. "Senate Republicans Block Lobbyist Reform Measure." *Washington Post,* October 6, A1, A4.

White, Joseph, and Aaron Wildavsky. 1989. *The Deficit and the Public Interest: The Search for Responsible Budgeting.* Berkeley, Calif.: University of California Press.

Williams, Marjorie. 1993. "Clinton's Mr. Inside." *Vanity Fair,* March 172-175, 207-213.

Wines, Michael. 1995. "Public Gives Congress Good Marks, But Is Mixed on Gingrich." *New York Times,* April 11, A22.

Wolfensberger, Donald R. 1992. "Comparative Data on the U.S. House of Representatives." Compiled by the Republican staff of the House Rules Committee, November 10.Yang, John E. 1991. "Budget Battle Set to Begin on New Terrain." *Washington Post,* February 3, A12.

Yang, John E., and Steven Mufson. 1990. "Package Termed Best Circumstances Permit." Washington Post, October 29, A4.

INDEX